The Assessment of Criminal Behaviours of Clients in Secure Settings

Edited by
Mary McMurran and John E. Hodge

Jessica Kingsley Publishers
London and Bristol, Pennsylvania

First published in the United Kingdom in 1994 by
Jessica Kingsley Publishers Ltd
116 Pentonville Road
London N1 9JB, England
and
1900 Frost Road, Suite 101
Bristol, PA 19007, U S A

British Library Cataloguing in Publication Data

Assessment of Criminal Behaviours of Clients in
Secure Settings
I. McMurran, Mary II. Hodge, John
364.3

ISBN 1-85302-124-5

Printed and Bound in Great Britain by
Cromwell Press, Melksham, Wiltshire

Contents

Acknowledgements

The Editors would like to thank Ray St Ledger for his helpful comments on the manuscript, and Steve Winstanley for preparing the graphics.

Introduction

MARY MCMURRAN AND JOHN E. HODGE

Assessment is the first, and arguably the most important, stage in any attempt to change a person's behaviour. It is only when the nature of the problem is clearly understood by the professional that appropriate, and therefore effective, intervention programmes can be designed. This understanding is based upon the interpretation of information collected from a variety of sources including formal records, the client (interviews, observation, and psychometric tests), and significant others. The type of information that the professional will seek is influenced by three major factors: (1) the theoretical approach adopted; (2) knowledge of the research literature concerning the specific problem area; and (3) practical issues.

This book is concerned specifically with the assessment of offending behaviour with clients who are detained in secure settings, such as prisons, special hospitals, and regional secure units. Assessment of offenders, particularly those who have committed serious offences and are therefore likely to be detained in a secure setting, is particularly challenging for the professional: observation of the offending behaviour *per se* is not ethically possible; many other relevant behaviours, for example drinking alcohol, are not open to observation because they are not permitted; and social and psychological factors which may be important to the understanding of the offending are simply not present in the unnatural environment that is the secure hospital or prison.

These difficulties undoubtedly exist, yet valid assessment of criminal behaviour is of paramount importance since assessment findings and consequent recommendations may contribute to a variety of decisions which are of major significance to society. Courts may use offender assessments to decide upon culpability and best disposal options, for example supervision in the community versus placement in an institution, or a treatment order versus a prison sentence. Assessments of offenders in institutions may be taken into account in the decision-making process of those bodies holding the power to recommend continued detention or release – the Parole Board, Mental Health Review Tribunals, and the Home Office. Clearly, there is a responsibility on the part of the professional to ensure that members of society, who are the potential victims of crime, are served well by valid assessments and appropriate recommendations. The professional also has a responsibility to the offender, since assessment may form the basis on which his or her future is decided. Only recommendations based upon valid assessment are in the best interests of the offender in suggesting ways of reducing the likelihood of further crime.

In assessment, it is important that all the relevant information is collected diligently and interpreted intelligently. The validity of assessment will depend upon the professional giving due consideration to the areas mentioned above – theoretical approaches; current research knowledge; and practical issues. These are the areas covered in the chapters of this book, specifically in relation to the assessment of criminal behaviour of clients in secure settings.

Information relevant to selecting a useful theoretical approach for understanding criminal behaviour comes from the work of various researchers and commentators who have reacted against the so-called 'nothing works' doctrine. This pessimism with regard to the effectiveness of offender rehabilitation derived from a review of correctional programmes by Martinson (1974), who concluded that 'the rehabilitative efforts that have been reported so far have had no appreciable effect on recidivism' (p.25). The view that 'nothing works' with offenders was readily adopted by policy-makers of the time, and a swing toward a justice model, and away from a rehabilitation model, of dealing with offenders followed. The rehabilitation model did, however, undergo a revival in the 1980s, and this has been augmented recently by a new methodology for examining the research evidence for effectiveness of rehabilitation programmes.

As Izzo and Ross (1990) point out, Martinson's review simply aggregated a large number of diverse outcome studies and presented a summary statement of whether rehabilitation worked. This type of 'this one works, that one doesn't' procedure obviously fails to do justice to the complexity of the issue. In reality, the question that should be asked is 'what works with which offenders and under what circumstances?' This question can be addressed by the statistical procedure known as meta-analysis which, as Izzo and Ross (1990) explain, is 'a technique that enables a reviewer to objectively and statistically analyse the findings of many individual studies by regarding the findings of each study as data points' (p. 135).

Recently, several meta-analyses of offender rehabilitation programmes have been conducted (e.g. Andrews *et al.*, 1990; Izzo and Ross, 1990). Of particular interest here are the findings that: (1) programmes are more likely to be effective if they are explicitly based on a theoretical principle (Izzo and Ross, 1990); and (2) the most effective programmes are based on behavioural, cognitive-behavioural, and social learning approaches (Andrews, 1990; Andrews, *et al.*, 1990). This suggests that a broadly behavioural perspective has considerable utility in working with offenders.

These conclusions have, however, been based upon studies of correctional programmes for 'normal' offenders. As we have stated, the subject matter of this book is intended to apply to offenders detained in psychiatric hospitals as well as prisons. The former are 'mentally disordered' offenders detained under the terms of the Mental Health Act (1983) under one of three possible classifications: mental illness, psychopathic disorder, and mental impairment.

An offender who is classified under the Mental Health Act is likely to be sent to hospital for treatment, rather than to prison as punishment.

Hollin (1989) points out that the relationship between mental disorder and crime may be either causal or correlational. That is, mental disorder may *cause* crime, or mental disorder and crime may *co-exist* independently of each other. Also, in some cases crime may be the cause of mental disorder. The form of treatment for mentally disordered offenders may be psychiatric, including drug treatments. For example, 'voices' may tell the schizophrenic to offend, and when the voices are controlled by drugs then the likelihood of crime may be vastly reduced. However, for many offender-patients psychological interventions are also appropriate. This is especially true for those with classifications of psychopathic disorder and mental impairment; there is no strong rationale for psychiatric treatment in such cases. Even for the mentally ill offender, control of the symptoms may not 'cure' the crime, and psychiatric treatment should be overlaid by behavioural approaches. It is our contention, therefore, that psychological approaches are relevant to most offenders, irrespective of Mental Health Act classification or psychiatric diagnosis.

The first chapter by J. Michael Lee-Evans provides the background to behaviour analysis. In emphasising the importance of this chapter to professionals, it is necessary only to refer back to the finding by Izzo and Ross (1990) that 'programs that were based on a theoretical principle were an average of five times more effective than those that had no particular theoretical basis' (p. 138). It behooves us all, then, to have a clear understanding of the theoretical principles on which we base our programmes.

This book is concerned with assessment of offending behaviour with clients detained in secure settings. In many respects, the secure setting is not the ideal environment in which to work. Andrews *et al.* (1990), in their meta-analysis, found that rehabilitation programmes conducted in residential facilities were less effective than those conducted in the community. Secure settings also present many obstacles to valid assessment; indeed, it may be precisely because valid assessment is problematic that there exists a difficulty in determining appropriate, and therefore effective, interventions. Andrews *et al.* (1990), like ourselves, are realists; they say that 'Institutions and group homes, however, remain important components of correctional systems and hence active but thoughtful service is indicated' (p. 386). A major aim of this book, therefore, is to tackle some of the problematic issues in assessment.

Several major sources of error in assessment have been described by McMurran (1991). Two of these relate to the basic approaches used by professionals in conducting assessments. First, there is a prevalent assumption that offenders *always* give distorted accounts of their behaviour in order to minimise the seriousness of their actions and their degree of responsibility for them. This assumption, along with other judgmental attitudes, can in practice lead to the use of aggressive confrontational techniques which are unlikely to elicit the desired honesty and openness required of the offender. Second, when working within the constraints of an institution, professionals often choose the easiest assessment methods, opting for interviews which can be conducted in the comfort of their own offices. To ignore the range of information available from archival sources, other people with knowledge of the offender, observation of behaviour, and analogue assessments can only be to the detriment of the assessment. These sources of error must be minimised, and methods of doing this are addressed in the second chapter on setting the scene for assessment by David M. Gresswell and Ilona Kruppa.

Many offenders detained in secure settings have committed serious offences, which are frequently seen as a priority for assessment and intervention. Three major offence types have been included in this book – sexual offending, violence, and arson. This is not to suggest that other types of offence should be ignored. Indeed, there is a strong case for paying attention to individuals who commit a large number of 'less serious' offences. Burglary of a domestic property, for example, can have profound consequences for victims, who often feel violated and insecure after an intrusion into their personal territory. Another obvious example is that of car crime; apart from the obvious dangers caused by reckless driving, members of certain communities have recently come to feel that joyriders have the upper hand and chaos reigns.

Serious offences, although they affect fewer people, obviously remain important and it is such offences that shall be addressed in this book. As stated earlier, it is important that the professional has an understanding of current knowledge relating to what factors should be focused on in assessment of any specific problem. To this end, David I. Briggs describes assessment of sexual offenders; Cynthia McDougall, Danny A. Clark, and Martin J. Fisher outline a procedure developed in prisons for the assessment of violent offenders; and Howard Jackson deals with fire-setters.

The information gathered in assessment will usually be used to recommend an appropriate disposal and/or intervention plan for the offender. However, the professional conducting the assessment may not be the person who holds the power to decide the future of the offender. This may be in the hands of a diverse number of groups or individuals such as the court, the Parole Board, the Home Office, a psychiatrist, or a prison governor. It is imperative in such cases that the professional has the ability to present assessment information cogently and persuasively in a written report. Andy Benn and Carol Brady provide guidance on report writing in Chapter 6.

Based on assessment and a written report, the professional may be required to present evidence in court as an expert witness. Many psychiatrists and other professionals are quite used to this, whereas psychologists are only now beginning to find their evidence admissible and even sought after. In the final chapter, Gisli H. Gudjonsson presents information and advice relevant to this emerging area.

This book is written by psychologists and is, therefore, naturally based on psychological theories and methods. This does not mean that the book is relevant only to psychologists. We believe that a number of professional disciplines could benefit from reading the information presented here, either simply to inform themselves of the way psychologists work, or to influence their own assessment practices. This book will be of particular interest to forensic psychiatrists, probation officers, social workers, forensic nurses, and prison personnel. Indeed, in recognition of this wider appeal, we have largely avoided the use of the designation 'psychologist' in favour of the generic term 'professional'. Since we hope that our professional readers will come from the various disciplines mentioned, and will therefore be working in a number of different types of secure setting, we have avoided use of the terms 'patient' and 'prisoner', preferring instead 'offender' or 'client'.

References

Andrews, D.A. (1990) 'Some criminological sources of anti-rehabilitation bias in the Report of the Canadian Sentencing Commission'. *Canadian Journal of Criminology*, 32, 511–524.

Andrews, D.A., Zinger, I., Hoge, R.D., Bonta, J., Gendreau, P., and Cullen, F.T. (1990) 'Does correctional treatment work? A clinically relevant and psychologically informed meta-analysis'. *Criminology*, 28, 369–404.

Hollin, C.R. (1989) *Psychology and Crime*. London: Routledge.

Izzo, R.L., and Ross, R.R. (1990) 'Meta-analysis of rehabilitation programs for juvenile delinquents'. *Criminal Justice and Behavior*, 17, 134–142.

Martinson, R. (1974) 'What works? Questions and answers about prison reform'. *The Public Interest*, 35, 22–54.

McMurran M. (1991) Assessment of criminal behaviours of clients in secure settings. Paper presented at the First Joint Spanish-British Conference on Psychology, Crime, and the Law, Pamplona, Spain.

CHAPTER 1

Background to Behaviour Analysis

J. MICHAEL LEE-EVANS

For most practitioners working with offenders, the key purpose of assessment is to provide an explanation of the individual's presenting problems. This process of identifying those factors relevant to explaining the offence and to preventing relapse is necessary for selecting relevant treatment targets, appropriate interventions and indices of change (Mash and Hunsley, 1990).

The *manner* in which we seek to explain (and subsequently treat) the offender's problems will be determined by the theoretical approach we take to understanding human behaviour. A wide variety of theories can be found in both the criminological and clinical literatures (Hagan, 1987; Hollin, 1989; Patterson, 1986). Most chapters in this volume reflect what has been described generically as the 'behavioural approach', which would embrace procedures variously described as 'behaviour therapy', 'behaviour modification', and 'cognitive behaviour-modification'. This approach has been widely adopted by clinical psychologists, and over recent decades it has assumed increasing influence in the treatment of delinquents and offenders (Morris and Braukmann, 1987). However, despite its popularity with clinical psychologists, it is an approach that has not been widely adopted by other professions (Wolpe, 1989). It is also one that remains liable to serious misunderstandings and misrepresentations (Cullen, 1991; Eysenck, 1987; Poppen, 1989). These range from the conclusion that the behavioural approach has only very limited relevance to the explanation and treatment of psychiatric disorders (Marks 1976), to the fear that it involves assumptions and procedures that are dehumanising and potentially unethical (Todd and Morris, 1983; Young and Paterson, 1981). Such fears have been fuelled by examples of 'behavioural treatment' programmes that have either pursued questionable goals (Emery and Marholin, 1977) or clearly involved major infringements of both client's rights and professional ethics (Risley, 1975).

Any potential for misunderstanding and misrepresentation has probably been compounded by the fact that the behavioural approach has itself rapidly developed and diversified in a manner that now reflects mixed and apparently contradictory points of view, to the point that its distinguishing characteristics may seem blurred. Kazdin and Wilson (1978) have concluded that:

> 'Contemporary behaviour therapy is marked by a diversity of views, a broad range of heterogeneous procedures with different rationales, and open debate about conceptual issues, methodological requirements and evidence of efficacy. In short there is no clearly agreed upon or commonly accepted definition of behaviour therapy' (p.1).

Indeed, there is evidence that not only are the diverse 'schools' within behaviour therapy poorly understood by those outside the field, but also that the different schools are themselves liable to misunderstand and misrepresent each others' approaches (Branch, 1987; Poppen, 1989). A potential consequence is that the present complexity of the field may not allow a clear correction of misunderstandings and indeed may even encourage these, so that the approach continues to be regarded with suspicion, if not overt hostility (Krasner, 1990).

The purpose of this chapter is to help the reader understand the key features of the behavioural approach, and their implications for assessment. Discussion of the origins and diversity of the behavioural approach will, it is hoped, enable the reader to recognise and refute some common misunderstandings. It is organised in two main sections: (1) origins and diversity; and (2) implications for assessment.

The diversity of the present behavioural approach is also reflected by a lack of consistency regarding terminology. Thus the terms 'behaviour modification' and 'behaviour therapy' have been used on the one hand to refer to different behavioural procedures, and on the other hand as generic terms to refer to all behavioural procedures. Similarly, the term 'behavioural analysis' has been defined variously as: 'a branch of experimental psychology, the object of which is to discover laws describing the behaviour of animals' (Rachlin, 1991); 'the process of gathering and sifting information to be used in the conduct of behaviour therapy' (Wolpe, 1982); and as being 'composed of basic applied and conceptual programmes of research which are technically and respectively the experimental analysis of behaviour, applied behaviour analysis, and the conceptual analysis of behaviour (e.g. radical behaviourism)' (Morris, 1991). In this chapter 'behaviour therapy' will be used be used as a generic term to refer to all behavioural treatment procedures, whilst 'behavioural analysis' will be used to refer to the process of assessing behaviour for the purpose of explaining a disorder and planning a relevant intervention.

Origins and Diversity

In order to appreciate both the defining characteristics of the behavioural approach, and the origins of common misunderstandings, it is important to understand the development of behaviourism. Behaviourism emerged as a reaction against earlier philosophies within general psychology. It provided the basis for the behavioural approach applied in clinical practice, which emerged as a reaction against the over-generalisation of the 'disease model' within psychiatry. After considering their origins, the apparent differences between the 'schools' of behaviour therapy will be discussed. Fundamental to this discussion are competing views over (a) the extent to which it is productive to invoke mental events and processes to explain behaviour; and (b) the manner in which 'personality' should be construed.

The development of behaviourism

In his account of the history of behaviour modification, Krasner (1990) comments that: 'Defining the nature of behaviourism is both a game and a large projective technique... An entire book could be written on the various attempts to delineate just what it is and is not and mutual contradictions abound' (p.5). Lee (1988) has listed 12 different forms of behaviourism and warns against treating 'behaviourism' in a global manner. However, all their origins can be traced to classical behaviourism, which emerged as a reaction against psychology's preoccupation with the study of mental events by means of introspection and the assumption that behaviour is to be explained in terms of the influence of mental processes. Much of earlier psychological enquiry had involved the use of introspection toward the goals of either describing the components of thoughts (e.g. ideas, images), or of defining the operation of thought processes (e.g. perception, memory). Such approaches reflected the assumptions of 'mentalism', that is, 'the practice of taking mental and psychological state to be causes of behaviour' (Zettle, 1990).

Mentalism is of course compatible with the common lay-view that ideas and thoughts cause actions. However, a number of objections can be raised to mentalism as a basis for the scientific study of behaviour. Two specific objections are most relevant to this discussion. The first is that inferences about mental states are subjective and therefore can be unreliable. Thus the same neurotic symptoms might be taken to result from quite different mental processes (e.g. substitute satisfaction of sexual urges, or attempts to avoid such satisfaction). The second objection is that mentalistic explanations can involve circular reasoning and thereby give a misleading impression of completeness. For example, anti-social behaviour may be explained by a mental disorder called 'psychopathy', which is in turn inferred from the anti-social acts it is invoked to explain (after Craighead *et al.*, 1981). It is these two issues – the level of inference involved and the adequacy of the causal explanation – that are at the heart of the debate within the behavioural approach about the precise significance that should be attached to mental events.

Classical behaviourists argued that psychology would be advanced better through the experimental study of *observable* behaviours and that explanations should be sought by assessing the impact of environmental influences on behaviour. J. B. Watson (1878–1958) is conventionally regarded as one of the principal promulgators of this movement away from introspection towards scientific method. Watson was heavily influenced by developments in the understanding of classical conditioning and argued that human behaviour could be understood in terms of learning theory in general, and of conditioning in particular. Most influential in this respect was the work of Ivan Pavlov (1849–1936) who investigated classical conditioning in a series of controlled experiments with dogs.

It is this emphasis on scientific method and on understanding behaviour in terms of principles of learning that have remained distinctive features of all subsequent behavioural approaches (Lee, 1988). However, the drawback to Watson's particular legacy has been the false conclusion that three of his additional assumptions have also remained part of contemporary behavioural approaches. First was the assumption that mental events should be excluded *completely* from the study of behaviour because they are not publicly observable and therefore elude experimental investigation. The second assumption Watson made was that complex human behaviour (including thinking) could be understood by reducing it to combinations of conditioned stimulus-response reflexes. A third assumption, perhaps erroneously accredited to Watson, is that human behaviour can be accounted for essentially in terms of learning and not in terms of inherited dispositions. In an attempt to assert the significance of learning against the instinct theories that were prevalent at the time, Watson may have been prone to exaggerate his position. Hence his famous claim that if he were given a healthy child and sufficient environmental control, he could determine what kind of adult the child would become, simply through environmental manipulation and no matter what the child's ancestry. In fact, Eysenck (1982) concludes that Watson did attach more significance to inherited dispositions than this claim might suggest; however, it is in these assumptions that one can see the origins of certain misconceptions that have persisted about the contemporary behavioural approach. These include the erroneous beliefs that it refuses to consider mental events by viewing organisms as 'black boxes'; that it is based essentially on the behaviour of non-human animals; and that it is totally environmentalistic (Todd and Morris, 1983).

Watson's assumptions can be understood when viewed against the background of his time: first as a reaction against former subjective methods of introspection and mentalistic explanations of behaviour; and second in the context of the prevailing emphasis on classical conditioning within experimental psychology. However, they have subsequently appeared overly simplistic and mechanistic because they ignore the significance and preclude the study of mental processes. As Valentine (1992) comments:

> 'A strict S-R approach, which deals only with observable stimuli and responses, has a very limited range of application. Sooner or later, the unpalatable fact becomes apparent that behaviour cannot be predicted on the basis of the stimulus alone. The same stimulus does not give rise to the same response, either across individuals or on different occasions within the same individual. It becomes necessary to postulate some processes intervening between stimulus and response'. (p.117)

We shall see below that one of the ways of understanding the subsequent diversification of the behavioural approach is in terms of different ways of accommodating the study and significance of mental events, whilst as the same time retaining the original emphasis on experimental method and on psychological theories of learning.

The emergence of Behaviour Therapy

The development of behaviour therapy can be regarded as the extension of the behaviourist emphasis on both scientific method and theories of learning to the explanation and treatment of abnormal behaviour. As such, it has been regarded as a paradigm shift within this field, which had previously been dominated almost exclusively by an extension of the medical model into what has been termed the 'intrapsychic disease model' of abnormal behaviour (Kazdin, 1978). Given the present diversity of models within the behavioural approach, it is arguable that their shared assumptions and distinct characteristics are still best understood by contrasting these with the key assumptions of the intrapsychic disease model.

The medical model of abnormal behaviour had previously done much to benefit the treatment of the 'mentally ill', first by demonstrating that in certain cases abnormal behaviour could be traced to disease processes such as infections or trauma (e.g. syphilis, head injury) and second by replacing former demonological explanations and associated punitive 'treatment' practices. However, the medical model became extended and altered to account for abnormal behaviour for which no underlying physical disease process is known to exist. In this 'intra-psychic disease model', abnormal behaviour is assumed to result from underlying psychological processes or disorders (e.g. repressed unconscious impulses). The intra-psychic disease model has been closely linked to traditional models of personality which have assumed first that there is a high degree of consistency within in an individual's behaviour, and second that this consistency can be traced to either fundamental biological and psychological needs or critical childhood experiences. McFall and McDonel (1986) described these assumptions as follows:

> 'The common underlying principle was that human beings could be best described, predicted and understood, in terms of a critical set of specific attributes within each person. While the different theorists disagree strongly about which intrapsychic attributes were critical, they all agreed that the critical attributes were intrapsychic'. (p.202)

A major impetus for intra-psychic disease model explanations of abnormal behaviour was the work of Sigmund Freud (1856–1939) and subsequent psychoanalytic schools. Three features of the intra-psychic disease model are: (a) the assumption that the behaviour that constitutes the disorder has to be regarded as a symptom of an underlying conflict; (b) the requirement that this conflict has to be identified and resolved if the symptom is to be removed; and (c) the greater significance attached to the historical (rather than current) determinants of behaviour. Craighead *et al.* (1981) outlined the implications of the intra-psychic disease model for an individual seeking treatment for social anxiety as follows:

> 'The focus is not on specific situations that appear to precipitate anxiety. Assessment focuses on the client's psycho-dynamics of personality attributes to which the anxieties assume to be traceable. Through psycho-dynamic assessment, the psychologist attempts to provide global descriptions of personality; to reconstruct the individual's psychological development; to determine how the person reacted to important psychological impulses, such as sex and aggression in the past; to determine what defence mechanisms have developed; and to determine what basic characteristic traits or psychological defects account

> for behaviour. Assessment searches for the psychological processes that are considered to be the sources of behavioural problems'. (p.101)

Kazdin (1978) summarises the sources of dissatisfaction with the intra-psychic disease model that contributed to the opportunity for the emergence of behaviour therapy. These included: (a) the inadequacies of psychoanalytic theory as a *scientific* theory, that is one that lends itself to testable (and refutable) hypotheses; (b) the lack of evidence to support the assumed relationship between the particular critical childhood experiences and adult behaviour; (c) the inadequacy of 'projective tests' and associated assessment methods in predicting behaviour; and (d) the failure of traditional psychotherapies to prove their effectiveness.

In the 1960s, it was customary to assert a range of sharp distinctions between the assumptions of the intrapsychic disease model approach and those of the behavioural approach (Eysenck, 1959). However, with the developments within both approaches, some of these former distinctions now appear less clear. For example, the original assumption that, unlike the behavioural approach, the intrapsychic disease approach would always predict symptom substitution if the treatment focused simply on the presenting problem alone now seems less tenable. Nowadays the intra-psychic disease model would not *always* predict symptom substitution in such cases. Moreover, behaviour therapists are becoming increasingly cautious about purely symptomatic treatment, and aware of the side-effects (both positive and negative) that can result from behavioural interventions (Kazdin, 1982a). Similarly, whilst it was previously customary to assume that, unlike the intrapsychic disease approach, the behavioural approach did not concern itself with the unconscious, this too now appears less defensible (Jaremko, 1986). Moreover, there have been increasing efforts in some quarters to integrate psychodynamic and behavioural approaches (Martin, 1991).

Even if such developments have served to erode some of the sharp differences previously supposed to exist between these general approaches, it is possible to define certain characteristics that continue to make the behavioural approach distinctive. However, in most cases the difference between the behavioural approach and alternative approaches (and indeed between the various schools within the behavioural approaches) is not absolute, but more one of degree and emphasis. Three defining features are most relevant to this discussion.

(1) AN EMPHASIS ON EXPERIMENTAL METHOD

The direct legacy of classical behaviourism for the behavioural approach is its emphasis on experimental method and the applications of the findings of experimental psychology, particularly principles of learning (Craighead *et al.*, 1981; Kazdin and Wilson, 1978). Levis (1990) concludes:

> 'Although the term behaviour therapy actually encompasses a variety of different techniques and theoretical justifications, each can attribute its origin to an attempt to extrapolate to the applied area basic research principles established in the learning and conditioning literature. As a result, the uniqueness of this approach is reflected in its emphasis on behaviour and its measurement, in its isolation of relevant environ-

> mental variables, in its attempt to develop precise definitions and specifiable operations, and its stress on experimental control'. (p.28)

As this quotation suggests, one of the consequences of the emphasis on experimental method is a requirement to define the presenting problem and the targets of treatment in precise and measurable terms. A second is the requirement to define the treatment procedure in sufficiently clear and precise terms to allow replication (Kazdin, 1982b).

Intrinsic to the emphasis on the application of the principles of learning to the explanation and treatment of abnormal behaviour is the assumption that behaviour disorders can be understood in terms of the same processes of learning that help to explain normal behaviour. Thus behaviour disorder can be seen as the result of a failure to learn adaptive behaviours, or of learning maladaptive behaviours, or of a combination of the two. Behaviour therapists do, of course, accept that physical attributes (including disease processes) influence the individual's capacity for learning and adaptation. However, they assume that the individual typically remains responsive to the physical and social environment, and therefore that care must always be taken to help promote adaptive, rather than maladaptive, learning. Thus when physical disease processes are known to exist, the task of the behaviour therapist is to identify how the consequences of the disease process interfere with the learning process, and thereafter to structure learning opportunities to make allowances for this. In this way behaviour therapists have contributed significantly to the habilitation and rehabilitation of people with learning disabilities and brain disorder.

However, behaviour therapists take issue in two respects with what they would regard as an overgeneralisation from the physical disease model. First, given that abnormal behaviour may be no more than the product of learning, they believe that it may be neither necessary nor useful to suspect an underlying causal physical disease process when none can be identified. Second, as is shown below, they specifically reject certain assumptions intrinsic to the intrapsychic disease approach.

(2) REJECTION OF TRADITIONAL PERSONALITY THEORY

Behaviour therapists depart from traditional personality theorists (and the associated assumptions of the intrapsychic disease approach) in two main ways. First, they place far more emphasis on the relevance of *situational* influences, rather than personality, in determining behaviour. The movement away from an emphasis on personality determinants to an emphasis on situational determinants owes much to the seminal works of Mischel (1968) and Peterson (1968) which revealed a major weakness in the traditional personality theory assumption that there is a high degree of consistency in an individual's behaviour across situations. They reviewed experimental evidence which showed that, with the exception of cognitive and ability measures, other traditional personality trait measures have been found to account typically for only 10–15 per cent of the cross-situational variance in behaviour. Although such evidence may appear contrary to our subjective impression that people do behave consistently, we are warned that there may be a number of reasons why we tend to over-estimate behavioural consistency in others.

These include the facts that human observers have a natural bias to observe consistency, and that they typically form impressions based on a limited sample in situations where their own presence alone can make for greater consistency of behaviour in others (McFall and McDonel, 1986).

As an initial reaction against the former over-emphasis on personality as a determinant of behaviour, there was a tendency within behaviour therapy to minimise the role of personality factors and to suggest that behaviour was largely, if not totally, situationally determined. Whilst this might have seemed most evident amongst radical behaviourists, even they acknowledged some degree of behavioural consistency which they explained in terms of the individual's previous learning history. However, such an extreme view is rarely taken now. Most behaviour therapists subscribe to an 'interactionist' view, which assumes that behaviour is the product of the interaction of both situational and individual influences.

This leads to the second point at which behaviour therapists differ from traditional personality theorists. In attempting to account for the way in which past learning experiences might bring about some degree of behavioural consistency across situations, they subscribe to models of 'personality' which are more understandable in terms of basic learning principles. For example, Eysenck's theory of personality makes reference to global personality constructs such as extraversion and neuroticism, originating in genetically determined biological dispositions and understandable in terms of how they contribute to individual differences in reactions to learning situations, that is, conditioning (Eysenck, 1987). Other behaviour therapists seek to explain the consistency that is found in behaviour more specifically in terms of the impact of the individual's previous experience of similar situations. Thus Mischel (1973) and Bandura (1977) suggest that the impact of past experience can be assessed by considering the cognitive and behavioural skills and the values and beliefs that the individual brings to bear on similar situations. Similarly, Staats (1986) suggests that the consistency that is observed in behaviour can be understood in terms of the impact of past experience on three basic behavioural repertoires: the language-cognitive repertoire, the sensory-motor repertoire, and the emotional-motivational repertoire. The assumption is that these repertoires develop from past experience and that these, in conjunction with the present environmental influences, will determine the individual's reactions to the present situation. Indeed Staats (1986) probably goes further than most behaviour therapists in redressing the balance between situational and 'personality' (or learning history) influences on behaviour, when he asserts:

> 'Increasingly, as the child acquires basic behavioural repertoires, what the child experiences and learns, and how the child responds, in any situation will be determined typically to a larger and larger extent by what the child brings to the situation rather than the conditions in the situation itself. To predict how a person will behave in a situation demands knowledge of that person's basic behavioural repertoires'. (p.252)

(3) A GREATER EMPHASIS ON CURRENT RATHER THAN HISTORICAL DETERMINANTS OF BEHAVIOUR

In contrast to the intrapsychic disease approach, the behavioural approach makes a careful distinction between those past experiences that may have helped explain why a problem first developed and those that currently maintain it. Whilst it may be helpful for both the patient and the therapist to be able to understand in learning terms why a problem originated, it is more important to consider how it is *currently* being maintained. Indeed, too much attention to tracing historical causes may be misleading for two reasons. First, it is difficult to validate assumptions about historical causes: given the general problems of memory and retracing the past, how can one be sure that one's recall of past events is accurate? Second, too much emphasis on tracing historical causes serves to detract attention from an analysis of those factors that currently maintain the problem behaviour. Thus the reasons why a problem started, and why it continues can be quite different. Implicit in the importance attached to this distinction is the assumption that treatment will be more effective if it focuses on identifying and modifying those factors currently maintaining the problem behaviour, rather than on identifying and somehow 'resolving' its historical determinants. Recall the example of social anxiety given previously in which the intrapsychic disease approach would attach considerable importance to identifying and resolving the historical causes of the social anxiety. One would expect the behaviour therapist to focus far more on identifying the current determinants of social avoidance, including the critical characteristics of the situations that provoke anxiety, the attitudes and skills that the individual brings to bear on such situations, and the consequences of the avoidance behaviour.

Contemporary 'Schools' of Behaviour Therapy

The main point of divergence between contemporary schools of behaviour therapy lies not in whether or not mental events should be part of a behavioural analysis, but in the manner in which they should be conceptualised and in their precise causal significance in explaining behaviour.

Kazdin and Wilson (1978) have identified four principal conceptual models within contemporary behaviour therapy. These are: (1) the Neo-behaviouristic mediational S-R model; (2) Social learning theory; (3) Cognitive behaviour modification; and (4) Applied behaviour analysis.

(1) THE NEO-BEHAVIOURISTIC MEDIATIONAL S-R MODEL

This draws heavily on principles of classical conditioning and is derived from the original work of Wolpe and Eysenck in explaining and treating anxiety-based neurotic disorders. This approach makes extensive use of assumptions about mediating cognitive states and processes, and emphasises the importance of genetically determined personality traits. Proponents of this approach are at pains to point out that mental events have always been part of a behavioural analysis, as evidenced by the focus on subjective reports of anxiety and mental imagery, and in the recognition that neurotic problems should be analysed in terms of a tripartite response system comprising behavioural, physiological, and cognitive responses (Lang, 1970). Equally, it is emphasised that the application of classical conditioning principles to human behaviour has to take special account of the role of language and thinking and should be understood not simply in terms of generating new stimulus-response connections, but in terms of the acquisition of knowledge (Eysenck, 1987). However, within this approach inferences about mental states are closely linked to operational definitions involving observable behaviours. The influence of mental events is regarded as being understandable in terms of the same processes of conditioning that apply to overt behaviour, and mental states are not assigned any independent causal status.

(2) SOCIAL LEARNING THEORY

This derives from the work of Albert Bandura (1977) and provides a more comprehensive theory of human behaviour in general, which draws upon three types of learning: classical conditioning, operant conditioning, and imitation learning. Social learning theory emphasises the importance of cognitive processes (such as attention and perception) in determining why people react differently to the same situation on different occasions, and in explaining how past experience influences future behaviour. Bandura assigns a greater degree of causal status to cognitive processes, assuming a 'reciprocal interaction' between the environment and the individual whereby the environment influences the content of mental processes on the one hand, and these in turn influence how the individual reacts and subsequently alters his environment. Bandura assigns particular causal significance to the construct of 'personal efficacy'. This refers to the belief that one is competent to deal effectively with the demands of a particular situation. Bandura argues that it is this belief that directs behaviour and that successful therapies achieve their effects by modifying this belief. However, whilst Bandura concedes that self-efficacy might be altered by therapies that attempt to tackle directly such beliefs through 'verbal persuasion', he assumes that performance-based treatments which encourage the individual to develop and experience mastery in coping with the problem situation will be significantly more effective.

(3) COGNITIVE BEHAVIOUR MODIFICATION

Although interventions derived from social learning theory might be regarded as one example of cognitive behaviour modification, the latter term has been used to refer to a wider range of procedures that similarly attach causal significance to mental events and processes, but place even greater emphasis on attempts to alter *directly* cognition as a means of changing overt behaviour. Although cognitive behaviour modification has been criticised as having no cohesive underlying theory, an attempt to articulate defining characteristics has been made by Ingram and Scott (1990). This includes the assumption that cognition mediates emotional and behavioural dysfunction; that at least some of the methods and techniques of treatment should be aimed specifically at cognitive targets; and that, whilst treatment might also include behavioural therapeutic tactics, the latter are also aimed at altering cognitions. Here they cite Beck's approach to depression in which homework assignments (a behavioural therapeutic tactic) are used, but intended to help modify dysfunctional thoughts or beliefs (Beck *et al.*, 1979).

COMMENT

The preceding 'schools' of behaviour therapy can be seen as different forms of contemporary methodological behaviourism. This is because they seek to use the experimental analysis of publicly observable behaviours to make inferences about mental processes or events. Thus, behaviour is taken to be a manifestation of mediating constructs such as personality traits, and cognitive states or processes. However, there are at least two significant points of divergence amongst the schools. The first is the level of inference that is made about cognitive processes and the second concerns their causal significance. S-R neo-behaviourists attempt to keep the level of inference about mental events as low as possible and continue to regard behaviour as being largely determined by conditioning processes. On the other hand, adherents of cognitive behaviour modification make relatively greater levels of inference and assign inferred cognitive constructs a far greater causal significance.

(4) APPLIED BEHAVIOUR ANALYSIS

Applied Behavioural Analysis refers to the applications of radical behaviourism in clinical practice. Radical behaviourism derives from the work of B. F. Skinner and has more recently been articulated as contemporary behaviourism by Morris *et al.* (1987). Skinner is most widely known for his experiments involving the principles of operant conditioning, that is, demonstrating that it is the influence of the *consequences* of behaviour in a particular situation that are most helpful for the tasks of explanation and prediction. Thus Radical Behaviourism shares the behavioural emphasis on experimental method and on understanding behaviour in terms of principles of learning.

However, radical behaviourists emphasise that their approach departs significantly from other behavioural approaches, not simply in terms of its focus on operant conditioning principles but, more important, in terms of its philosophy of science. Two distinctions are relevant here. First they argue that their purpose is to show not only how behaviour can be explained and predicted, but also how it can be *controlled*. They regard a preoccupation with mental states as a potentially misleading diversion, since this simply helps one explain the organisation and operation of human behaviour, and may lead to a neglect of environmental factors that for the purposes of control are more directly influential and easier to manipulate (Hayes and Brownstein, 1986). In this sense, radical behaviourists remain suspicious of the need to invoke hypothetical intervening variables to help explain behaviour. They fear that this will promote a preoccupation with inner 'mentalistic' causes and detract from the identification of the ultimate environmental causes of behaviour that will allow more effective control.

The preceding argument gives rise to the common misconception that radical behaviourists refuse to acknowledge the relevance of cognitive events such as thoughts and feelings. However, a second key feature of radical behaviourism is its argument that cognitive processes are no more than another form of behaviour (albeit 'covert') that should be understandable in terms of the same principles of learning as overt behaviour. The task for radical behaviourism is to explain in learning theory terms how cognitions become established and how they then come to influence behaviour. Thus the influence of cognitions is not denied but what is emphasised it is the need to identify the *environmental events* that give rise to and perpetuate cognitions and cause them to influence behaviour.

COMMENT

Given the present diversity within behaviour therapy, many behaviourally orientated clinicians resort to an 'eclectic' approach whereby they will draw on any of the wide range of behavioural and cognitive techniques proposed by the different schools according to which has most face validity in any particular case. Whilst Branch (1987) applauds such 'technical eclecticism', he cautions against any 'theoretical eclecticism' for fear that this will fail to produce both theoretical and technical advances:

> 'Eclecticism can be seductive. It is often characterised as exemplifying 'open mindedness', but it just as well can be characterised as exemplifying ignorance, or, worse yet, intellectual cowardice. Developing and understanding a theoretical position is hard work, but it is just such work that leads to scientific (and therefore technological) advancement'. (pp.79–80)

The growth of cognitive behaviour modification over recent years has been very rapid, to the point that its protagonists have described it as a paradigm shift within behaviour therapy, overtaking neo-behaviouristic and radical approaches. However, the cognitive approach has also been subject to serious criticisms. These include the fact that cognitive behaviour modification has yet to demonstrate any superior effectiveness over more conventional behavioural approaches, with the implication that any successful effects are due more to the behavioural than the cognitive components of its treatment procedures (Latimer and Sweet, 1984; Sweet and Loizeaux, 1991). Perhaps an even more important criticism that can be levelled at cognitive behaviour modification is its lack of a clear and cohesive theory and its consequent vulnerability to the criticisms of 'theoretical eclecticism' outlined above. Thus Eysenck (1982) concludes quite unequivocally that:

> '... it is quite erroneous to talk about cognitive theory or social learning theory. Neither theory exists as such, even in the least rigorous sense of the term "theory"... For a theory to exist, there must be a consistent body of propositions from which testable deductions can be made; furthermore these deductions should be different from those made by alternative and better established theories. No such body or proposition exists, and no such firm predictions can be made'. (pp.237–238)

Eysenck argues that in the treatment of anxiety disorders the beneficial treatment effects of cognitive behaviour modification methods are readily understandable in classical conditioning terms.

Radical behaviourists also argue that much of cognitive behaviour modification is understandable in basic learning theory terms. They use the term 'rule-governed behaviour' (Hayes, 1987) to describe behaviour that is primarily under the influence of thoughts, beliefs or values. Rules can be maintained, either because they are found to be accurate and useful or because compliance has been socially reinforced. It is argued that the processes of rule-forming and rule-following are themselves learned: children are explicitly encouraged to describe beliefs and feelings that are congruent with their overt behaviour. Exponents of radical behaviourism can argue that much of what is currently understood in terms of cognitive behaviour modification can be reformulated in terms of rule-governed behaviour (Jaremko, 1986; Zettle, 1990). More important, they also emphasise the dangers of pursuing cognitive explanations to the neglect of environmental determinants. For example, Biglan (1987) has argued that Bandura's attribution of causal significance to the construct of 'self-efficacy' is potentially misleading, since it is ultimately environmental influences that have established and will maintain any correspondence between an individual's 'self-efficacy' beliefs and his subsequent behaviour.

Possibly one of the consequences of the move towards cognitive behaviour modification has been the acknowledgement by radical behaviourists of their failure to address fully the implications of rule-governed, as opposed to contingency-shaped, behaviour. However, they are now paying increasing attention to these implications, for the purpose not only of demonstrating that cognitive behaviour modification effects can be explained in operant conditioning terms, but also of generating alternative treatment interventions (Hayes *et al.*, 1989; Hayes and Melancon, 1989; Poppen, 1989).

Implications For Assessment

Amongst the sources of dissatisfaction with more traditional projective and personality tests was their failure not only to predict behaviour, but also to generate relevant implications for the design of treatment interventions. Because of such shortcomings, the behavioural approach has been associated with an alternative approach to assessment, generically described as behavioural assessment. Although behavioural assessment may have a wide variety of purposes, including determining the cause of the client's problem (diagnosis), generating predictions about future behaviour (prognosis), and assessing treatment outcome (evaluation), this discussion will focus on its core function of gathering information relevant to planning appropriate interventions (i.e. behavioural analysis).

Behavioural assessment has a number of characteristics that can be recognised from the previous discussion. These include the need to define problems in terms of specific behaviours that can be observed and measured; the assumption that presenting problems do not have to be regarded as a symptom or sign of an underlying pathology; and the requirement that particular attention has to be paid to current situational influences that help maintain the problem.

Based upon the belief that presenting problems are the result of the complex interaction between biological make-up, previous learning history and current situational influences is the assumption of *aetiological heterogeneity*. This allows not only that different kinds of problem may have different determinants, but also that the same problem may have different determinants in different individuals, and even within the same individual on different occasions. This contrasts sharply with assumptions that different behavioural problems may all reflect a common aetiology, for example that many types of problem stem from psychosexual conflicts, or that the same kind of problem invariably has the same aetiology, for example that paranoia is invariably rooted in sexual identify conflict (after Haynes, 1986). Where assumptions of a common aetiology are made, treatment intervention follows in a straightforward manner from a description or classification of the presenting problem. However, within behavioural analysis no such assumptions of a common aetiology should be made and instead a careful analysis is required to identify the particular determinants of the behaviour disorder in each particular case. Thus one of the hallmarks of behavioural analysis should be individual tailoring of treatment interventions to the precise circumstances of each client (Mash and Hunsley, 1990).

The key to identifying the precise determinants of the given behaviour lies in the principle of adaptation to environmental influence that is fundamental to the behavioural emphasis on learning. This suggests that explanations of behaviour should be sought in terms of the *functions* it serves in a particular context. Thus behaviours that may appear structurally or topographically similar (e.g. different variations of verbal abuse) may require quite different explanations because they serve different functions for different individuals (e.g. demand avoidance or instrumental gain); or even different functions for the same individual in different contexts. Conversely, behaviours which appear to be topographically dissimilar (e.g. verbal abuse and crying) may have a similar explanation if the individual has learned that they can have the same functional value (e.g. gaining individual attention or reassurance). In the latter case, the two topographically dissimilar behaviours would be described as falling in the same *functional response class*. One of the implications of a functional response class is that treatment which focuses simply on reducing one inappropriate response (verbal abuse) could result in the increased frequency of a second functionally-related inappropriate response (crying) if no attempt has been made to teach a new and more appropriate way of achieving the desired goal.

This distinction between the topography (or appearance) of a behaviour and its function provides an important contrast between traditional and behavioural diagnostic systems. Within a traditional approach, diagnosis depends on the *appearance* of the symptoms (anxiety, depression, thought-disorder, etc.) and patients are allocated to diagnostic categories that are assumed to have implications for aetiology, prognosis and treatment. However, within a behavioural approach, such assumptions appear questionable since the same symptoms may serve quite different functions and therefore require quite different intervention strategies. Thus Haynes (1991) asserts that: 'Intervention programmes cannot be based solely on a diagnostic or classification category such as 'depression', 'substance abuse', 'hyperactivity' or 'hypertension', because such topographically based diagnoses do not identify which of many possible determinants are operational for a particular person' (p.435).

The term 'functional analysis' is applied to this process of identifying the precise determinants of a client's problems, with a special emphasis on those that may be manipulated as part of a treatment programme (Haynes and O'Brien, 1990). The task of the analysis is to understand the behaviour disorder in terms of the particular functions it serves. Consequently, the task of treatment becomes either to reduce the functional value of the maladaptive behaviour or to facilitate a more adaptive means of achieving the same end. Strictly speaking, functional analysis can be independent of any particular theoretical approach (Owens and Ashcroft, 1982). The assumption is that any functional analysis is validated in terms of the accuracy of the predictions it generates concerning the most effective means of altering behaviour. Nonetheless, the practice of functional analysis in clinical psychology has been associated most with the behavioural approach wherein the provision of a functional analysis is regarded as one of the primary aims of behavioural assessment.

A framework for functional analysis

A number of different models have been proposed as a framework for identifying sources of information relevant to conducting a functional analysis (see Barrios, 1988; Mash and Hunsley, 1990). Each involves an elaboration of the core assumption that any behaviour can be best understood in terms of its relationship with preceding and consequent events (or stimuli). This is the A:B:C unit of analysis, that is, Antecedent : Behaviour : Consequence. One of the more popular models is described under the acronym SORC (Goldfried and Sprafkin, 1976; Nelson and Hayes, 1981, 1986; see Table 1.1). Here, R refers to the response or behaviour of interest; S (antecedent stimuli) and C (consequences) refer to the immediate environmental controlling variables; and O refers to variables involving the state of the organism, including physical factors, physiological status and past learning history.

Table 1.1: The SORC framework

S *Antecedent Stimuli*	*O* *Organism Variables*	*R* *Response Variables*	*C* *Consequent Stimuli*
Setting Events Trigger Events	Physiological Factors; Behavioural Skills; Cognitive Skills; Beliefs, values, needs	Frequency; Intensity; Duration; Relationship to other behaviours	Immediacy; Probability

S: ANTECEDENT STIMULI

Although it is relevant to consider both distal (i.e. historical, distant) and proximal (i.e. recent, close) antecedent events (Herbert, 1987), more significance is usually attached to the latter. Antecedent events may, through classical conditioning, come to elicit conditioned emotional responses such as anxiety, anger or sexual arousal. At the same time they may, through operant conditioning, have developed power as discriminative stimuli, that is as sources of information concerning the probability that a particular behaviour is likely to be followed by certain consequences. Relevant antecedent stimuli may include specific observable triggers (actions or events), and/or more general setting conditions that increase the probability of behaviours occurring. These might include external conditions such as an impoverished or over-crowded environment, or internal setting conditions such as fatigue or mood state. The task in functional analysis is to specify as clearly as possible the precise antecedent stimulus conditions that are associated with the target behaviour.

O: ORGANISM VARIABLES

These require us to take account of the various physiological factors that influence the individual's development and behaviour. These can include inherited dispositions, physical capacities and appearance, the sequelae of illness or injury, and the physiological consequences of acquired habits or preferences (e.g. eating disorders, smoking or drug abuse). It is by consideration of such influences on adaptation that a functional analysis would take account of the full range of physical factors (identified within the medical model) which are of potential relevance to any given disorder.

An important set of organism variables concerns the impact of the individual's past learning history on the experience he or she brings to bear on a given situation (i.e., the behavioural conception of 'personality' referred to previously). These include the individual's repertoires of knowledge, cognition and behavioural skills, and also beliefs, needs and values. Of particular relevance will be the individual's capacity for social reasoning, for realistic self-evaluation, and for adopting strategies for effective self-control.

R: RESPONSES

The tradition within functional analysis has been to focus on discrete target responses and on determining the precise conditions under which they occur. Thus presenting problems have to be defined precisely in terms of behaviours that can be observed and measured. Typical measures of target responses include frequency, intensity, and duration.

Increasing concern is being shown for understanding the manner in which the individual's responses (or behaviour) may be internally organised and the implications of this for assessment and intervention.[1] One approach recognises that any problem may have cognitive, physiological and motor components which may not always be consistent or in synchrony with each other. Thus there may be a discordance between a phobic patient's overt-avoidance behaviour, self-report of anxiety and physiological measures of arousal. The implication is that a comprehensive functional analysis should include an

1 Where relationships between behaviours can be determined, one may have to consider the potential positive or negative 'side-effects' of altering one behaviour on those other behaviours related to it. Alternatively, one might entertain the possibility of altering an inaccessible target behaviour indirectly by seeking instead to alter a second more accessible behaviour that is functionally related to the first.

assessment of the target behaviour across all three response modalities. Although this tripartite response system is now a commonly-accepted framework for investigating response co-variation, the precise significance of asynchrony remains a matter of speculation and debate (Nelson and Hayes, 1986). Moreover, fears have been expressed that the tripartite response system may be an over-simplification and substantially misrepresent the potential complexity of behavioural organisation (Strosahl and Linehan, 1986).

Other frameworks have been proposed for conceptualising the manner in which an individual's responses may be organised (e.g. Evans, 1985; Kanfer, 1985; Voeltz and Evans, 1982). These include the concept of *functional response class* where it is assumed that behaviours can be related because they serve similar functions. It was noted above that decreasing the frequency of one inappropriate behaviour could lead to an increase in the frequency of a second related inappropriate behaviour if no other means of achieving the desired goal have been taught. Similarly, once a new, more appropriate response has been taught and is naturally reinforced, then it could be hypothesised that any additional steps taken to reduce the frequency of one inappropriate behaviour may also reduce the frequency of the second functionally-related inappropriate behaviour.

A second model of response co-variation involves the assumption that certain behaviours will emerge in a standard sequence or *response chain*. This model is typically incorporated into relapse prevention programmes with offenders, wherein it is assumed that the offence may represent a final step in a predictable sequence (or sequences) of behaviour. For example, it might be discovered that one client's sexual offences have typically been preceded by a sequence involving an aversive interaction with an adult female; resulting in feelings of resentment and anger; leading to the client walking the neighbourhood alone; then to walking through parks or children's play areas; and then to sighting a potential victim; and then committing the offence. When such chains can be identified, one aim of treatment can be to substitute an earlier response in the chain (e.g. teaching assertiveness skills and alternative means of anger control) to prevent the subsequent responses from occurring.

A third model for considering the possible organisation of behaviour involves the notion of *skill hierarchies*, that is, the assumption that certain skills have to be acquired as prerequisites to the acquisition of others. This requires consideration of the organisation of behaviour from a developmental perspective and is receiving increasing attention (Masten and Braswell, 1991). Finally, in an attempt to gain a better understanding of the organisation of behaviour and its implications for assessment and intervention, behavioural assessors are paying increasing attention to formal psychiatric classification systems (e.g. DSM 111-R). These systems assume that certain symptoms or behaviours occur together within particular diagnostic categories, and therefore provide a source of hypotheses about possible behavioural relationships (Mash and Hunsley, 1990; Nelson and Hayes, 1986).

The preceding discussion is only a brief overview of some of the more common models for considering the manner in which behaviour might be internally organised. (For a more thorough discussion see Evans 1985; Kanfer 1985.) This literature makes clear the obligation for the therapist to consider carefully the possible relationship between the client's target behaviours and other behaviours. However, this often has to be conducted at the level of informed speculation as clear models and guidelines are often lacking. As Haynes (1991) concludes: 'Despite their importance and potential clinical utility, little is known about which behaviours tend to co-vary together, the degree of co-variance among behaviours in the same response class, the generality of response classes across people, or the factors that control covariation among behaviours' (p.439).

C: CONSEQUENCES

Here one needs to consider the consequences that maintain the inappropriate behaviour, which may include positive reinforcement (i.e., gaining a reward) or negative reinforcement (i.e., escape or avoidance). The reinforcing events do not have to occur on every occasion to control the behaviour; once the behaviour has been acquired, occasional or intermittent reinforcement can be sufficient to maintain it.

The immediate or short-term consequences of a behaviour typically exert greater control than more distant or remote consequences. Behaviours that are anti-social or otherwise perceived as problematic or self-defeating (e.g. stealing, social avoidance, drug-taking) typically have both short-term reinforcing consequences and longer-term punishing consequences. The problems typically persist because the client's behaviour is controlled more strongly by immediate reinforcers. Thus many offenders have been found to display impulsive behaviour, inability to defer gratification, and to be poor at anticipating the longer-term consequences of their behaviour. Equally relevant to understanding the impact of consequences on problematic behaviour is their probability. The power of more immediate reinforcing consequences becomes all the greater in controlling behaviour if the punishing longer-term consequences have a low probability of occurrence. Thus an offender's behaviour might be maintained by the high probability of immediate reinforcement, particularly when the punishing consequences of being caught are perceived as being remote in time and low in probability (Wilson and Herrnstein, 1985).

Both Bandura (1968) and Kanfer and Grimm (1977) have proposed systems for categorising the possible determinants of problem behaviour that might be identified by a functional analysis. Kanfer and Grimm have also made suggestions concerning the general treatment strategy that might be indicated by each category. These systems are by no means comprehensive and focus exclusively on the SOC components of the SORC framework, that is, they do not consider possible issues arising from response co-variation. Equally, they do not consider in detail the relevance of physiological factors. Nonetheless, within these limitations they do provide some useful illustrations of possible issues that might arise in a functional analysis. These include the following:

(1) ANTECEDENT STIMULI

(A) DEFECTIVE STIMULUS CONTROL

This refers to generalisation problems. In the case of over-generalisation, a behaviour which is appropriate in certain situations also occurs in situations where it is inappropriate. An example of over-generalisation might be engagement in overly familiar behaviour with a relative stranger due to failure to discriminate between cues that signal polite friendliness and those that signal more intimate interest. In some cases it is possible that physical or sexual assault are associated not with selective attention to and enjoyment of the victim's distress (i.e. sadistic enjoyment) but more with the failure to attend to or discriminate on the basis of relevant social cues.

In the case of failure to generalise, a behaviour occurs in certain situations where it is appropriate but fails to occur in other situations where it is also appropriate. Failure to generalise adaptive behaviour is a common problem in treatment interventions. Unless deliberate steps are taken to promote generalisation, adaptive behaviours that have been acquired and practised within an artificial treatment setting, may fail to generalise to the natural environment (see for example Kazdin, 1989, Chapter 11).

(B) INAPPROPRIATE STIMULUS CONTROL

Through the process of classical conditioning, the fortuitous association of neutral stimuli with intense emotional experiences can lead to stimuli eliciting inappropriate responses. This is most evident in the case of phobias where innocuous stimuli come to elicit totally irrational fears. To return to the example of sexual violence, one possibility is that the client has experienced (either directly or vicariously) situations involving anger and violence as an antecedent to sexual intimacy. In such circumstances, it is possible for the violent situation itself to develop sexually arousing properties, particularly in view of the potential for misperceiving the different states of anger and sexual arousal (see below).

(C) ENVIRONMENTAL LIMITATIONS

Here the main problem may be that the client's social environment does not provide opportunities for the development of adaptive behaviours. For example, particular lifestyles or situations may not afford adequate opportunities for the development of adaptive social and sexual relationships. Some institutional environments may not afford sufficient or adequate opportunities to express anger or frustration or to gain personal support and reassurance in legitimate ways.

(D) DEFECTIVE 'INTERNAL' STIMULUS CONTROL

The preceding examples really relate to problems arising from the 'external' environment. However, as a result of experience, people develop beliefs and expectations that can also serve to mediate or prompt their own behaviours. Thus certain problems could be due to maladaptive self-prompting, for example 'I am helpless'; 'I am unattractive'; 'I mustn't offend other people'. Similarly, ruminating on possible catastrophes or perceived insults may mediate inappropriate emotional responses, raising anxiety and anger levels. In some instances individuals may lack the ability to discriminate (and therefore correctly attribute) their emotional feelings, for example confusing anger for anxiety; excitement for fear, and so on.

2. ORGANISM VARIABLES

In addition to the limitations imposed by physiological factors, one can consider the adequacy of the client's existing behavioural repertoires for dealing more adaptively with the problem situation. Kanfer and Grimm (1977) have listed a potential range of behavioural deficits including:

(a) A lack of relevant information or knowledge, for example, knowledge of social or sub-cultural norms.

(b) A lack of social interaction skills, for example social skills, assertiveness skills.

(c) A lack of 'self-directing' skills, that is, an inability to organise one's time and activities and plan ahead.

(d) Self-reinforcement deficits, that is, an inability to self-evaluate realistically.

(e) Self-monitoring deficits, that is, a lack of awareness of the precise circumstances under which given behaviours occur and the reasons for this.

(f) Self-control deficits, that is, the inability to exercise self-controlling responses – for example 'calming'; resisting temptation by means of avoidance; focusing on longer-term consequences or competing cognitive imagery.

(g) A lack of sensitivity to reinforcers, that is, because of lack of exposure to activities or situations, potential reinforcers that exist in the client's social environment may have lost their incentive value; for example, through prolonged deprivation or non-attendance, a client may have lost interest in engaging in a range of social or recreational activities that previously served to relieve the states or boredom or social isolation that typically precede his offending behaviour.

(h) Deficits in living skills, that is, an inability to deal with the normal demands of independent living – for example domestic skills, transport, shopping.

Implicit in the above classification are a range of cognitive or social reasoning skills which have been considered far more explicitly and systematically by those working with offender groups. It has been suggested that offenders can exhibit particular deficits in their ability to consider and evaluate the consequences of their actions, to consider a range of alternative solutions to social dilemmas or problems, and to plan how a particular solution might be executed. Deficits in perspective-taking have also been identified. These and other cognitive deficits and their implications for treatment have been considered in detail by Ross and Fabiano (1985).

3. CONSEQUENCES

The relevance of inappropriate self-generated consequences (i.e., self-evaluation) has already been considered above. Self-evaluation styles are themselves typically the product of the social reinforcement that the client has previously received (and continues to receive) from valued others. For example, the belief that it is manly and therefore good to be physically aggressive when provoked is likely to have been the product of past modelling and encouragement received within family or peer group settings.

Other problems that could be associated with the consequences of a behaviour include: (a) the failure of the natural environment to offer sufficient encouragement for appropriate behaviour, for example resolving problems through reasoned discussion ceases because of a partner's failure to respond; and (b) encouragement of undesirable behaviour; for example, within a delinquent sub-culture, anti-social acts may receive explicit peer group approval. Kanfer and Grimm (1977) also point out how encouragement for appropriate behaviour can prove ineffective if the form of the encouragement is not valued or if the encouragement is offered inconsistently.

The focus of Functional Analysis

To summarise, functional analysis is based on the premise that a problem behaviour serves a particular *function* for the individual. Consequently, successful treatment involves first understanding the nature of that function and then ensuring either that the behaviour ceases to have functional value, and/or that it is replaced by more adaptive behaviour with the same functional value. In conducting a functional analysis it is therefore useful to consider not only the various determinants that help maintain a problem behaviour, but also those determinants that might prevent an alternative, more appropriate behaviour from developing. One possibility is that there has been little opportunity for the adaptive behaviours to occur. Another is that the individual does not have the necessary skills or confidence to perform the adaptive behaviour successfully. The third possibility is that the individual's social environment does not encourage and may even punish what would normally be regarded as adaptive behaviour. For example, a functional analysis of a client's sexual offending may reveal that sexual interest has been prompted by pictures, films and fantasies depicting young children and reinforced through masturbation. The same sex offender may fail to develop the kinds of social and intimate relationships that might lead to the development of more acceptable sexual interests, either because he has no opportunities to do so, or because he lacks the skills and/or confidence to do so successfully, or alternatively because such relationships are actively discouraged. Thus, in conducting a functional analysis of a presenting problem, it is useful to address two issues: what is maintaining the occurrence of the inappropriate behaviour? and what is maintaining the non-occurrence of more adaptive behaviour?

So far, functional analysis has been considered as a means of gaining an understanding of the determinants of a client's problem behaviour that will identify issues relevant to planning treatment intervention and assessing change. However, a functional analysis can be applied to understanding *any* behaviour, not simply the presenting problem. As part of a comprehensive pre-intervention assessment, it is also relevant to consider a functional analysis of those behaviours which are required for an individual to become and remain fully engaged in the treatment programme. These will include the appropriateness and accessibility of treatment services, the individual's acceptance of a need for treatment, and any expectations held concerning the proper nature and likely benefits of this. The last two are likely to have been influenced significantly by past experiences. It will also be important to consider whether the client has the appropriate cognitive and social skills to engage fully in the proposed treatment procedure. Similarly, one should consider carefully what both the short- and long-term consequences of engaging in treatment are likely to be. Again in those cases where it is not possible to conduct a functional analysis of the presenting problem, and/or where it is not considered feasible to offer effective treatment, it will nonetheless be useful to consider as potential targets those behaviours relevant to co-operating with support and supervision. (This is because such behaviour may allow the offender to be moved to a less secure setting.) Here one might consider what kinds of setting conditions and events are relevant for prompting and maintaining the client's co-operation; what kinds of cognitive and behavioural skills the client might require to benefit from supervision; what kinds of beliefs and values are relevant to the client's acceptance of the need for this; and what consequences are necessary to ensure that co-operation and compliance occur.

The practice of Functional Analysis

It is clear that functional analysis calls for a detailed knowledge of the precise circumstances under which the target behaviour occurs. Given the acknowledgement that behaviour varies across situations, a critical issue in behavioural assessment is that the more dissimilar the assessment situation is from that in which the target behaviour normally occurs, the less confident one can be that the information obtained is relevant and valid. For this reason, behavioural assessment has traditionally emphasised the need whenever possible to observe directly the target behaviour in the natural situation, either by an independent observer and/or by the client keeping an ongoing personal record. However, in many circumstances such direct observation is not possible and consequently behavioural assessors will also use structured and unstructured interviews with the client and key members of his social environment, as well as checklists, questionnaires, psychophysiological tests and analogue tests such as role-play. As part of the reaction against traditional approaches to personality and assessment, behavioural assessors initially rejected the relevance of traditional tests. However, there is now an increasing willingness to entertain the potential relevance of some traditional testing methods (particularly measures of cognitive abilities) and similarly there is growing awareness of the need to establish formally the reliability and validity of behavioural assessment methods (Mash and Hunsley, 1990).

Despite the central role of functional analysis in behavioural assessment, several authors have commented on what can be a significant gap between theory and practice. Thus Haynes (1986) has suggested that: 'Despite the importance attached to pre-intervention assessment in behavioural construct systems, there is significant variability in the degree to which behavioural intervention programmes are dependent on or reflect the results of pre-intervention assessments' (p.388).

In a review of a 156 behavioural case studies published between 1985 and 1988, Haynes and O'Brien (1990) found that treatment decisions were based on pre-intervention data on functional relationships in only 20 per cent of the cases. Similarly, Hawkins (1986) has expressed doubts that observational assessment procedures are used to any large extent outside academic settings.

There appear to be two principal reasons for this discrepancy between theory and practice. First, it has to be acknowledged that, within the practical constraints of most clinical practice, undertaking a comprehensive behavioural assessment can be impractical because its requirements seem too costly and time-consuming and significantly delay the onset of treatment. Therefore when a functional analysis is attempted, it can often be hasty and superficial (Haynes, 1991). A second reason why a functional analysis may not be undertaken may be because of its anticipated utility. Haynes (1986) points out that in those circumstances where individuals present with similar problems, that typically share a similar functional explanation (e.g. a simple phobia maintained by escape and avoidance), and where a powerful treatment is known to exist (e.g. systematic desensitisation), it may not seem necessary or useful to undertake a comprehensive functional analysis since this might not add significantly to the intervention design or to its effectiveness.

It is probably because of both the preceding considerations (practicality and utility) that there has been a tendency to develop standardised behavioural treatment programmes, for example programmes for stress management, anger control, and sexual offending. Whilst the authors of such programmes will typically emphasise the need for a careful pre-intervention assessment before allocating clients to such programmes, it can be all too tempting for the busy clinician to curtail the pre-intervention stage and to allocate the client uncritically to existing programmes. Haynes (1986) emphasises the need to weigh carefully the social and personal consequences of what are legitimate cost-effectiveness decisions:

> 'The social and personal significance of benefits associated with pre-intervention assessment varies across behaviour problems. A 10% failure rate for a standardised intervention programme for nail-biting may not warrant extensive pre-intervention assessment to design individualised intervention programmes that would reduce the rate to 5 per cent. However, more extensive pre-intervention assessment may be warranted by a proportionate increase in the effectiveness of interventions for suicidal, self-mutilatory or socially violent behaviours'. (p.393)

Conclusion

The practical problems of adopting a behavioural approach within secure settings have previously been reviewed by Laycock (1979) and Lee-Evans (1982). From the previous discussion one can anticipate that the main areas of difficulty in conducting an adequate functional analysis will include:

(1) The fact that the client may be a poor informant either because of low motivation, difficulty in verbalising his feelings and experiences, or inadequate memory for past events; and

(2) The fact that it is not possible to observe directly relevant target behaviours within the natural environment and that any

observations conducted with the artificial environment of the institution may be very misleading.

Such difficulties have been well-documented by Crawford (1980) in his account of work in a secure hospital:

> 'The dictates of security mean that we cannot generally expose the patient to his problem situation or to problem stimuli. Patients are not allowed alcohol so one has no way of knowing whether patients with a history of excessive drinking have changed...contact with female patients is only under controlled and supervised conditions so that we cannot assess whether sex offenders have learnt to exercise self-control... Conversely there may be some behaviour problems which are precipitated by the hospital but which disappear once the patient is released. Problems such as institutionalisation, reaction against authority, some forms of aggression and sexual frustration, may be caused by the unnatural and artificial nature of the secure environment. There is a danger that such behaviour will be misinterpreted as evidence of the unsuitability of the patient for discharge'.

Such considerations oblige the clinician to be concerned as much with altering and improving the social environment of the secure setting as with assessing and modifying the behaviour of clients within it. Nonetheless there will inevitably remain a significant discrepancy between the artificial environment of any secure institution and the natural environments where offences have previously occurred and to which the client will eventually return. It is because of such a discrepancy that behavioural assessors are obliged to consider adopting either of two tactics:

(1) Placing particular reliance on the use of psycho-physiological and analogue measures (e.g. role-play tests of social skills); or

(2) Making assumptions about the internal organisation or co-variance of responses within the client, in the hope that target behaviours which do have a direct relationship to the offending behaviours can be identified and assessed within the institution.

This latter approach usually involves one of two assumptions. Either (a) a cognitive approach is adopted, whereby it is assumed that the offending behaviour has been mediated by underlying beliefs or attitudes which can be validly assessed and modified within the institutional setting; or (b) it is assumed that the offending behaviour has occurred because the individual has significant cognitive or behavioural deficits which have prevented the development of more adaptive behaviours. Such an assumption underlies the common emphasis found within offender programmes on teaching educational, vocational, social and problem-solving skills (Braukmann and Morris, 1987).

With both the above general approaches, important validation questions are raised. For example, are the psychophysiological or analogue measures used reliable in discriminating between offender and non-offender groups and in predicting future behaviour? How valid is the assumption that identifying and altering fundamental beliefs or values or teaching new adaptive skills will decrease the propensity for offending behaviour? To what extent will the client's present and future environments naturally maintain such changes?

This chapter opened by referring to the misunderstandings and misapplications that have been associated previously with the behavioural approach. Part of the misunderstanding has been based on confusion concerning definitions and scope. This confusion can include errors of over- as well as under-inclusion. Over-inclusion errors assume that the approach embraces other behaviour change interventions, such as electro-convulsive therapy, psycho-surgery or brain-washing (Young and Patterson, 1981). Under-inclusion errors assume that it has only restricted scope and is limited to a range of basic anxiety management and reward and punishment procedures. The latter misunderstanding can also be associated with the assumption that behavioural treatments are essentially 'common sense' and easy to apply.

It is hoped that this chapter will have served to make clear the distinguishing characteristics of behavioural analysis, and shown that it represents a comprehensive approach towards understanding complex human behaviour. This chapter is intended to illustrate the promise that behavioural analysis holds out as a conceptual model for analysing offending behaviour, and for planning treatment interventions. However, in most cases offenders do not present with discrete, homogeneous problems for which powerful and obvious treatments already exist. Moreover the problems of working within the artificial constraints of a secure environment are clear. Therefore the costs of any superficial grasp of behavioural analysis, inadequate functional analysis, or hasty pre-intervention assessment could be heavy.

References

Bandura, A. (1968) 'A social learning interpretation of psychological dysfunctions'. In P. London and D. Rosenham (eds) *Foundations of Abnormal Psychology*. New York: Holt, Rinehart and Winston.

Bandura, A. (1977) *Social Learning Theory*. Englewood Cliffs, New Jersey: Prentice Hall.

Barrios, B.A. (1988) 'On the changing nature of behavioural assessment'. In A.S. Bellack and M. Hersen (eds) *Behavioral Assessment: A Practical Handbook, Third Edition*. New York: Pergamon Press.

Beck, A.T., Rush, A.J., Shaw, B.F. and Emery, E. (1979) *Cognitive Therapy of Depression*. New York: Guilford Press.

Biglan, A. (1987) 'A behaviour-analytic critique of Bandura's self-efficacy theory'. *The Behavior Analyst*, 10, 1–15.

Branch, M.N. (1987) 'Behaviour analysis: A conceptual and empirical base for behaviour therapy'. *The Behavior Therapist*, 4, 79–84.

Braukmann, C.J. and Morris, E.K. (1987) 'Behavioural approaches to crime and delinquency'. In. E.K. Morris and C.J. Braukmann (eds) *Behavioral Approaches to Crime and Delinquency*. New York: Plenum Press.

Craighead, W.E., Kazdin, A.E. and Mahoney, M.J. (1981) *Behavior Modification: Principles, Issues and Applications, Second Edition*. Boston: Houghton Mifflin.

Crawford, D. (1980) Problems in the assessment and treatment of sexual offenders in closed institutions: And some solutions. Paper presented to the British Psychological Society Conference, London.

Cullen, C. (1991) 'Radical behaviourism and its influence on clinical therapies'. *Behavioural Psychotherapy*, 19, 47–58.

Emery, R.E. and Marholin, D. (1977) 'An applied analysis of delinquency: The irrelevancy of relevant behaviour'. *American Psychologist*, 32, 860–873.

Evans, I.M. (1985) 'Building systems models as a strategy for target behaviour selection in clinical assessment'. *Behavioral Assessment*, 7, 21–32.

Eysenck, H.J. (1959) 'Learning theory and behaviour therapy'. *Journal of Mental Science*, 105, 61–75.

Eysenck, H.J. (1982) 'Neo-behaviouristic (S-R) theory'. In E.T. Wilson and C.M. Franks (eds) *Contemporary Behaviour Therapy*. New York: Guilford Press.

Eysenck, H.J. (1987) 'Behaviour therapy'. In H.J. Eysenck and I. Martin (eds) *Theoretical Foundations of Behaviour Therapy*. New York: Plenum Press.

Goldfried, M.R. and Sprafkin, J.N. (1976) 'Behavioural personality assessment'. In J.T. Spence, R.C. Carson, and J.W. Thibaut (eds) *Behavioral Approaches to Therapy*. New Jersey: General Learning Press.

Hagan, J. (1987) *Modern Criminology: Crime, Criminal Behaviour and its Control*. Singapore: McGraw-Hill.

Hawkins, R.P. (1986) 'Selection of target behaviours'. In R.O. Nelson and S.C. Hayes (eds) *Conceptual Foundations of Behavioural Assessment*. New York: Guilford Press.

Hayes, S.C. (1987) 'A contextual approach to therapeutic change'. In N.S. Jacobson (ed) *Psychotherapists in Clinical Practice: Cognitive and Behavioral Perspectives*. New York: Guilford Press.

Hayes S.C. and Brownstein, A.J. (1986) 'Mentalism, behaviour-behaviour relations and a behaviour-analytic view of the purposes of science'. *The Behavior Analyst*, 9, 175–190.

Hayes, S.C. and Melancon, S.M. (1989) 'Comprehensive distancing, paradox and the treatment of emotional avoidance'. In L.M. Ascher (ed) *Therapeutic Paradox*. New York: Guilford Press.

Hayes, S.C., Kohlenberg, B.S. and Melancon, S.M. (1989) 'Avoiding and altering rule-control as a strategy of clinical intervention'. In S.C. Hayes (ed) *Rule-Governed Behavior: Cognition, Contingencies and Instructional Control*. New York: Plenum Press.

Haynes, S.N. (1986) 'The design of intervention programmes.' In R.O. Nelson and S.C. Hayes (eds) *Conceptual Foundations of Behavioral Assessment*. New York: Guilford Press.

Haynes, S.N. (1991) 'Behavioural assessment'. In M. Hersen, A.E. Kazdin, and A.S. Bellack (eds) *The Clinical Psychology Handbook, Second Edition*. New York: Pergamon Press. York

Haynes, S.N. and O'Brien, W.H. (1990) 'Functional analysis in behaviour therapy'. *Clinical Psychology Review*, 10, 649–668.

Herbert, M. (1987) *Behavioural Treatment of Children with Problems: A Practice Manual*. London: Academic Press.

Hollin, C.R. (1989) *Psychology and Crime: An Introduction to Criminological Psychology*. London: Routledge.

Ingram, R.E. and Scott, W.D. (1990) 'Cognitive behaviour therapy'. In A.S. Bellack, M. Hersen, and A.E. Kazdin (eds) *International Handbook of Behavior Modification and Therapy, Second Edition*. New York: Plenum Press.

Jaremko, M.E. (1986) 'Cognitive behaviour modification: The shaping of rule-governed behaviour'. In W. Dryden and W.C. Golden (eds) *Cognitive Behavioural Approaches to Psychotherapy*. London: Harper and Row.

Kanfer, F.H. (1985) 'Target selection for clinical change programmes'. *Behavioral Assessment*, 7, 7–20.

Kanfer, F.H. and Grimm, L.E. (1977) 'Behavioural analysis: Selecting target behaviours in the interview'. *Behavior Modification*, 1, 7–28.

Kazdin, A.E. (1978) *History of Behavior Modification*. Baltimore: University Park Press.

Kazdin, A.E. (1982a) 'Symptom substitution, generalization and response co-variation: Implications for psychotherapy outcome'. *Psychological Bulletin*, 9, 349–365.

Kazdin, A.E. (1982b) 'History of behaviour modification'. In A.S. Bellack, M. Hersen, and A.E. Kazdin (eds) *International Handbook of Behavior Modification and Theory, First Edition*. New York: Plenum Press.

Kazdin, A.E. (1989) *Behavior Modification in Applied Settings*. California: Brooks/Cole Publishing Co.

Kazdin, A.E. and Wilson G.T. (1978) *Evaluation of Behavior Therapy: Issues, Evidence and Research Strategies*. Massachussetts: Bollinger.

Krasner, L. (1990) 'History of behaviour modification'. In A.S. Bellack, M. Hersen, and A.E. Kazdin (eds) *International Handbook of Behavior Modification and Theory, First Edition*. New York: Plenum Press.

Lang, P. (1970) 'Stimulus control, response control and the desensitization of fear'. In D. Lewis (ed) *Learning Approaches to Therapeutic Behavior*. Chicago: Aldine.

Latimer, P.R. and Sweet, A.A. (1984) 'Cognitive versus behavioural procedures in cognitive behaviour therapy: A critical review of the evidence'. *Journal of Behavior Therapy and Experimental Psychiatry*, 15, 9–22.

Laycock, G. (1979) 'Behaviour modification in prisons'. *British Journal of Criminology*, 19, 400–415.

Lee, V.L. (1988) *Beyond Behaviorism*. New Jersey: Lawrence Erlbaum Associates.

Lee-Evans, J.M. (1982) 'The adult offender'. In R.E. McCreadie (ed) *Rehabilitation in Psychiatric Practice*. London: Pitman Books.

Levis, D.J. (1990) 'The experimental and theoretical foundations of behaviour modification'. In A.S. Bellack, M. Hersen, and A.E. Kazdin (eds) *International Handbook of Behavior Modification and Theory, First Edition*. New York: Plenum Press.

Marks, I.M. (1976) 'Current status of behavioural psychotherapy: Theory and practice'. *American Journal of Psychiatry*, 133, 253–261.

Martin, P.R. (1991) 'Theoretical and empirical foundations of behaviour therapy'. In P.R. Martin (ed) *Handbook of Behavior Therapy and Psychological Science*. New York: Pergamon Press.

Mash, E.J. and Hunsley, J. (1990) 'Behaviour assessment: A contemporary approach'. In A.S. Bellack, M. Hersen, and A.E. Kazdin (eds) *International Handbook of Behavior Modification and Theory, First Edition.* New York: Plenum Press.

Masten, A.S. and Braswell, L. (1991) 'Developmental psychopathology: An integrative framework'. In P.R. Martin (ed) *Handbook of Behavior Therapy and Psychological Science.* New York: Pergamon Press.

McFall, R.M. and McDonel, E.C. (1986) 'The continuing search for units of analysis in psychology: Beyond persons, situations, and their interactions'. In R.O. Nelson, and S.C. Hayes (eds) *Conceptual Foundations of Behavioral Assessment.* New York: Guilford Press.

Mischel, W. (1968) *Personality and Assessment.* New York: Wiley.

Mischel, W. (1973) 'Towards a cognitive social learning reconceptualisation of personality'. *Psychological Review,* 80, 252–283.

Morris, E.K. (1991) 'The contextualism that is behaviour analysis: An alternative to cognitive psychology'. In A. Still and A. Costall (eds) *Against Cognitivism.* Hemel Hempstead: Harvester Wheatsheaf.

Morris, E.K. and Braukmann, C.J. (eds) (1987) *Behavioral Approaches to Crime and Delinquency.* New York: Plenum Press.

Morris, E.K., Higgins, S.T., Bickel, W.K. and Braukmann, C.J. (1987) 'An introduction to contemporary behaviourism: History, concepts and a system of analysis'. In E.K. Morris and C.J. Braukmann (eds) *Behavioral Approaches to Crime and Delinquency.* New York: Plenum Press.

Nelson, R.O. and Hayes, S.C. (1981) 'Nature of behavioural assessment'. In. M. Hersen and A.S. Bellack (eds) *Behavioral Assessment: A Practical Handbook, Second Edition.* New York: Pergamon Press.

Nelson, R.O. and Hayes, S.C. (1986) 'The nature of behavioural assessment'. In R.O. Nelson and S.C. Hayes (eds) *Conceptual Foundations of Behavioral Assessment.* New York: Guilford Press.

Owens, R.G. and Ashcroft, J.B. (1982) 'Functional analysis in applied psychology'. *British Journal of Clinical Psychology,* 21, 181–189.

Paterson, C.H. (1986) *Theories of Counselling and Psychotherapy.* New York: Harper Collins.

Peterson, D.R. (1968) *The Clinical Study of Social Behavior.* New York: Appleton-Century-Crofts.

Poppen, R.L. (1989) 'Some clinical implications of rule-governed behaviour'. In S.C. Hayes (ed) *Rule-Governed Behavior: Cognition, Contingencies and Instructional Control.* New York: Plenum Press.

Rachlin, H. (1991) *Introduction to Modern Behaviorism, Third Edition.* New York: Witt, Freeman and Co.

Risley, T.R. (1975) 'Certify procedures, not people'. In W. Scott-Ward (ed) *Issues in Evaluating Behavior Modification.* Champaign, Illinois: Research Press.

Ross, R.R. and Fabiano, E.A. (1985) *Time to Think: A Cognitive Model of Delinquency, Prevention and Offender Rehabilitation.* Johnson City, Tennessee: Institute of Social Sciences and Arts Inc.

Staats, A.W. (1986) 'Behaviourism with a personality: The paradigmatic behavioural assessment approach'. In. R.D. Nelson and S.C. Hayes (eds) *Conceptual Foundations of Behavioral Assessment*. New York: Guilford Press.

Strosahl, K.D. and Linehan, M.A. (1986) 'Basic issues in behavioural assessment'. In A.R. Ciminero, K.S. Calhoun, and H.E. Adams (eds) *Handbook of Behavioral Assessment, Second Edition*. New York: Wiley.

Sweet, A.A. and Loizeaux (1991) 'Behavioural and cognitive treatment methods: A critical comparative review'. *Journal of Behavior Therapy and Experimental Psychiatry*, 22, 159–185.

Todd, J.T. and Morris, E.K. (1983) 'Misconceptions and miseducation: Presentations of radical behaviourism in psychology textbooks'. *The Behavior Analyst*, 6, 153–160.

Valentine, E.R. (1992) *Conceptual Issues in Psychology*. London: Routledge.

Voeltz, L.M. and Evans, I.M. (1982) 'The assessment of behavioural inter-relationships in child behaviour therapy'. *Behavioral Assessment*, 4, 131–165.

Wilson, J.Q. and Herrnstein, R.J. (1985) *Crime and Human Nature*. New York: Simon and Schuster.

Wolpe, J. (1982) *The Practice of Behavior Therapy*. New York: Pergamon Press.

Wolpe, J. (1989) 'The derailment of behaviour therapy: A tale of conceptual misdirection'. *Journal of Behavior Therapy and Experimental Psychiatry*, 20, 3–15.

Young, L.D. and Patterson, J.N. (1981) 'Information and opinions about behaviour modification'. *Journal of Behavior Therapy and Experimental Psychiatry*, 143, 315–320.

Zettle, R.D. (1990) 'Rule-governed behaviour: A radical behavioural answer to the cognitive challenge'. *The Psychological Record*, 40, 41–49.

CHAPTER 2

Special Demands of Assessment in a Secure Setting

Setting the Scene

David M. Gresswell and Ilona Kruppa

The assessment of offending behaviour has much in common with the assessment of other classes of behaviour. The professional is faced with a number of key tasks, namely to produce an accurate description of the behaviour in question; to develop an understanding of its history and aetiology, including the interaction between the client and the environment in which the behaviour took place; and to determine the function the behaviour served for the individual. Beyond these common goals, however, there are a number of ways in which working with offenders may differ markedly from work from other client groups. In this chapter these key differences will be discussed under three broad headings: (1) Practical problems arising from the secure setting in which assessment takes place; (2) Motivational issues arising from the involuntary status of the offender; and (3) Emotional issues for the professional.

Practical Problems

This first section presents practical advice about approaching the assessment of offenders in secure settings, including a discussion of the preparatory work that should precede the first contact with the offender, the range of sources of information available to the professional, and advice on ordering the large volume of information that can be involved.

The behaviour in question – the offending – is unlikely to be directly observable at the time of assessment, and as a result, the professional is reliant upon indirect sources of information for a description of the events surrounding the offence, with consequent difficulties in terms of assessing the validity and reliability of these sources. Since the professional is unable to observe changes in offending behaviour directly, he or she must rely upon behaviours that are hypothesised to be functionally related to offending. These behaviours are likely to include private events, for example sexual or violent fantasies, and the professional will often be reliant upon the offender's self-report as a measure of change.

1. Preparation

When working in secure settings it is extremely unlikely that the professional's first interview with an offender will be the first time that the offender has described details of the offence. In fact, it is likely that the offender will have repeated his or her account on numerous occasions and the initial response to contact with the professional may be an expression of irritation at having to answer the same questions about the offence yet again. Unfortunately, numerous repetitions of offence details provide the opportunity for the offender to consolidate an account of the offence that includes distortions. The offender may even thoroughly convince himself or herself of the preferred version of events. The many opportunities presented to the offender to rehearse his account may well, therefore, decrease the likelihood of producing the degree of validity required in order to design appropriate interventions. Furthermore, since rehearsal can dampen affect, consideration must be given to whether any lack of emotional tone in recounting the offence reflects genuine lack of feeling or is the result of a degree of detachment achieved through constant repetition. This is especially important when the professional is asked to express an opinion about the degree of remorse displayed by the offender. Although remorse is a complex phenomenon, it has received little attention in the literature. It is as well to be aware that expressions of remorse are likely to vary across time, between situations, and as a product of the relationship between offender and interviewer.

Two types of preparation are important before the initial interview; the first involves accessing the relevant information on file. In approaching the assessment of an offender, as a rule the professional is likely to have been furnished with at least a brief description of the offence, plus the background or historical details. The professional has then to decide whether to approach the offender from this comparatively naive position, or to take up the option of researching the offender more thoroughly. The advantage of the first approach is that the professional is able to approach the assessment free from the influence of others' perceptions of events. The advantage of the second approach is that, by informing the offender that you have had access to alternative sources of information, you may be able to enhance the validity of self-report early on. This decision is likely to reflect the professional's personal style, or differing requirements of the interview depending on circumstances; there is no right or wrong approach.

Given that the offender's version of events cannot be accepted unquestioningly, reference must be made to other sources for corroboration at some stage in the assessment. In most cases, when offenders have been either charged or convicted, the investigating police force will have collected a series of witness statements, transcripts of interviews with the offender, and the offender's statements. These reports, known as depositions, often contain valuable information that can be used to verify the offender's account of events. The depositions, if not already available on file, can generally be obtained from the client's solicitor and, occasionally, depending on the referral source, from the Crown Prosecution Service (CPS) or the Home Office.

The professional may also find it helpful to obtain information about the client's previous offences from the Criminal Records Office (CRO). This is available from the same sources as the depositions, though probation departments can additionally be helpful. The CRO sheet usually contains details of offence type and disposal details. Other useful sources, though less easily obtainable, are transcripts of the trial (these may have to be paid for if obtained directly via a court), judges' summaries, and the Senior Investigating Officer's (SIO) summary for the CPS. Further consistency checks can also be made through consideration of other professionals' reports held on hospital or prison files.

Additional information which may enhance the professional's understanding of the offence behaviour can be obtained from an interview with the SIO or the arresting police officer who may have information or theories about the offence which are useful, but not written in official reports. Relatives who may have been witnesses or even victims of an offence can also be helpful, though such contacts will require careful preparation and attention to confidentiality. Rare for the professional assessing an individual, but insisted upon by most crime scene personality profilers, is a visit to the scene of the crime. Such visits can provide additional information or impressions that are difficult to retrieve from reports alone (for example, in relation to the privacy of the surroundings and the role of 'opportunism'). To some professionals, however, a visit to the scene of the crime might be regarded as in poor taste, reflecting a morbid curiosity or as playing 'amateur detective'. In many cases maps, photographs, or diagrams provided as part of police evidence are adequate.

The second type of preparation is familiarity with the relevant academic literature. The wide range of available models of offending can provide a useful guide to interviewing. For example Briggs (1991) has suggested a model of the cycle of offending displayed by sex offenders. Alternatively, a number of functional analyses have been developed for different types of offending: arson (Jackson, Glass, and Hope, 1987); delinquency (Jones and Heskin, 1988); and sexual homicide (Burgess, Hartman, Ressler, Douglas, and McCormack, 1986). These provide both a useful survey of the literature and interesting pointers to formulation.

These models can be used to generate hypotheses about processes that may have contributed to the offending and may therefore shape the questions that are posed to the offender. In constructing an account of the offence, the '5 WH' model described by McGuire and Priestley (1985) provides a useful guide to the type of information to be gathered and how to order it in the early stages of assessment. The key questions are: 'who, what, where, when and how', which lead to the generation of hypotheses about the 'why' question. The '5 WH' approach has been adapted for violent offenders by Gresswell and Hollin (1991), as shown in Table 2.1.

Table 2.1: '5 WH' questions (from Gresswell and Hollin, 1991)

Who	Who was the victim? What did they look like? Who do they remind you of? Who were your accomplices?
How	How did you plan the offence in your mind before hand? Had you acted or tried out any parts of the offence previously? How did you get control of the victim? How did you come to get caught?
Where	Where did you pick up the victim? Where did the major part of the offence take place? Where did you leave the victim's body?
What	What were you doing before the offence took place? What did you do to the victim? How did the victim die?
When	When did you make the decision to attack the victim? What sort of mood were you in? When did the offence occur?
Why	What sense do you make of what happened here; how would you explain it? What were the important factors for you?

Models of offending, such as the examples mentioned above, have prompted some authors to produce lists of assumptions to test when working with offenders. Wyre (1988), for example, has produced a list for working with sex offenders, presented in Table 2.2, which can be modified for use with other types of offender.

Table 2.2: Hypotheses to test in an interview (after Wyre, 1988)

1. The offence was premeditated.
2. The perpetrator's role was conscious.
3. The offence was rehearsed in fantasy.
4. The offender perceived the victim as an 'object' or devalued the victim.
5. The victim was specifically targeted.
6. The offender 'groomed' the environment. (i.e., prepared the scene to facilitate the offence.
7. A repetitive cycle of behaviour has developed.
8. The offender's account includes denial/minimisation.

2. *Ordering material*

For some offences, hundreds of pages of statements are not uncommon, and such a wealth of material, combined with the information obtained directly from the offender, can result in major organisational problems. A useful way to start ordering this material is to produce a summary sheet with events organised chronologically and referenced to page numbers within other reports. An example of this is given in Table 2.3. With the evidence organised in this way, sources of error (for example dates, names, witnesses, descriptions) quickly become apparent. At this point, the professional can choose to sort out discrepancies, for example by referring back to the SIO report, or go for the 'best fit', accepting that witnesses to crimes are liable to make errors.

Table 2.3: Organising deposition material

Time	*Page*	*Summary of the depositions*
4.30pm	75	Fred Smith was spotted by Bill Jones walking away from the High Street.
Between 4.30pm and 5.00pm	71	Fred Smith went to the Blue Fish Cafe and had a cup of tea. He stayed approximately 20 minutes. According to Mrs Smith, her son came back to the house around 5.00pm. Jane Smith (wife of Fred) says he came back before 5.00pm. He was not wearing a jacket.
5.05pm	66	According to his mother and wife, Fred Smith left the house to go for a walk.
5.20pm	131	Mr Hall spots Fred Smith on Rectory Court. He is also seen by and acknowledges Peter West.
5.30pm	60–61	Paul Cary sees a man walking up the steps of 60 Rectory Court. The front door was open, as usual, but the inner doors were closed. The man was wearing dark trousers and 'I think a blue jacket of light material'. The man's right hand was behind his back and covered by the flap of his coat. The man is described as having blond hair and being in his twenties. Mr Cary would not say if it was Fred Smith or not.
Just before 5.30pm	23, 43	Mrs Cook receives a phone before call from her daughter, Jean Cook, who has decided to catch the bus over to her mother's house.
6.00pm	5, 8	Jean Cook is stabbed to death.

There are as many models for the formulation of offences as there are professionals working with offenders (Bromley 1986; Gresswell and Hollin, 1992), therefore this section does not advocate a particular style of formulation, but will examine instead common pitfalls for the professional that apply particularly in relation to the assessment of serious offences.

The professional needs to be aware of the tendency for people, including experienced professionals, to make internal attributions of causality, that is to blame the person rather than the circumstance for more serious behaviours (Walster, 1966). An action resulting, for example, in the death of another person is more likely to be seen as the responsibility of the actor than is a similar behaviour with non-fatal consequences. When considering a behaviour with less serious consequences, the observer is more likely to look for reasons within the environment. The professional may find, therefore, particularly with very serious offences, that insufficient attention has previously been awarded to environmental conditions which may have contributed to an offence and which may be vital factors in determining appropriate intervention strategies and in assessing dangerousness.

The professional needs to be aware that certain cognitive distortions displayed by the offender in the course of assessment may be a consequence of committing an offence rather than an antecedent or contributory factor. Research with violent offenders, for example, indicates that both the perpetrator's and the victim's attitudes may be changed by their experience (Siama, 1985). The perpetrator may come to justify what he has done by believing that the victim deserved it, while the victim may equally and irrationally adopt a self-blaming attitude. The need to believe in a just and fair world, rather than in a world where people are attacked at random, is as pervasive amongst offenders as amongst other people.

The professional also needs to be aware of base rates, particularly when assessing dangerousness. Although it is beyond the scope of this chapter to examine the assessment of dangerousness in any depth, the following illustration of this issue is included.

> 'Assume that one person out of a thousand will kill. Assume also that an exceptionally accurate test is created which differentiates with 95 per cent effectiveness those who will kill from those who will not. If 100,000 people were tested, out of the 100 who would kill, 95 would be isolated. Unfortunately, out of the 99,900 who would not kill, 4995 people would also be isolated as potential killers. In those circumstances, it is clear that we could not justify incarcerating all 5090 people'. (Howells, 1987, quoting Livermore *et al.* 1968)

Finally, if the professional hopes that the results of an intervention are to influence decisions about the offender's progress towards rehabilitation in the community, it is important to elicit from the decision-makers, for example the Parole Board and the Home Office, their views about what constitutes acceptable change. If the intervention is likely to result in changes that cannot easily be observed within a secure setting or depend heavily upon self-report, then the professional needs to negotiate with decision-makers to ensure that self-report evidence will be acceptable as a measure of change. As a guide, a list of questions commonly asked by the Home Office when considering the cases of restricted (compulsorily detained) patients is presented in Table 2.4.

Table 2.4: Checklist of points considered by the Home Office in examining restricted patients

1. Has any information come to light since the last report which increases understanding of the circumstances surrounding the index offence?
2. Is the motivation for behaviour that has put others at risk understood?
3. Is there any evidence that the patient has a persistent pre-occupation with a particular type of victim or a particular type of violent/sexual/arsonist activity?
4. What are the chances of circumstances similar to those surrounding the offence arising again and similar offences occurring?
5. In cases of mental illness, what effects have any prescribed drugs had? Do any symptoms remain? How important is the medication for continued stability? Has stability been maintained in differing circumstances? Does the patient have insight into the need for medication?
6. In cases of mental impairment, has the patient benefitted from training? Is the patient's behaviour more socially acceptable? Is the patient explosive or impulsive?
7. In cases of psychopathic disorder, is the patient now more mature, predictable and concerned about others? Is he more tolerant of frustration and stress? Does he now take into account the consequences of his actions? Does he learn from experience?
8. Does the patient now have greater insight into his condition? Is he more realistic and reliable?
9. Have alcohol or drugs affected the patient in the past? Did either contribute towards his offence?
10. How has the patient responded to stressful situations in the hospital in the past and how does he respond now – with physical aggression or verbal aggression?
11. If the patient is a sex offender, has he shown in the hospital an undesirable interest in the type of person he has previously been known to favour as his victim? What form has any sexual activity taken? What have been the results of any psychological tests?
12. What views do members of the clinical team have about the patient's continuing dangerousness.
13. Is it considered that the patient should/should not continue to be detained? For what reasons?
14. If so, is it considered that detention in conditions of special security is necessary.

Source: Home Office, C3 Division

Motivating the Offender to Disclose Information

In establishing a working relationship with clients who are subject to compulsory detention, a key issue arises and needs to be faced immediately: how to maintain a working alliance with a client whom the professional believes may never be able to disclose full details of his problems. Offending can be a rewarding experience, providing increased material wealth, status, excitement, sexual pleasure, or relief from negative mood states. The offender may have a long history of gaining these rewards through offending, without being detected, and may be an unwilling participant in a process that could reveal information leading to a custodial sentence, an indeterminate stay in hospital, or a delay in his return to the community. Consequently, many offenders will employ the defences of denial, minimisation and rationalisation to avoid recognising or admitting the full extent of their offence behaviour. Failure to work through these issues may be detrimental to the offender in the long-term and hinder progress towards rehabilitation.

Motivating the client to disclose

Not all offenders deny or attempt to avoid the consequences of their actions. Some will openly admit their offences and a few, for idiosyncratic reasons, will admit to offences they have not committed. The professional will, however, face offenders who are secretive and protective about their offence behaviour. Such clients will not spontaneously abandon the cognitive distortions, rationalisations, and practices that support their offending, and the professional must be prepared to tackle such behaviour as and when it arises or risk colluding with the offender. Many professionals, particularly those starting out in work with offenders, feel that confronting denial conflicts with their previous training which has often emphasised warmth, unconditional acceptance, and allowing the client to work at his or her own pace. For some, confrontation implies berating or belittling the offender. However, an understanding of the processes which lead offenders to deny aspects of their offending and a strong armoury of techniques to challenge this denial without engaging in conflict can dramatically improve the quality of assessment.

Understanding denial

Denial is often thought of as a binary phenomenon, that is, that an offender will either deny or admit to the whole truth. Generally this is not the case: offenders will typically describe part of their offence and related behaviour. As Salter (1988) notes, this can be very puzzling to the professional who may be at pains to explain why major aspects of offences are admitted but details refuted. Despite obvious temptations, however, the professional cannot assume, because an offender has made some major admissions, that he or she is necessarily innocent in any area vociferously denied. As Salter (1988) states, 'offenders make idiosyncratic distinctions in degrees of blame often unintelligible to the outside observer'. Salter argues that denial is best considered as a spectrum with a number of different components including: (a) denial of details of the acts themselves, for example type and period of time over which they occurred; (b) denial of the role of fantasy and planning, for example fantasy rehearsal, and 'grooming' the environment or victims; (c) denial of responsibility for the acts, for example blaming illness, alcohol or stress, blaming the victim, or redefining the behaviour (e.g.. construing child sexual abuse as educating children about sex or as an appropriate display of affection); and (d) denial of the seriousness of the behaviour, such as the consequences for the victim.

Part of the professional's job is to sort out different types of denial, for example distinguishing the 'public denier' who is aware that he or she is lying and is deliberately trying to avoid the consequences of his or her actions, from the 'internalised' denier who may have convinced himself or herself that he or she is telling the truth and who may genuinely lack awareness.

The different components of denial apply differently according to specific circumstances. The route from committing the offence through arrest, pre-trial investigation, court appearances, and sentence create a number of different conditions in which the offender may be rewarded or punished for disclosing the different aspects of his offence. Denial may also be exposed and recognised in some social interactions and not others, often as a function of the relationship between the offender and the interviewer.

In considering how denial may arise and be maintained we have drawn upon Bandura's (1977) social learning theory. According to this theory there are three crucial components in understanding a behaviour: acquisition, instigation and maintenance. Denial is explained within this framework.

1. ACQUISITION

Offenders may acquire denial behaviours through direct experience and observing others. Most people, both offenders and non-offenders, have experienced being 'let off' by parents or teachers after having denied and lied about minor misdemeanours. Some offenders will have avoided previous convictions by denying offences to the police. Many offenders may have seen or heard of people being committed to trial, and subsequently punished, solely on the basis of their own confession. Disclosure may also have been directly punished during previous institutional experiences; sexual offenders in particular may have experienced the censure of their fellow offenders. Most offenders will therefore have experience of disclosure being punished and denial rewarded.

2. INSTIGATION

Preparation for denial may begin at the time of the offence when victims may be threatened or coerced into not disclosing and other attempts are made to prevent detection. After arrest, the police offer prompts about the risks of disclosure when informing the offender of his rights – 'anything you say may be taken down and used in evidence against you'. Solicitors may also prompt denial by advising their clients to maintain their right to silence during police interviews. When a professional attempts to instigate disclosure, the offender will be making conscious evaluations of the possible outcomes of admitting or denying.

In secure settings, issues of confidentiality influence the likelihood of motivating the client to disclose information. It is important at the outset to delineate the special limits to confidentiality that exist. Professional staff have a responsibility to report to the relevant bodies all information that is pertinent to the question of continued dangerousness. The 'inexperienced' offender may assume that a level of confidentiality exists which is identical to that between a general practitioner and his patient, or between the therapist and his voluntary client in the community. There is often, therefore, a need to make it explicit that in a secure setting the professional's allegiance is split and consequently confidentiality has severe limitations. Naturally, these limitations on confidentiality can instigate denial.

3. MAINTENANCE

The admission of details of offences may have adverse consequences, for example further prosecutions, extension mental health detentions, or postponement of transfer to lower security institutions. The client may also find it emotionally painful, and therefore extremely punishing, to accept responsibility for the damage he has done to himself and others and may therefore avoid disclosure. Obviously, the rewards for disclosure may seem thin in comparison to the possible penalties.

Offender denial is best viewed as a non-static behaviour which may change across time, situation, and as a function of the relationship between the offender and the interviewer. The management of denial therefore depends on addressing the issue of what is denied and why. This leads to the view that denial-behaviour, like any other behaviour, should be assessed in terms of its antecedents and consequences, and tackled like any other problem behaviour on the basis of this assessment.

Progress through denial towards rehabilitation

Even the most skilled and experienced professional will rarely help an offender move to a full admission of responsibility in one step. Offenders will often go through a series of steps from denial of the acts, to minimising their extent, to admitting the extent of the behaviour but denying the seriousness of the consequences and the need for intervention. Offenders may then learn to accept the seriousness of their offences but continue to externalise responsibility. Finally, a stage is reached at which they are able to admit to the offences, the seriousness of the consequences, and accept personal responsibility for them.

Salter (1988) provides the following illustration of the sex offender who has reached the stage of 'full admission of responsibility and guilt':

- Offender admits the extent of his sexual deviancy
- Offender is able to describe the antecedents to the offence including thoughts, fantasies, other victims, and other forms of deviancy.
- Offender acknowledges fantasy rehearsal and 'grooming' of the environment and victim(s).
- Offender is aware of current deviant fantasies and the temptation to relapse.
- Offender appreciates the seriousness of the consequences to the victim(s).

- Expressions of guilt and remorse are related to an appreciation of the harm caused and not simply to the consequences to the offender of public disclosure.

The need to work through the offender's denial can create discomfort. The professional needs to be aware of the offender's attempts to divert or distract attention from offence issues and of any impulse to collude with such behaviour. Offenders are often reluctant to abandon defenses and may be far from grateful for the attempts at exposing the true nature and extent of their difficulties. However, there are a number of techniques that can be employed to encourage the offender to abandon denial and to increase the offender's motivation to change.

Motivational techniques

Motivational techniques can be effective in encouraging the offender to contemplate change, to work at change, and to maintain change. A useful model of stages of change has been described by Prochaska and DiClemente (1986). The motivational tasks for the professional vary depending on the stage the offender is at (see Table 2.5). A comprehensive review of motivational techniques is beyond the scope of this chapter, and for a more detailed description we refer the reader to the work of Miller and Rollnick (1991). However, a number of simple techniques are outlined below.

Table 2.5: Stages of change and the therapist's tasks (Miller and Rollnick, 1991)

Client Stage	*Therapist's Motivational Tasks*
Pre-contemplation	Raise doubt. Enhance the offender's perception of risks and problems with continued offending.
Contemplation	Tip the balance. Elicit reasons to change and the risks of not changing. Reinforce the offender's belief in his ability to change.
Determination	Help the offender determine the best plan of action to take in seeking change.
Action	Help the offender move toward change.
Maintenance	Help the offender identify and use strategies to prevent reoffending.
Relapse	Help the client to restart the processes of contemplation, determination, and action, without becoming stuck or demotivated because of relapse.

(1) **Provide Information:** Describe the limits of confidentiality, the nature and purpose of any assessment being undertaken, the professional's role, available treatments and the requirements for entry into treatment.

(2) **Communicate Understanding:** It is helpful for the professional to convey an empathic understanding of the possible reasons for denial or dissimulation (e.g. loss of self-esteem, difficulty in self-labelling, fear of the consequences of disclosures). The professional may wish to describe the consequences of persistent denial (e.g. being found unamenable to treatment, the risk of re-offending) and the loss of the opportunity to participate in promising treatment approaches.

(3) **Use Open-ended Questions:** Allow the offender to describe his offences in free-flow as a first stage to narrowing the focus. Closed questions tend to inhibit disclosure by encouraging minimal, unelaborated responses.

(4) **Use Assumption-led Questions:** Kinsey *et al.* (1948) found that by asking subjects questions such as 'Do you ever…?', 'Have you ever…?', interviewers obtained less information about their subject's sexual behaviour than when the questions were framed in the form of assumptions, such as 'How often have you…?', 'When was the last time that you…?'. This finding can be applied to the assessment of offenders. For example, asking questions such as 'Tell me about your rape fantasies' or 'How often do you fantasize about rape?' of a sex offender may be more effective than 'Do you ever fantasise about rape?' Caution must be exercised in employing this technique, however, in order to avoid leading suggestible clients, particularly if the client is on remand and the assessment results are intended for presentation in court (see Gudjonsson, 1992, for a fuller discussion of these issues).

(5) **Use 'Cognitive Interviewing' Techniques:** Geiselman and Fisher (1989), in their work on enhancing eyewitness testimony, suggest reinstating the context in which the event occurred, recounting aspects of the event in more than one order, and recounting the event from the point of view of others present. Gaining a description of the offence through all sensory modalities, that is, what the offender could see, hear, smell and touch, and asking for a report from the victim's perspective, can be powerful aids to memory, facilitate engagement, and make it far harder for the offender to 'fake' an account of his actions.

(6) **Use Reframing:** One example provided by Garland and Dougher (1991) is of a sex offender who claims that his sexual offending occurred spontaneously and without premeditation in the form of fantasy rehearsal or behavioural 'try-outs'. The professional can re-frame this by pointing out how unpredictable, and therefore dangerous, this position identifies the offender as being.

(7) **Use Paradox:** This strategy can be used throughout the course of an intervention programme to increase the offender's motivation. It consists of explaining the value of treatment but expressing mild doubts about the offender's ability to maintain motivation and follow through with treatment. This strategy places the offender in the position of needing to provide self-

motivating statements to convince the professional of his or her motivation to change.

(8) **Use Assessment Results:** Assessment information can be used as an indirect challenge to offender denial. Inconsistencies between the offender's presentation and, for example, official documentation (e.g. victim's statements) or physiological measurement of sexual arousal patterns can be used to advantage. Rather than adopting a confrontational approach, the offender should be encouraged to correct any inconsistencies in his account through the acknowledgement that stress may have muddled his thinking, which allows the offender to alter his account without losing face.

(9) **Reduce the Desirability of the Offending Behaviour:** The most significant aspect of strengthening the offender's motivation to change is to reduce the desirability of the offending behaviour and to make it discrepant with the offender's beliefs, feelings, and self-image. A variety of interventions are useful for this purpose, including cognitive re-structuring, victim empathy training, and relapse prevention approaches (Laws, 1989; Marlatt and Gordon, 1985; Pithers, 1990).

Emotional Issues for the Professional

Problems in empathising with offenders

Listening to offenders recount the details of their offences can be emotionally disturbing. Emotional responses are natural and common, but are often hard to predict; professionals may work unperturbed with offenders for years and then unexpectedly experience an adverse emotional reaction. Perhaps it is the way a certain client presents or talks about his offences, or that a victim reminds the professional of a member of his own family, or that some unexpected feature brings the offence too close to home. Emotional reactions to this type of work may also be influenced by seemingly unrelated life experiences, so that at times when affected by other stresses the professional is less able to retain the desired degree of detachment.

A number of writers have commented on the difficulty in trying to empathise with the offender when simultaneously feeling repulsed by the offence behaviour. It is often difficult to separate the sinner from the sin. This situation is often eased when the professional begins to explore the offender's life history. Experiences of victimisation and deprivation are met with great frequency. This can, however, present the unexpected danger of over-empathising and subsequent collusion with the offender's attempts to deny or externalise responsibility on the basis of their own victimization experience. There is also the danger that, having established a therapeutic relationship after a long period of time, the professional can lose sight of the offender's potential dangerousness and allow personal feelings to influence assessments of risk. It is important to achieve a balance between accepting the offender and rejecting his or her offending behaviour.

The professional needs to develop a degree of emotional detachment. To an extent, this can be achieved by remaining 'task-orientated', that is by concentrating on the range of information sought, and focusing on the offender's reactions to the process. Supervision and peer support are also important.

The professional's motivation

Although the importance of treating serious offenders is increasingly being recognised, punitive attitudes towards offenders are still pervasive. Many regard the only feasible option as being long-term incarceration and take a pessimistic view of the likelihood of any positive response to treatment; serious offenders are often seen as 'untreatable'. Faced with repeated questioning of the value and effectiveness of interventions, professionals working with this group are likely to feel their work to be both unappreciated and misunderstood by the public and colleagues alike. They may even, at times, lack confidence in the value of their own contribution. Indeed, many professionals will be familiar with having their motivation for choosing this specialism questioned, often with the implicit suggestion that it reveals unhealthy interests or needs. To some extent, these misunderstandings can be alleviated by sharing ideas across specialisms; an understanding of the treatment of offenders can be valuable to the professional treating victims, and *vice versa*.

Historically, professionals working in secure settings, such as prisons and special hospitals, have found themselves isolated from colleagues in other settings and have not easily found allies in the health service or community forensic settings. This position is not immutable; formal and informal contacts with colleagues in Probation, Social and Health Services can be beneficial. Many probation departments run support groups for those who work with offenders and are typically very welcoming to other disciplines. Participation in research and research interest groups, peer supervision networks, and attending conferences can all help to maintain enthusiasm.

In addition, the professional's motivation can be influenced by personal biases towards certain offender types or behaviours. Roundy and Horton (1990) have identified a number of specific personal biases that can be detrimental to working effectively with offenders.

(1) 'WILLINGNESS TO TREAT'

The first of these issues is defined by Roundy and Horton (1990) as a 'willingness to treat'. It may seem paradoxical to include this here, but the professional who has entered this field, presumably having resolved to work with offenders, may still experience reservations about particular individuals or offender types. The professional who embarks upon a therapeutic relationship with a particular offender must be committed to treatment as the best course of action for this individual. To maintain a therapeutic relationship with an offender with the concurrent belief that this individual is 'untreatable' or that long-term incarceration is the only solution to the individual's problems may sabotage the effectiveness of the treatment process, leaving all concerned with the false impression that the offender has been successfully treated when this is not the case.

Often there may be pressure from other members of the team to continue to intervene with an individual who is clearly not responding to treatment. It is important to resist this pressure because others may view that offender as having been successfully treated and therefore no longer constituting a significant risk to the public, even though he or she has, in fact, merely 'gone through the motions'. However, it is equally important that professionals are aware that in defining the individual as 'untreatable' they are not responding to individual biases or prejudices and have good grounds for making this judgement. Treatability is best viewed not as a trait of the client, but as partly influenced by the relationship between the offender and the professional, and the individual's responsivity to treatment may vary across time and situation.

(2) AMBIVALENCE REGARDING THE RESPONSIBILITY OF VICTIMS AND SIGNIFICANT OTHERS

Even experienced professionals may partly adhere to 'pop psychology' theories about the behaviour of victims: that children may behave seductively or willingly participate in sexual contacts with offenders; that rape victims are partially responsible if they were dressed in certain ways or were travelling alone after dark; that victims of violence may have behaved in a provocative manner; or that a sexually unresponsive partner may be to some degree responsible for sexual deviance. These are all commonly held opinions, despite a lack of empirical foundation. The professional with biases regarding the victim's role is at risk of colluding with the offender's attempts to deny or redirect responsibility for offending. Working with offenders therefore requires that professionals should be willing to examine their own biases which may create 'blind spots' unless faced and appropriately dealt with.

(3) THERAPEUTIC PESSIMISM

Unrealistic expectations for success in working with offenders can lead professionals to experience frustration, self-doubt, or discouragement. The key to maintaining motivation is to establish realistic goals and to learn to measure success in small increments. Maintaining an awareness of the literature on offending helps. Hollin (1991) and Blackburn (1988) have written reviews which indicate that cognitive-behavioural strategies can be effective with difficult offender populations and which help the therapist apply interventions where they will be most effective.

Summary of practical guidelines for dealing with emotional issues

The following practical guidelines are offered for the professional considering working with offenders (based on Roundy and Horton 1990):

- Be prepared to accept that this work may not be for you.
- Accept the offender's denial as a stage in the process towards rehabilitation, not as a trait common to all offenders.
- Be prepared to face indifferent and negative motivation, to encourage in treatment, and to develop strategies to circumvent this.
- Attempt to address personal issues/biases.
- Establish realistic expectations of success.
- Learn to measure success in small increments.
- Establish adequate supervision and support networks.

- Acknowledge the value of your role.

Summary

This chapter has examined the special demands presented by the assessment of offenders in secure setting in three domains: practical issues arising from the secure setting; the involuntary status of the offender; and emotional issues for the professional.

It is acknowledged that assessment within the confines of a secure environment presents unique difficulties for a number of reasons. The behaviour in question – the offending – is unlikely to be observable at the time of assessment and, therefore, the professional is reliant upon indirect sources of information. The professional may be able to observe changes only in behaviour hypothesised to be functionally related to offending.

Some practical advice for overcoming these difficulties has been presented in this chapter, including a discussion of the preparatory work that should precede the first contact with the offender, information about the range of sources of information available to the professional, advice on ordering the large volume of information that can be collected, and a discussion of the common pitfalls that impede the professional when approaching the assessment of offenders in secure settings.

The involuntary status of the offender has obvious implications for the development of an effective working relationship between the professional and offender, compounded by the need that often arises to confront or challenge the offender's version of events and the limited confidentiality that the professional is able to offer to the offender.

Personal issues for the professional include low morale arising from the general lack of appreciation or understanding of the work done in this field, difficulty empathising with the offender, discomfort associated with discussing offence behaviour, and pessimism about the likelihood of a positive response to treatment. Personal biases, related to the treatability of certain offence types and the role of the victim, can interfere with the professional's ability to work effectively with this group, unless properly acknowledged and addressed.

Acknowledgement

The authors wish to thank Home Office C3 Division for permission to use Table 2.4.

References

Bandura, A. (1977) *Social Learning Theory*. New York: Prentice Hall.

Blackburn, R. (1988) Cognitive-behavioural approaches to understanding and treating aggression. In K. Howells and C. Hollin (eds) *Clinical Approaches to Aggression and Violence*. Issues in Criminological and Legal Psychology, No 12. Leicester: The British Psychological Society.

Briggs, D.I. (1991) Relapse prevention with sexual offenders. Paper presented at the 'Addicted to Crime?' Conference, Rampton Hospital, Retford.

Bromley, D.B. (1986) *The Case Study Method in Psychology and Related Disciplines.* Chichester: John Wiley and Sons.

Burgess, A.W., Hartman, C.R., Ressler, R.K., Douglas, J.E. and McCormack, A. (1986) Sexual homicide: A motivational model. *Journal of Interpersonal Violence, 1,* 251–272.

Garland, R.J. and Dougher, M.J. (1991) Motivational intervention in the treatment of sex offenders. In W.R. Miller, and S. Rollnick (eds) *Motivational Interviewing: Preparing People to Change Addictive Behaviour.* New York: Guilford Press.

Geiselman, R.E. and Fisher, R.P. (1989) The cognitive interview technique for victims and witnesses of crime. In D.C. Raskin (ed) *Psychological Methods in Criminal Investigation and Evidence.* New York: Springer.

Gresswell, D.M. and Hollin, C.R. (1991) Multiple homicide interview proforma and checklist. Unpublished.

Gresswell, D.M. and Hollin, C.R. (1992) Towards a new methodology for making sense of case material: An illustrative case involving attempted multiple murder. *Criminal Behaviour and Mental Health, 2,* 329–341.

Gudjonsson, G.H. (1992) *The Psychology of Interrogations, Confessions, and Testimony.* Chichester: John Wiley and Sons.

Hollin, C.R. (1991) Designing effective rehabilitation programmes for offenders: Empirical findings and practical suggestions. Paper presented at the First Spanish-British Conference on Psychology Crime and the Law, Pamplona, Spain.

Howells, K. (1987) Forensic problems: Investigation. In S.J.E. Lindsay and G.E. Powell (eds) *A Handbook of Clinical Adult Psychology.* (pp.649–668) Aldershot: Gower.

Jackson, H.F., Glass, C. and Hope, S. (1987) A functional analysis of recidivistic arson. *British Journal of Clinical Psychology, 26,* 175–186.

Jones, R.S. and Heskin, J. (1988) Towards a functional analysis of delinquent behaviour: A pilot study. *Counselling Psychology Quarterly, 1,* 35–42.

Kinsey, A.C., Pomeroy, W.B. and Martin, C.E. (1948) *Sexual Behaviour in the Human Male.* Philadelphia: W B Saunders.

Laws, D.R. (ed) (1989) *Relapse Prevention with Sex Offenders.* New York: Guilford Press.

McGuire, J. and Priestley, P. (1985) *Offending Behaviour: Skills and Stratagems for Going Straight.* London: Batsford.

Marlatt, G.A. and Gordon, J.R. (eds) (1985) *Relapse Prevention.* New York: Guilford Press.

Miller, W.R. and Rollnick, S. (eds) (1991) *Motivational Interviewing: Preparing People to Change Addictive Behaviour.* New York: Guilford Press.

Pithers, W.D. (1990) Relapse prevention with sexual aggressors: A method for maintaining therapeutic gain and enhancing external supervision. In W.L. Marshall, D.R. Laws and H.E. Barbaree (eds) *Handbook of Sexual Assault: Issues, Theories, and Treatment of the Offender.* (pp.343–361) New York: Plenum Press.

Prochaska, J.O. and DiClemente, C.C. (1986) Towards a comprehensive model of change. In W.R. Miller and N. Heather (eds) *Treating Addictive Behaviours: Processes of Change.* (pp.3–27) New York: Plenum Press.

Roundy, L.M. and Horton, A.L. (1990) Professional and treatment issues for clinicians who intervene with incest perpetrators. In A.L. Horton, B.L. Johnson, L.M. Roundy and D. Williams (eds) *The Incest Perpetrator: A Family Member No-one Wants to Treat.* Newbury Park: Sage.

Salter, A.C. (1988) *Treating Child Sex Offenders and Victims.* Newbury Park: Sage.

Siama, G. (1985) *Accounting for Aggression: Perspectives on Aggression and Violence.* Boston: Allen and Unwin.

Walster, E. (1966) Assignment of responsibility for an accident. *Journal of Personality and Social Psychology, 3,* 73–9.

Wyre, R. (1988) Assumptions to test when working with sexual offenders. Unpublished material. Birmingham: The Gracewell Clinic.

CHAPTER 3

Assessment of Sexual Offenders

David I. Briggs

For several years the author of this chapter, with colleague Jean Jones, has run group-based programmes for the assessment and treatment of sexual offenders in an English Special Hospital. Most of our work has been with male offenders and the words 'he', 'his', and 'him' will be used in this chapter. It is becoming apparent, however, that women also commit sexual offences, though the assessment and research of the phenomenon of female perpetration lag several years behind that of male perpetrators. In addition, we have been involved in the training of multi-professional groups of practitioners working in prisons who have been developing their skills in sex offender management. This experience is drawn upon in determining the content of this chapter.

The assessment of clients in secure settings is an activity fraught with difficulty. Issues of the reliability and validity of assessment techniques are crucial since much of importance rests upon assessment decisions. For example, is our sex offender client capable of behavioural control? If a client discloses ongoing sexual fantasies of pubescent boys, are these a predictor of the likelihood of his reoffending? If a rapist shows no response to material portraying sexual aggression in the laboratory, what should we make of this finding?

One goal in assessing sex offenders in secure settings is that of obtaining evidence of dangerousness sufficient to inform the offender's progress through the system to discharge or transfer. Where therapeutic resources are available, assessment provides information necessary for determining therapeutic targets and evaluating outcome. For those offenders to be released from incarceration, assessment is used to set an agenda for their rehabilitation in the community.

The Process of Intervention

We view our work with sexual offenders in institutions as a series of steps along which therapeutic targets are defined and clarified. These steps can be summarised as follows:

- referral
- initial assessment
- motivational interventions
- educational interventions
- eclectic therapies
- relapse prevention
- monitoring

Following the referral of the client to the professional, we see it as important to engage the client in work explicitly designed to address the issue of motivation. It is important not to treat motivation as implicit: we cannot assume that because the client agrees to work with us that his motivation is optimal or that he is engaged upon a path of work for the right reasons.

The education of our clients is also seen as an important aspect of our work. Attitudes toward various sexual practices, knowledge of issues pertaining to intercourse, conception and contraception, the consideration of gender roles and sexuality, issues of health and sexually transmitted disease, and the law relating to sexual behaviour have to be addressed.

On the basis of motivational and educative work it is then appropriate to engage the client in those specific therapies designed to assist the client in gaining eventual control over sexual urges, fantasies and behaviour. These might include behaviour therapies targeting inappropriate sexual arousal, management of sexual fantasies, challenging rationalising cognitions and excuses, and victim empathy training. Such interventions are best anchored upon a rigorous functional analysis of previous offending, both known convictions and others. A point to be made here is that we have relatively little research evidence to identify which technique will achieve maximum impact with which client and with which problem behaviours. We are in the position of offering a potentially over-inclusive range of interventions in the hope that something works!

In this chapter, assessment in the areas mentioned above will be described: motivation; knowledge and attitudes; sexual arousal; sexual fantasies; rationalising cognitions; and victim empathy. The longer term maintenance of self-control has to be targeted in the relapse prevention phase. This is work which will have to be continued by those who support the offender upon discharge or release from the institution, as will the longer term monitoring of that person.

Assessment using penile plethysmography (PPG) is not addressed in this chapter, despite the importance of this method. The reason for this omission is quite simply that we view PPG as a highly specialised technique which should be used only by those professionals trained to do so. It would be misleading to suggest by including a section within this chapter that PPG is within the competence of any professional working with sex offenders. For further reading, refer to Pratt (1986).

Assessment of Motivation

One of the fundamental aspects of work with sexual offenders is that of sustaining their motivation to engage in those potentially long-term, demanding, and intrusive interventions designed to facilitate self-control and avoid relapse. Motivation is not a static trait inherent within the perpetrator, but a dynamic, fluid state which is responsive and reactive to environmental factors and agents. The assessment of motivation, therefore, although very relevant to work with perpetrators at the outset of any intervention, is something which should occur throughout the perpetrator's stay within the institution, and should be revisited at regular intervals during the treatment or sentence plan.

Our preference in assessing motivation is to avoid the use of questionnaire measures and to exploit the personal interaction of interviewer and interviewee. It is hoped that the subtleties of attitude and values encompassed in this concept of motivation can thereby be discerned.

Our assessment of motivation is organised around a structured interview, presented below.

(a) Instructions to the interviewer

It is suggested that after some degree of rapport has been established with the client, and the purpose of the interview has been made explicit, the following questions be asked of the client. It is recommended that the worker at this stage adopt a questioning rather than confrontational interviewing style, and bear in mind that the purpose of the interview is to obtain information which will help understand the client's attitudes. Interviewers are encouraged to use whatever probes are necessary to facilitate discussion, and to pursue questions in detail, using an assumption-free manner.

(b) Questions

- What have you been told about the sort of treatment and counselling that might be offered to you here?
- The staff may have told you about the need for you to make changes in your life; is this so? If you have been told that you need to make changes, what changes are these?
- One of the main reasons for you being here is because of committing sexual offences. Have you tried to control your behaviour in the past? If so, what did you try to do to stop yourself offending? Why do you think you were not successful in controlling your behaviour?
- Some people become demoralised and feel quite helpless when they get sent to a place like this. Has this happened to you? Do you feel that you will ever be able to control your behaviour in the future? What will be the most difficult thing for you to achieve?
- Who are the staff who have responsibility for helping you? Can you list these people, one by one? For each, tell me in what ways they are helpful to you, and also in what ways they are not helpful.

- Are there other people who help you, perhaps people who do not necessarily have any responsibility for you? How do these people help you?
- Who wants you to change? Why?
- Who does not want you to change? Why not?
- If you were to commit yourself to work to help you control your sexual behaviour, what benefits do you think this will bring you both short-term and long-term? List as many of these as possible. Similarly, what disadvantages do you think you might experience, both in the short-term and the long-term, if you started to work on your offending behaviour?
- How long do you think it will be necessary to work on your reasons for committing sex offences? A month, up to six months, a year, longer?
- When we think about your offences, are there issues that you find it very difficult to talk about? How could this be made easier for you?
- If we were to draw up a contract for our work together, what expectations would you have of me? What would it be fair for me to expect of you?
- Where do you think you will be living two years from now,... five years from now,... ten years from now? Tell me why.

It is recommended that a careful record be made of the substance of this interview against which any changes can be monitored. Again, it will be important for the client to be informed of the purpose of the record, and, if copies are to be circulated, who will have access to them. It is recommended that as a matter of routine the client be offered a copy of any notes taken at interviews such as this. This will signal openness on the part of the professional and a spirit of therapeutic collaboration. It is likely that several sessions will be needed to work through the above list, and opportunities should be given to clients to add to or amend their replies.

Assessment of Knowledge and Attitudes

The majority of sexual offenders we have worked with in our Special Hospital setting have experience of disturbed and abusive childhoods. They have been exposed to parental neglect, physical or sexual abuse, inconsistent management by parents, and so forth. The consequences of this are that often our clients have quite distorted attitudes towards relationships, and are misinformed or ignorant about quite crucial matters.

Heinz, Gargaro, and Kelly (1987) have outlined a sex education curriculum for juvenile sex offenders cared for in a residential setting. This can usefully be extrapolated to adult offenders in secure settings. The assessment of knowledge, attitudes, and beliefs might be structured around the following topic areas.

- Attitudes towards sex roles, including stereotyping and sexism.

- Attitudes towards intimacy, including understanding of the notion of choice within relationships.
- Knowledge of the developmental changes associated with adolescence and early adulthood, including physical, emotional, and cognitive changes.
- Knowledge and beliefs regarding sexuality, including sexual orientations.
- Attitudes towards developing relationships and 'dating'.
- Knowledge of the mechanics and responsibilities associated with reproduction and contraception.
- Attitudes towards sexual health, and knowledge of safe sex (to include assessment of the awareness of sexually transmitted diseases and mechanisms of transmissions).
- Knowledge of the law relating to sexual behaviour.
- Attitudes towards masturbation, masturbatory practices, and sexual fantasy.

Much of the above is best achieved through clinical interviews. The point to be made here is that a full assessment of sexual knowledge and attitudes is time-consuming and requires careful planning. It is our experience that this phase of assessment is one which is easily neglected or conducted in a somewhat perfunctory manner.

Assessment of Sexual Arousal

Many sexual offenders, not surprisingly, report being sexually aroused by images or reminders of the targets of their offending. Within institutions our clients have little opportunity to reoffend, yet they remain sexual: they masturbate; they have sexual daydreams; they may form sexual relationships with other patients or inmates. It is important for those working with sexual offenders in institutions to assess fully those events, objects and materials used by the offender to sustain or develop both appropriate and inappropriate sexual arousal.

The offender may use fairly obvious strategies to maintain arousal to inappropriate stimuli. For example, the offender might have access to pornography depicting images of children and sexual violence. More likely such 'pornography' will be self-constructed: the offender may have collections of images of children, for example gathered from magazines and newspapers; may show an interest in photographs of children of members of staff to be found in some offices; or may enjoy watching children's programmes on television. It is worthwhile asking quite specific questions of the client about their use of pornography. In addition to ascertaining the general class of stimuli used (pubescent girls, toddlers, etc.), detail should be sought of fetishistic interests (attractions to particular garments or fabrics, for example), and also detail of how the material is incorporated into fantasy (for example, does the client superimpose images of violence upon the stimulus; does the client fantasise about being irresistible to the model in the picture?).

The reporting of sexual violence in the media is noteworthy. The client might have saved press cuttings of 'headline' cases, for example those depicting child abduction, multiple rape, or sexual murder. It is interesting that it is not unknown for the offender to draw these to the attention of staff, and to show a desire to discuss the events. Staff should be alert to apparently casual conversations which have a sexual motive in this respect, serving to titillate the offender.

Television programmes can also be drawn upon to stimulate the sex offender's arousal. Access to images of rape and sexual degradation is relatively straightforward for many institutionalised clients. The regular coverage of rape and sexual assault in the media, and the use of such images in drama on film and television provide adequate fuel for an offender motivated to sustain sadistic interests. For those offenders with a history of sexual violence towards adults, again it is important to log the detail of their viewing habits.

Less commonly, offenders will seek to reinforce their interests through swapping details of their offending with other inmates and patients. This is perhaps more likely when we consider an inmate housed under the conditions of Rule 43 in prisons than a patient within a secure hospital setting. (Rule 43 conditions in prisons can apply to vulnerable prisoners such as those with a history of sexual offending where there may be a threat from other inmates. Prisoners subject to this 'rule' are segregated for their own protection.)

Paradoxically, one of the richest sources of fantasy stimulation for the incarcerated offender is that of therapy. Within our prisons and secure hospitals, examples are to be found of group-based interventions for sexual offenders which aim to impact on the sexual offending of clients. Within these groups, men will listen to detailed descriptions of other men's sexual offences. These descriptions then have the potential to feed the sexual fantasy lives of those who have heard them. This is not to be alarmist about therapeutic work with sexual offenders, but rather to suggest to professionals the need to enquire of their client, after each session, whether they have been aroused by the material they have been exposed to within sessions and whether they are likely to recall this material for their subsequent sexual gratification. If this is the case, then the professional is obliged to offer techniques to help the client gain control over their arousal.

Some clients may be motivated to write their own pornographic material. One of the important features of such writing is that the material generated can be highly idiosyncratic. Furthermore, if the client is motivated to hide the content of these descriptions from others, then specific acts and practices can be given code names as a disguise. The diaries of clients are also worth reading in this respect, if made available.

It should be evident from the above that motivated sexual offenders within our institutions will have no difficulty in maintaining inappropriate sexual arousal. Rather than provide a checklist for workers of key stimuli, it is hoped here to encourage the careful observation, questioning, and checking of clients. This is a long-term exercise. Clients' interests may remain apparently dormant for many years only to resurface at times of stress, for example the stress of an impending discharge from the institution. Furthermore, the assessment of those stimuli serving to sustain inappropriate arousal is a skilled exercise depending not least on the imagination and perceptions of the assessor. Impressions and 'gut feelings' should not be ignored, but shared and explored with colleagues in the multi-professional team.

Assessment of Sexual Fantasies

For the inmate starved of intimate contact, it is not unusual that he should resort to sexual fantasy to stimulate sexual arousal. Indeed, as noted above, there are many opportunities to stimulate sexual fantasies within institutions. Why is it important for workers to assess the content of those most personal thoughts and sexual fantasies?

The association of images of offending with the arousal of masturbation and ejaculation has been considered to contribute to the maintenance of inappropriate behaviour through simple conditioning procedures. The pleasure of masturbation is linked to fantasies of offending. For the habitual offender, sexual fantasy is something which is often activated at times of stress and strong negative emotional states. The offender retreats into his world of sexual fantasizing, rather like an alcoholic might return to drink.

We must consider what it is we are assessing when we talk of sexual fantasies. Sexual fantasies are mental events. The ability to produce mental images is a skill like any other, and some people are able to produce clear and vivid images at will, whilst others struggle to do so. Some are able to absorb themselves in the content of these images, whilst others can only achieve the status of mental voyeur. Some people can generate sensory experiences in tactile or auditory images. Students of imagery have long asserted that to assess imagery attention must be paid to the subject's ability to control and achieve clarity of imagery across the sensory modalities. This is to be recommended when we consider that subset of imagery, sexual fantasy.

It is recommended that prior to direct questioning of the offender as to the content of his or her sexual fantasy life that some time be spent in education and scene-setting. We have found it useful to explain to our clients that both masturbation and sexual fantasising are normal human activities. Concerning the former, masturbation should not be viewed just as an alternative to sexual intercourse, but rather another outlet of a person's sexuality and one that many people, men and women, use on a regular basis. Furthermore, when we consider sexual fantasies, many people (perhaps the majority) regularly use more than one sexual fantasy to stimulate themselves. Sometimes several fantasies may be used within a single masturbatory episode. Sometimes fantasies will represent re-enactments of past relationships; sometimes these fantasies will involve known partners but feature practices and behaviours that have not been indulged in; and sometimes these fantasies will be of offending. It is probably more realistic to target the control of such fantasies of illegal acts than to promise their eradication.

A simple way of gathering information of sexual fantasies is the use of a 'masturbatory log', similar in construction to the 'drink diaries' used by colleagues working in the addictions field (see Figure 3.1). It is important when asking the client to keep such a record that attention is paid to those factors which will enhance his motivation to do so. Clients will be concerned about who will gain access to the record, where it will be stored, whether their masturbatory practices may be seen as unusual, and what opinion will be formed if fantasies of offending are reported. If the records are to be used within the context of group therapy, the client will be concerned about how much detail he will be required to share with other inmates or patients. The job of the assessor here is to provide clear guidance and answers to these questions.

Instructions:

Please keep a record of the number of times you masturbate over the next week. This can be recorded on the sheets enclosed. As well as recording how often you masturbate it would be helpful to know what fantasies you use. Please identify a trigger to the fantasy; record details of the type of person you think about (e.g. boys, girls, women, men); and record whether the fantasy contained elements of violence. The main purpose of the record is to help you. If you are too embarrassed to keep the record then it would be better for you to leave it blank and talk about it at the next session, rather than make something up.

Fantasy Record Sheet

Date: ....

Number of times you masturbated: ....

Descriptions of fantasies used:

Trigger?

Subject? (boys, girls, women, men)

Content?

Did you try to change the fantasy?

Comments:

Figure 3.1: Example of a Masturbatory Log

Another tool we have used to examine the content of masturbatory fantasy has been the 'masturbatory pie chart'. The name is drawn from the use of pie charts in simple statistics and graphics to represent the relative distributions of frequencies of events or activities. Clients are asked to consider the last one hundred times they have masturbated and to think about the range of different fantasies they have used. They are then asked to display the relative frequency of each fantasy as a segment of the pie chart. Again the exercise is preceded by discussion of the phenomenon of fantasizing, and the fact that many people, offenders and non-offenders, use different fantasies across time.

An example of a masturbatory pie chart is given in Figure 3.2.

The client here had an index offence of rape and a history of assaultive sexual behaviours escalating in intensity and frequency. Using the pie chart method described above, he reported that his main fantasy was rape of new victims. Approximately one in four of his current fantasies were of his previous offence behaviour, and one in four of consenting (non-sadomasochistic) intercourse. His least used fantasies were those of sadomasochistic practices with a consenting partner. The pie chart provides an opportunity then for the client to elaborate upon descriptions of each area.

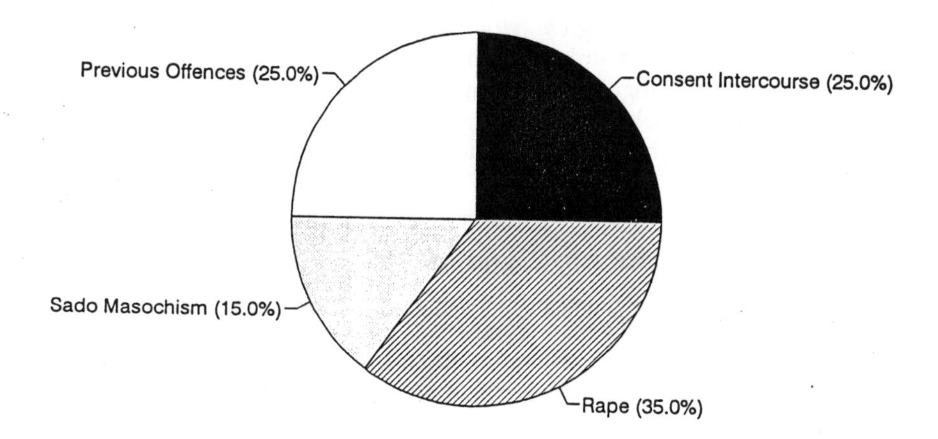

Figure 3.2: Example of a Masturbatory Pie Chart

The value of these 'pies' is not in the accuracy of the segmentation. Indeed, in our experience, it is difficult for many clients to recall accurately the content of their masturbatory fantasies across the previous weeks, even if they were motivated to do so. Rather the value of these charts is in the opportunity it affords to the offender to disclose undesirable material (fantasies of offending) in a relatively non-threatening way. Furthermore, for those clients who are not literate it is a non-demanding tool in terms of reading skills.

In discussing sexual fantasy with our clients we have a checklist of questions we ask ourselves of the clients:

- Has the client been willing to talk about his sexual fantasies?
- Has the client co-operated with recording exercises, for example masturbatory logs or pie charts?
- Has there been any change in the content of the client's fantasies? If so, what is this change attributed to?
- Can the client explain why it is important to focus on sexual fantasy in his therapy?

- Are there any indicators of events or stimuli which trigger the use of fantasies of offending?
- Has the client shown any ability to control the content of his sexual fantasy life? If so, how has this been achieved?
- Are there influences which have countered the aims and objectives of our sessions?
- How can improvements be consolidated and maintained?

It is worth pointing out here, as a caution to the professional, the potential double-bind that disclosure of sexual fantasies may create for the offender. Disclosure of sexual fantasies of illegal acts may be taken as an indicator of therapeutic engagement; if the client is able to disclose inappropriate fantasies then he must be making progress. However, using disclosure of fantasies as an index of motivation can place the offender in a no-win situation. If the offender discloses the ongoing use of fantasies of unlawful acts, then he may be considered to be at risk of re-offending. If he does not make such disclosure, then he can be thought to be withholding information and therefore not motivated to change.

Assessment of Rationalising Cognitions

It is clear from talking to many professionals that the excuses offenders use to support their offending behaviour are considered to be worthy and necessary targets for therapeutic intervention. It is assumed that the offender who continues to deny the extent or severity of his offending behaviour cannot be properly engaged in the true therapeutic purpose and therefore is at risk of reoffending as a consequence. Finkelhor *et al.* (1984) talk at a theoretical level of rationalising cognitions serving to disinhibit controls over inappropriate sexual drives. The centrality of this notion of excuse-making at both practice and theoretical level has unfortunately sometimes been reflected in professionals assuming heavily confrontational and judgmental approaches with their clients, often to the detriment of the therapeutic process.

In assessing rationalising cognitions, it is clear that some definition is required. Denial may take the form of simple non-acceptance of committing the offence(s). For example, 'Yes, I know that the little girl was assaulted, but I didn't do it, even though I got blamed for it'. More commonly, denial is about non-acceptance of responsibility for the offence: 'Yes I did it, but you can't blame me. If my wife hadn't left me none of this would have happened'. Sometimes denial will take the form of denial of harm to the victim: 'When I had sex with my daughter I knew at the time it was my responsibility but I didn't hurt her; she never asked me not to do it; it was a loving thing'. The perpetrator may deny the risk of future offending: 'It won't happen again'. Associated with this is the denial of ongoing sexual or personal problems.

It will be clear from the above that we are not describing a unitary phenomenon. Furthermore, what is equally clear is the dynamic nature of denial. Denial may change as a function of time and circumstance. For example, prior to sentencing, offenders often 'come clean', not surprisingly, in an attempt to win the sympathy of the courts and those who might be preparing reports for the courts. Following sentence and incarceration, attitudes harden and survival for the offender becomes paramount. Denial may also fluctuate in relation to the interviewer. It may be more problematic for the offender to disclose ongoing sexual difficulties to someone who is central to decision-making about transfer or discharge from the institution than to make such disclosures to less important players.

To summarise, when assessing rationalising cognitions and denial it is recommended that we make explicit just what is being observed or recorded, how the attitude has been manifest, to whom, and under what circumstances (see Figure 3.3).

Denial of:	*Yes/No*	*How manifested*
Committing an offence		
Responsibility for the offence		
Damage to victim		
Ongoing sexual problems		
Risk of re-offending		

Figure 3.3: Record of Denial

Denial and excuse-making can be assessed in several ways including the use of questionnaire measures, and direct observation of the offender's behaviour, for example in group discussion. One of the most straightforward ways of gaining access to excuse-making is that of asking the offender simply to describe the antecedents to and consequences of their offending.

For example, the following was recorded from a client who had been receiving group therapy for about six months and had been educated about the forms of denial and excuse-making. When asked to describe his index offence to a new group member, he said: 'I abused Joanne at a time when my wife had left me and I was very depressed. The abuse involved the touching of her breasts and vagina, and masturbation. I am to blame for the abuse, and it is lucky for Joanne and me that it was disclosed before it progressed'.

In the example above, it is clear that the client does not deny committing an offence. There is, however, still the suggestion of blaming others ('my wife'), of depersonalising the action ('the abuse involved'), and possibly of denial of victim damage ('it is lucky for Joanne'). The fact that this was obtained after six months of work with the client serves to emphasise the resistance to therapeutic input.

Assessment of Victim Empathy

The concept of empathy is referred to frequently by practitioners. The development of victim empathy for the offender's own victim or victims and also potential victims is a fundamental goal of many contemporary treatment programmes. Although the word empathy is much used, there is a lack of clarity as to its meaning. Theorists have debated distinctions between cognitive empathy (an intellectual understanding of the feelings of others without necessarily experiencing any emotional change oneself), and emotional empathy (vicariously experiencing the emotion of others in response to their situation and feelings). It seems that when professionals talk of victim empathy training, what is often referred to is the confrontation of clients with images or materials depicting the suffering of victims. This is done in the hope that the client's experience of pain in the controlled setting of the clinic or professional's office will then generalise to settings where empathy is more relevant, that is, scenarios in which reoffending is a risk. In addition, clients are often educated as to the short-term and long-term consequences of abuse for victims with distinctions drawn between physical and psychological sequelae.

The assessment of empathy in institutional settings is especially difficult. As a consequence of institutionalisation, emotional responses and responsivity are often blunted. For some, survival within the institution entails an avoidance of emotional spontaneity, an almost narcissistic preoccupation with self-presentation, and calculated, well-rehearsed expressions of remorse. Unfortunately, some offenders fall into a double-bind. If they show feeling and talk of empathy for their victim they are judged not to be genuine; if they do not show such feeling they are judged callous and unemotional. For juvenile offenders, additional concerns are raised. If an adolescent offender does not show victim empathy we have a 'psychopath' in the making. Little consideration is given to the developmental stage of the adolescent and how adolescents display empathy. It is wrongly assumed that adolescents share the same emotional constructs as adults with respect to empathy. The point to be made here is that when we assess empathy within institutions we have to respect environmental influences upon the individual, those constraints and motivators contingent upon its display, and the developmental level or age of the client.

There are no pencil and paper measures of victim empathy that have been standardised for use with the institutional sex offender population. However, Bays, Freeman-Longo, and Hildebran (1990) have developed a workbook for offender clients, one chapter of which deals with enhancing empathy. The message to offenders is clear:

> 'The focus of empathy is not how you feel, it is how *others* feel. The only way you can understand the depth of their feelings is to feel deeply yourself and *then put yourself in the other person's place*. Think of how

you would feel if you were experiencing what they are experiencing' (p.42).

Bays, Freeman-Longo and Hildebran's assignments can be adapted for assessment purposes. In written or audiotaped exercises clients might be encouraged to describe the following:

- The physical feelings of their victims before, during and after each offence
- The thoughts of their victims before, during and after each offence
- The emotional feelings of their victims, before, during and after each offence
- The physical and emotional state of each of their victims now
- The impact of the offences upon the family members of each victim
- The physical and emotional state of those who dealt with the victims (e.g. police surgeon, social worker, friend).

The quality of empathy is to be inferred from the answers given.

Two other approaches to the assessment of empathy are to be found in contemporary practice, both of which are relatively unstructured. One involves observing the reactions, both verbal and non-verbal, of clients whilst viewing material depicting victim distress, or whilst in role-reversal exercises where the client has been instructed to adopt the persona of their victim. The other involves the 'victim letter' in which the client is asked to write a letter to his victim(s) expressing remorse or giving an explanation for the offence. Again the assessment of empathy is inferred.

Self-Assessment

To conclude this chapter it seems appropriate to emphasise the need for professionals to examine and assess their own attitudes and motivations for engaging in sex offender work. O'Connell, Leberg and Donaldson (1990) have written guidelines for the selection of therapists in working with sexual offenders. Furthermore, Roundy and Horton (1990) have written on professional issues for clinicians working with incest perpetrators. We can use these discussions of traits and abilities to derive questions for therapists:

- How am I coping with the stress of this work?
- Are there any aspects of sexuality and offending which I am having difficulty discussing?
- Am I maintaining objectivity?
- Am I being precise in my work so that treatment integrity is maintained?
- What assumptions am I making about each of my clients?
- Has any of the material I have been exposed to sexually aroused me, and if so how have I dealt with that arousal?
- What cultural, social, religious, and gender biases am I bringing to my work?

- What models am I using to help structure my work?
- Am I making best use of the resources within the institution to help my client?
- Am I communicating my work properly to members of the multi-professional team?

Co-work in the treatment of sexual offenders has long been recognised as the norm, although less so at the assessment stage. The questions above might usefully form part of the peer review that is implicit in co-work, so that we would encourage co-workers to ask these questions of each other and discuss the answers. Similarly, the questions might usefully be asked by supervisors or consultants supporting projects.

Bibliography

Finally, various texts and monographs have been published in recent years which cite useful questionnaire measures of relevance to sex offender assessment. Whilst many of these have been developed for use with non-institutional populations their applicability to incarcerated clients is apparent. Some recommended reading is described below.

Cook S. and Taylor J. (1991) *Working with Young Sex Offenders.* Liverpool: Barnado's North West.

Describes the assessment of sexual attitudes and beliefs about men, women, and children; the assessment of understandings of the abuse of power within relationships, and a Sexual Experience Questionnaire.

Faller K.C. (1990) *Understanding Child Sexual Maltreatment.* London: Sage.

Contains a checklist for assessing the severity of sexual abuse, harm to the child, and risk of future sexual abuse.

Griffiths D.M., Quinsey V.L. and Hingsburger D. (1989) *Changing Inappropriate Sexual Behaviour: A Community-Based Approach for Persons with Developmental Disabilities.* Baltimore, MD: Paul H Brookes.

Refers to the Edwards Assessment of Socio-Sexual Skills. The text also lists a bibliography of training materials in sex education, social competency training, relationship and responsibility training, and readings on sexuality and persons with learning disabilities.

Horton A.L., Johnson B.L., Roundy L.M. and Williams D. (eds) (1990) *The Incest Perpetrator, A Family Member No One Wants to Treat.* London: Sage.

Contains assessment guidelines for perpetrators, non-offending partners, children, and relationships within incestuous families, and is useful in primary prevention work.

Laws D.R. (ed) (1989) *Relapse Prevention with Sex Offenders.* New York: The Guilford Press.

A rich tome with many references to assessment tools serving the main theme of the text viz. relapse and its prevention.

Salter A.C. (1988) *Treating Child Sex Offenders and Victims: A Practical Guide.* London: Sage.

A comprehensive guide to a sex offender treatment programme. It also contains many assessment instruments: The Abel and Becker Cognitions Scale, the Spence Attitudes Toward Women Scale, The Burt Rape Myth Acceptance Scale, The Buss-Durkee Hostility Inventory, The Interpersonal Reactivity Index, The Michigan Alcoholism Screening Test, The Social Avoidance and Distress Scale, the Wilson Sex Fantasy Questionnaire, The Nowicki-Strickland Internal/External Scale, and The Fear of Negative Evaluation Scale.

Wanigaratne S., Wallace W., Pullin J., Keaney F. and Farmer F. (1990) *Relapse Prevention for Addictive Behaviours.* Oxford: Blackwell.

A general text, not specific to sex offenders, which contains useful appendices capable of adaptation for this population. These include examples of Craving Diaries, a Session Evaluation Questionnaire, a Relapse Prevention Group Evaluation Questionnaire, an adaptation of the McLellan, Luborsy, and Erdlen Addiction Severity Index, and a Problem Listing form.

References

Bays, L., Freeman-Longo, R. and Hildebran, D. (1990) *How Can I Stop? Breaking My Deviant Cycle: A Guided Workbook For Clients In Treatment.* Orwell: Safer Society Press.

Finkelhor, D., Araji, S., Baron, L., Browne, A., Peters, S.D. and Wyatt, G. (1984) *A Source Book on Child Sexual Abuse.* London: Sage.

Heinz, J.W., Gargaro, S. and Kelly, S.G. (1987) *A Model Residential Juvenile Sex-Offender Treatment Programme: The Hennepin County Home School.* New York: Safer Security Press.

O'Connell, M.A., Leberg, E. and Donaldson, C.R. (1990) *Working with Sex Offenders: Guidelines for Therapist Selection.* London: Sage.

Pratt, P. (ed) (1986) *Sexual Assessment: Issues and Radical Alternatives.* Issues in Criminological and Legal Psychology, No. 8. Leicester: The British Psychological Society.

Roundy, L.M. and Horton, A.L. (1990) Professional and treatment issues for clinicians who intervene with incest perpetrators. In A.L. Horton, B.L. Johnson, L.M. Roundy and D. Williams (eds) *The Incest Perpetrator: A Family Member No-one Wants to Treat.* London: Sage.

CHAPTER 4

Assessment of Violent Offenders

CYNTHIA MCDOUGALL, DANNY A. CLARK, AND MARTIN J. FISHER

Assessment of violent offenders has always been given a high priority in secure settings because of their potential danger to society, and sometimes to staff and other clients in the establishment. In the Prison Service, there is a clear responsibility to assess, mainly in connection with the parole and life licence system, where the consequences of granting early release to someone who is likely to re-offend can be dramatic.

More recently, in the Prison Service (England and Wales), interest in assessment has increased for two reasons. First, the Prison Service, through its Directorate of Inmate Programmes, has given priority to the development of national treatment initiatives including control of anger and aggression. As effective treatment programmes cannot be delivered without a clear understanding of the motivation for aggression and/or violence, assessment is crucial to this process. Second, the Criminal Justice Act (1991) requires changes in the process of review of discretionary lifers (i.e., those whose offence was other than murder and therefore a life sentence was not mandatory) and it is anticipated that this will be characterised by fully open reporting, and the possibility of legal representation for the life sentence prisoner. In such cases, assessment of risk of re-offending must be clearly explained, as it will be likely to be challenged by the offender and his legal representative. Assessment methods have therefore to become much more objective and supportable by evidence.

Although categorisation of offenders by their use of violence might be expected to be a simple procedure, violent offenders are as diverse a group of individuals as can be found in any population in terms of personality, background and behaviour. Motivations for violence are also diverse, with some violent acts being a reaction to a real or perceived provocation, while others may be sexually motivated, have a political basis, be committed as a means to an end such as robbery, or be related to a psychiatric condition. Violence in

The views expressed in this chapter are the authors' and do not necessarily represent those of the Home Office Prison Service itself cannot, therefore, be considered a unifying factor and these offenders must all be examined as individuals.

In assessment, most psychologists would adopt the principles of behavioural analysis, studying the idiosyncratic antecedents and consequences of the individual's behaviour, as described in Chapter 1. Whilst a thorough and individual assessment may be considered ideal, the numbers of violent individuals to be assessed, identified for treatment and progressed through the system by relatively few professionals, require standardised assessment methods to be developed.

In many settings, the Prison Service being no exception, much effort has been put into assessment, leaving few resources to meet the needs identified. The methods described here, however, attempt to meet the needs of the many by tailoring assessment to relate to the treatment options which are available. Current theories of anger and aggression have led to the development of a range of interventions which have been evaluated and shown to be effective with various populations, and our present assessment systems are therefore concentrated on these approaches. That is not to say, of course, that we should not always be seeking to develop new methods of intervention.

Anger and Aggression

Before discussing assessment of violent offenders, it is necessary first to define what is meant by the terms associated with violent behaviour, such as anger and aggression, which are often considered to be interchangeable. Howells (1988) attempted to differentiate between the emotional states of anger, hostility and aggression, by describing anger as a subjective state of emotional arousal, hostility as an attitude or a longer-term negative evaluation of people or events, and aggression as overt behaviour involving harm to another person, but he went on to acknowledge that the terms are inter-related. Aggression is not, however, always the behavioural expression of anger or hostility, and Blackburn (1985) emphasised the distinction between incentive-motivated and annoyance-motivated aggression. In the first, the aggression is secondary to some other goal – Blackburn gives the example of a robber striking a security guard in order to obtain the money in his care – while in the second, the injury to the victim serves directly to reduce an aversive emotional state. In the assessment of violent offenders we would therefore be seeking to distinguish between incentive-motivated aggression and angry aggression.

Bandura (1973) also made this distinction and described incentive-motivated, or instrumental aggression as it is sometimes called, in social learning theory terms, depicting it as a form of coping with environmental demands based on observational learning of its utility in avoiding frustration and achieving rewards. He emphasised that observation of reward for aggression may in fact be as powerful in strengthening such behaviour as actually experiencing it.

Most modern theories of angry aggression make cognitive appraisal the central determinant of whether anger will occur in a given situation. For example, if someone receives a critical comment and perceives it as a personal attack, he or she is likely to become angry. If, conversely, the criticism is seen as being helpful and constructive, the reaction is unlikely to be one of anger. Cognitive appraisal has therefore determined the reaction. This is the basis of cognitive theories of anger, from which Novaco (1975) derived his approach, which has been the most influential in the development of methods for controlling anger in the last decade. Novaco's theoretical model of anger has four components: external events which act as triggers for anger; cognitive processes by which they are appraised; physiological arousal associated with anger; and behavioural reactions. In such a model, cognitive processes would determine whether the behavioural reaction was violent.

Among offenders whose violence is considered to be motivated by angry aggression, there is the dichotomy between those whose violence is frequent and could be described as under-controlled (Megargee, 1966) and those who may have been convicted of only one offence, but of a very serious and sometimes fatal kind. In the latter case, the victim is often well known to the offender and may be a close relative, and these cases are often most difficult to assess. As pointed out by Blackburn (1982), research studies lead to the conclusion that past violent behaviour is the best predictor of future violent behaviour, and therefore a prediction of future violent reactions could be more easily made on the under-controlled offender, where the frequency allows patterns of reaction to be identified. Those offenders who commit a single act of violence may actually reflect a disposition *not* to behave aggressively, and as such are more difficult to assess.

Megargee (1966) proposed that these 'one-off' violent offenders were over-controlled and that their extremely violent offences were committed through a build-up of unexpressed emotion over many years being suddenly unleashed. Howells (1981) suggested, however, that evidence did not support the theory of cathartic expression of emotion, nor that frustration could persist over long periods of time independently of external stimulation or internal cognitions. Howells (1981) proposed an alternative cognitive view of the over-controlled offender. He found, using repertory grids (a method of eliciting personal constructs), that over-controlled offenders construed their victims in a more 'idealised' way than those who were under-controlled. He suggested that hostile evaluation might be submerged until, under stress, a shift was made to more hostile evaluations. This shift made violence possible, then afterwards the offender returned to his earlier idealised style. This theory is similar to that of Megargee, but attributes the violence to changed cognitive appraisal rather than a physiological build-up of frustration. More recent research, however, demonstrates that expression of aggression has the effect of reducing the physical tension which has been generated by internal stimuli (McDougall and Boddis, 1991). Howells (1981) has, however, questioned the statistics of the 'one-off' violent offender, and he recommends research into the unreported domestic, non-homicidal violence which may have preceded the offence.

The main theories of anger and aggression would appear to indicate some broad categories into which many of the diverse motivations can be grouped. The main division appears to be between angry and incentive-motivated aggression, and in both categories there is the further sub-division of whether the occurrence of the aggression is frequent or infrequent (see Table 4.1). In the category of angry aggression this indicates the theoretical models of under-and over-controlled offenders while, in the case of incentive-motivated aggression, the sub-categories could be seen as representing habitual aggression as a pattern of behaviour, or as a rare event associated with an offence.

Table 4.1: Categories of Aggression

	Angry aggression	*Incentive-motivated aggression*
Frequent	under-controlled	habitual
Infrequent	over-controlled	rare

Assessment Methods with Frequently Aggressive Offenders

Practical assessment methods can be described for each of the above categories but it is helpful first to link the methods by frequency of the event. This link is useful because, where frequency is a significant factor, the aggressive behaviour is likely to occur within the secure setting where it can be observed.

Where aggression and violence occur frequently, the two types of aggression can be mis-diagnosed. In a study of young offenders referred by prison officers for anger control training, self-report by the offenders showed them to be aggressive but not more angry than other young offenders (McDougall, Venables, Boddis and Roger, 1991). This would therefore place them in the incentive-motivated, non-angry aggressive category. An anger control training programme has been designed for use in the prison system (McDougall, 1988). This caters for both frequent angry and frequent non-angry aggressive offenders, since it incorporates an aggression control element. An economical way to use this programme in treating non-angry aggressive offenders would be a short course specifically targeting their aggression and leaving aside anger control (McDougall and Boddis, 1991). Selection can be based on psychometric testing which will be described later in the chapter. The distinction between angry and non-angry aggression may not always be clear cut, and it is probably more practical in some cases to combine the two groups, while being aware of their different needs within the course.

Where aggression occurs frequently in both the angry aggressive category and the incentive-motivated category, aggressive behaviour is the main criterion for prediction of future risk and the basis of referral for treatment. Frequency of violent behaviour, and not the motivation, is therefore the first assessment measure, and subjects for anger control training are referred on this basis. The next stage of assessment takes place within the training course, with assessment of triggers to anger and motivations being an integral part of the treatment programme, and their understanding being an essential step towards achieving behavioural change. It is necessary, therefore, to describe the treatment programme briefly to demonstrate the context in which the assessment occurs.

Anger Control Training

Research over the last 15 years has supported the proposition originally made by Novaco (1975) that a cognitive-behavioural approach is most effective in the control of anger. A study by Novaco (1975) found that cognitive self-control strategies with relaxation training methods were more effective than cognitive or relaxation methods alone in reducing self-reported and observed anger, and later Novaco (1978) added role-play of anger situations to the treatment programme. In later studies (Deffenbacher, Story, Stark, Hogg, and Brandon, 1987; Hazaleus and Deffenbacher, 1986; Kettlewell and Kausch, 1983; Moon and Eisler, 1983; Schlichter, 1978), programmes based on Novaco's approach have been evaluated with similar results, although Deffenbacher, Demm and Brandon (1986) demonstrated that relaxation techniques were significantly effective in reducing general and situational anger when compared with a non-treatment expectancy control group. In a later study, Glick and Goldstein (1987) included a moral development module in an attempt to deal with aggressive attitudes which were resistant to change, a problem which McDougall (1989) overcame using an approach in which offenders listed and emphasised 'negative consequences' of aggression for the aggressor.

The component of the treatment programme most relevant to assessment is the cognitive self-control element of the training, which proposes that negative self-statements are the determinants of angry behaviour. These should be elicited from course members, who are then encouraged to replace them with positive self-statements. When the self-statements are elicited in discussion of previous angry events and incidents from an anger diary, an analysis becomes possible of the nature of the cognitive appraisal which leads to anger. This can be related to Novaco's propositions about anger which include: becoming angry because of taking things personally; feeling threatened; feeling a loss of control of a situation; and always having behaved that way. Being aware of the cognitive appraisal assists in the understanding of the occurrence of violence and verbal aggression, and enhances our ability to predict its likely re-occurrence.

Evaluation of Treatment Effectiveness

Success of course members in learning anger control strategies is important to the assessment of future risk, and consequently evaluation of course effectiveness is essential to the individual assessment. Most usual evaluation methods, including those proposed by Novaco (1975), are: behavioural measures; psychometric tests; psychophysiological measures; observer- and self-ratings of responses to real provocation incidents; and ratings of performance in role-played anger situations. Of these, real provocation ratings have not been tested in a prison setting for the ethical reasons against deliberately provoking an offender to anger, and ratings of role-play were thought to be invalid, as role-play was already being used as a treatment method. Other evaluation methods have been examined as follows.

(1) Behavioural methods

Staff rating of behaviour can be seen as a valid method of evaluating change where aggression has been regularly exhibited in the establishment. Behaviour rating forms are given to prison officers to report on the aggressive behaviour of individual offenders in advance of anger control courses and after courses. Such ratings can give a useful indication of change, but it must be recognised that they have the disadvantage of being openly linked to the treatment programme and can be biased because of the officer's knowledge of the purpose of the ratings. To have a completely independent rating, it is necessary to obscure this link. A more objective evaluation method is to use the institutional disciplinary measure – Governors' Reports. Governors' Reports were calculated for a three-month period prior to an anger control course and for a three-month period after a course and compared with Governors' Reports over the same period for a waiting list control group (McDougall, Barnett, Ashurst and Willis, 1987).

Results of this study (see Table 4.2) showed that subjects who had been on an anger control course decreased significantly in Governors' Reports after the course (Sign Test, $p = <.05$) whilst there was no significant difference found for the control group. It is worth noting that these results were set against a background when the overall number of Governors' Reports in the establishment was rising. Subsequently, anger control training courses have shown consistent reduction in Governors' Reports following treatment (McDougall and Boddis, 1991) and this measure appears to be an effective independent means of assessing behaviour change for young offenders.

Table 4.2: Pre and Post Course Evaluation – Governors' Reports

	3 Months Prior to Course	*3 Months After Course*
Course (n=15)	25	8
Control (n=15)	18	22

It must be emphasised, however, that this independent measure is only appropriate in parts of the system where Governors' Reports tend to be administered on a regular and consistent basis. It has, for example, been found that with long-term dispersal prisoners Governors' Reports are not a good measure, since dispersal prison staff do not apply this sanction in anger incidents if it can be avoided. For this reason, other means of monitoring angry behaviour have been developed for such establishments and these are described later in the chapter under 'Assessment of over-controlled offenders'.

(2) Psychometric tests

Although psychometric tests of anger and aggression have sometimes been found to be reliable and valid when assessing large groups, they are rarely used for individual assessment except as an indication of type of anger, and then only in conjunction with other forms of assessment. In addition, some psychometric tests have not been validated on the population in question, in this case a secure establishment population and, therefore, although providing a valid measure in the community, would not be appropriate for use with incarcerated offenders. This is true of the Novaco Anger Inventory (Novaco, 1975). The inventory was validated on a sample of university students, teachers, and members of the community, and was in addition used as a before and after measure to evaluate anger control training. Although the inventory has subsequently been widely used in studies of anger, it has not been validated on a criminal population, and in a study of young offenders was found to be unrelated to their angry behaviour (McDougall *et al.* 1987). This has been acknowledged by Novaco himself in conference discussion.

There is also the option of measuring anger as a state or as a trait. Spielberger, Jacobs, Russell, and Crane (1983) made this distinction and the State-Trait Anger Scale (STAS) incorporated two scales to meet the distinction. The STAS was designed specifically to measure anger, and does not include, as some inventories do, hostility, aggression and angry behaviour. State anger is defined as an emotional state or condition that consists of subjective feelings of tension, annoyance, irritation, fury and rage, with consistent activation or arousal of the autonomic nervous system. Trait anger is defined in terms of individual differences in frequency of state anger over time. Trait anger, as defined by Spielberger in terms of frequency of angry states, might be expected to change as a result of anger control training. In fact, scores on trait anger following anger control training did not correlate with behaviour change, nor did the scale appear to differentiate clearly anger from other emotions (McDougall, 1989).

Similarly, in a study by Deffenbacher, Demm and Brandon (1986) which compared angry and non-angry subjects over a range of anger and anxiety measures, including the STAS and the State-Trait Anxiety Inventory (STAI; Spielberger, Gorsuch, and Lushene, 1970), general anxiety was found to be equally predictive of anger as general anger measures. It is proposed, therefore, that this measure is not appropriate for individual assessments, and it would not be likely to reflect changes in level of anger following training.

There is always a problem in finding self-report measures which co-vary with behaviour, and this is the case with the Hostility and Direction of Hostility Questionnaire (HDHQ; Foulds, Caine, and Creasy, 1960) which was developed as an index of whether hostility was directed inwards towards the self or outwards against other people and objects. The HDHQ has been used extensively in prisons, but the results have been equivocal: although offenders were reported to have higher overall hostility scores than normal controls (Caine, Foulds, and Hope, 1967), it has proved impossible to discriminate amongst incarcerated subjects according to degree or type of offence (Crawford, 1977). Scores on the HDHQ have also been found to correlate poorly with overt hostile behaviour (Oldham, McGurk, and Magaldi, 1976).

An inventory which does appear to be unaffected by the problems described for other inventories is the Situations-Reactions Hostility Inventory (SHRI) developed by Blackburn and Lee-Evans (1985; see Appendix 4.1). This inventory, based on an earlier inventory by Endler and Hunt (1968), was developed to take into account the situational component of angry incidents, and was developed for a Special Hospital population. Some situations were adopted from the Endler and Hunt scale, while others were derived from incidents known to provoke anger in an institutional setting. Reactions were also drawn from the Endler and Hunt scale. A principal component analysis of the situations produced two factors which Blackburn and Lee-Evans identified as Attack and Frustration. The 12 reaction items, when factor-analysed, identified three factors which were named Aggression, Anger and Arousal. A research study carried out on young offenders undergoing anger control courses showed the SRHI as being the only psychometric measure which demonstrated significantly reduced self-report of aggression and anger concurrently with reduction of the behavioural measure of Governors' Reports (McDougall, Venables, Boddis, and Roger, 1991). In addition, the three reactions scales were associated with different profiles on the Special Hospitals Assessment of Personality and Socialisation (SHAPS; Blackburn, 1982) and had independent psychophysiological profiles (McDougall, 1989).

These findings suggest that the SRHI can be recommended as a means of evaluating self-report changes following anger control courses.

(3) Psychophysiological measures

Novaco (1975) and others have used psychophysiological measures before and after anger control training as a means of evaluating the effectiveness of the training. The validity of this form of evaluation is, however, questionable. For example, skin conductance responses as an individual measure of anger can be unreliable due to the variety of factors which can influence the response, and the inability to standardise the provocation so that comparisons can be made. These concerns are illustrated in a pilot study carried out by McDougall (1989) to explore the feasibility of this form of evaluation and to investigate whether the Novaco methodology was appropriate with a secure residential population. Subjects were two inmates in a top-security dispersal prison who had a history of serious anger and violence. The pre-and post-anger course measures were frequency of skin conductance responses, as used by Novaco (1975), with a similar methodology, and these were recorded during imaginal and role-played anger incidents. Although one would expect fewer skin conductance responses after treatment, for both subjects more responses were measured post-treatment than pre-treatment, and both registered only one response during the entire pre-treatment session. During the post-treatment evaluation both subjects produced responses during a neutral role-play where there was no anger provocation. Neither subject produced responses during imaginal provocation scenes and only one subject produced responses during provocation role-plays.

Both subjects expressed subjective feelings of anger, but discussion afterwards suggested that anger was not always in response to predicted stimuli. It was found to be impossible to predict reliably subjective anger to a provocation or lack of it in neutral instances. In one situation, one of the subjects became angry at something completely unexpected in the role-play; in another, rather than becoming angry he became uncertain of himself. The amount of provocation cannot therefore be standardised, and it cannot be determined with certainty that responses are to a stimuli rather than spontaneous fluctuations.

In addition, interaction between the subject and presenter cannot be controlled. At one stage, one subject became angry because of the tone of voice of the presenter, rather than the subject matter of the role-play. This can be overcome in imaginal situations by using a pre-recorded presentation, but this cannot be overcome in role-play. This pilot study showed that artifacts may affect psychophysiological responding in an experimental design which includes imaginal and role-play anger provocation, and would therefore be invalid as a method of evaluating anger control treatment.

A further study by McDougall (1989) brought into question whether the frequency of skin conductance responses (SCRs) was in fact a measure of anger, and the associated assumption that reduction of these was evidence of reduction of anger. Since the pilot study described above demonstrated an inability to standardise anger provocation, the methodology was changed, with subjects being subjected to a series of recorded tones and the frequency of SCRs analysed in relation to scores on the SRHI. Results showed that the frequency of SCRs was associated more with high scores on self-reported arousal, which had been shown to be related more to anxiety than to anger. Reduction in frequency of SCRs might, therefore, in Novaco's (1975) experiment be related to a reduction in anxiety following anger control training. Research on SCR as a psychophysiological measure of anger, therefore, does not currently give confidence in its use as a method of assessment of effectiveness of anger control training and this is not recommended.

Summary of Assessment Process with Frequently Aggressive Offenders

The first stage in this assessment is a study of the aggressive/violent behaviour exhibited. This is a brief assessment based on frequency and patterns of behaviour drawn from past records, previous offence behaviour, disciplinary reports, interviews with prison officers who have frequent contact with the client, and a preparatory interview with the client to gain his or her agreement to undertaking treatment and to obtain his or her view of the angry behaviour and its motivation. The process of obtaining the inmate's view can be assisted by completion of the SRHI. This is a particularly useful instrument as it asks about reactions to specific situations and these can be analysed in terms of provocation by attack and/or frustration and, when examined individually, can be narrowed down to the specific kinds of situation which promote anger and aggression in that individual.

Further information on the situational components of anger can be obtained by asking the subject to complete an anger diary prior to a course and between course sessions. A typical anger diary is shown in Figure 4.1, and records where the incident occurred, who was involved, what it was that made the subject angry, and the subject's anger rating on a 1–5 scale, representing a 'slightly annoyed' to 'furious' reaction. This rating becomes an important part of anger management training by encouraging the subject to be more aware of the early signs of anger.

Date of incident ....

What happened?

Who was involved?

What made you angry?

How angry did you feel? (Circle a number)

1 .... 2 .... 3 .... 4 5

Slightly Annoyed *Furious*

Figure 4.1: Anger diary

Subsequently, the motivation for the angry behaviour can be assessed during anger control training by examining each incident recorded in diaries and eliciting cognitive self-statements. This process is achieved by encouraging the subject to think what was going through his or her mind before, during and after the incident. This part of the assessment may need patience on the part of the tutor, since subjects are frequently unaware of a thought process associated with their anger. This is, however, a crucial step in understanding the person's cognitive appraisal of events. Treatment methods follow on from this understanding by identifying distorted cognitions and modifying them by encouraging more appropriate positive self-statements which will assist anger control.

Evaluation of the effectiveness of the anger control programme in assisting the subject to control his or her anger and associated aggressive behaviour is measured by frequency of post-course aggressive events in comparison with pre-course frequency.

Case Study Example

Subject	Frequently on report for angry behaviour to officers, sometimes assault.
Diary Incident	Shouting abuse at work instructor because he thought his pay was wrong.
Elicited Cognitive Self-statements	
	My pay's wrong again.
	It's always wrong.
	I work hard but he doesn't think so.
	He doesn't like me.
	It wouldn't happen to John, because he's his favourite.
	He's making a fool of me.
	He'll try to get away with paying me less.
	He won't listen to me.
	He thinks I'm an idiot.
	I hate him.
	I should punch him.
	It would be worth it.
	Then he'd have to listen to me.
Reasons for Anger	1. Takes incident as a personal attack.
	2. Thinks he is being made to look stupid.
	3. Feels he has no control of the situation.
Positive Self-statements	My pay seems to be wrong but I might have made a mistake.
	I'll discuss it with him, he might have an explanation.
	Maybe he's made a mistake.
	There's more chance of him listening if I'm reasonable.
	There's no need to get annoyed, this can be sorted out.

Having learned to use positive self-statements, the subject may require social practice in handling situations in a different way, and encouragement that he can have more control if he handles the situation more calmly and skilfully. Relaxation training can be given to help him keep calm.

Assessment of Offenders with Infrequent Violent Behaviour

As stated earlier, assessment of subjects whose violence is a rare event, whether in the category of angry aggression or incentive-motivated aggression, cannot rely on evidence of previous violent behaviour being predictive of future behaviour. In the case of serious offenders, particularly murderers, the offences for which they were imprisoned are often their only violent offence and the past behaviour model would suggest that re-offending is unlikely to re-occur because of the infrequency of the event. With such serious offences, however, we cannot afford to rely on this model and need to look much more closely at individual cases to understand the nature of their offending. Traditionally, a thorough functional analysis would be undertaken by a psychologist, however the large number of offenders who require assessment does not always allow for this process. In addition, with the advent of open reporting on life sentence prisoners and on parole decisions, it is necessary to find a way of improving the assessment process in order to attempt to make assessments more objective.

An assessment model has therefore been developed to address the problems described, and in addition to address the problems inherent in a system of assessment where judgments are largely based on information and conclusions which have been drawn from interview. As a specialist, one is aware that things said in interview are often in complete contradiction to behaviour that is observed outside the interview room. An offender may say that he is never going to be in trouble again, but the prison officer may say that the offender is running all the extortion rackets on the wing. The offender says all he wants to do is get out of prison and make up to his wife and family for the damage done to them, while all the time he is writing to two or three other women. In such situations, one is more convinced by what the offender does than by what he says. In cases where behaviour supports the interview comments, however, confidence in the validity of the statements can be much stronger.

Prison officers are in the best position to observe behaviour, but often their observations are unfocused and not necessarily related to risk. A new approach to assessment seeks to draw on the rich source of behavioural information available to officers by observation and to give guidance on what should be observed in order to elicit information about risk.

It may seem at first that observation of behaviour in a prison setting cannot apply to assessment of risk in the community, since a prison environment is far removed from the situational context of a crime. In some cases, the type of victim who might be at risk is not present; that is there are few women and no young children in the prison. It is, however, surprising how persistent patterns of behaviour can be, despite situational changes, and how often offenders find themselves in similar situations in prison to those which occurred in their outside environment.

The assessment model seeks to identify the consistent behaviour patterns associated with risk of offending and monitor these as a more objective method of assessing level of risk. The model also seeks to focus more clearly on behaviour which should be targeted for intervention and behaviour change. The kinds of behaviour pattern which persist despite a changed environment can be illustrated in the following real case examples.

Prisoner A, who had murdered his father and claimed as a reason that his father was interfering too much in his life, began to exhibit the same behaviour with a fellow-inmate, complaining that the inmate was interfering in his life in a similar way. All the early complaints and threats made to and about his father were being displayed in the new situation. (This case study is described more fully in Appendix 4.2).

Prisoner B, whose sex offences against children were always linked with rows with adult women, succeeded in rowing with his female probation officer, various female prison visitors, and a female prison governor, and seemed adept at setting up relationships with females even in prison which resulted in conflict.

Prisoner C, a 50-year-old man, had murdered a 15-year-old girl whom he had befriended. He had encouraged her to come to his house, become fond of her, thought she returned his feelings, made sexual advances to her and when these were rejected, raped and murdered her. After 15 years of a prison sentence he was a model prisoner, doing all the correct things to appear ready for release. However, what began as a kind gesture in making a soft toy for the 14-year-old disabled daughter of another inmate, progressed to correspondence with her and then her school friends for whom he also began making soft toys. Soon he was having regular correspondence with a number of 14-year-old girls; a repetition of the kind of befriending behaviour which had led to his original offence.

Although many staff do take behaviour patterns into account when making an assessment, the model seeks to make this process more systematic and explicit, and to focus and co-ordinate the various assessments of a multi-disciplinary team. In practice, for each case the co-ordinator examines the behaviour associated with the offence, then, with reference to previous history and probation reports, attempts to discover whether a similar pattern of behaviour has been illustrated in the past, albeit in a less serious form. When the behaviour pattern has been identified, this is used to predict comparable kinds of behaviour in the prison environment.

An example might be someone whose murder offence was due to an adverse reaction to rejection. In the past, although never having committed a murder, there might be illustrations of a poor reaction to rejection, for example storming out of his job after being criticised, or family problems when refused something. The pattern for prison behaviour would then be predicted to include an angry reaction to refusals by officers, such as storming out of the office and slamming the door. This response to rejection could be monitored for change and interventions designed to assist behaviour change.

A preliminary validation has been carried out to see whether predicted behaviour is reflected in actual behaviour, using independent raters to examine prison reports and records, without reference to the offence detail and risk assessment, in order to identify actual behaviours observed in the prison. Other independent raters have compared actual behaviours with predicted behaviours for evidence of agreement. Early results showed 60 per cent accuracy of prediction compared with 23 per cent accuracy when behaviour predictions were carried out randomly. The validation process is described in more detail by McDougall and Clark (1991).

Behavioural Assessment in Practice

(From Risk Assessment Programme; Clark, Fisher and Thomas, 1991).

Instructions for carrying out a risk assessment are as follows and a worked example is shown in Appendix 4.2.

1. Complete Section 1 of the risk assessment proforma. Record background history and offence information solely from documented evidence: do not interview the inmate.
2. In Section 2, based on the factual information you have recorded in Section 1, extract the behaviours of greatest concern.
3. Having analysed the offence and selected risk factors (areas of greatest risk) you are now in a position to begin to predict how these risk factors may manifest themselves in the prison environment in Section 3 of the risk assessment pro forma.

For example, you could have identified lack of anger control, alcohol problems, poor ability to cope with stress as risk factors. Possible predictions of these risk factors could be:

Offence risk factor	*Institutional Behaviour*
Lack of anger control	Fights, assaults, arguments
Alcohol problems	Make illicit alcohol, drugs, debt
Poor ability to cope with stress	Drugs, debt, constantly seeks support from others.

4. Once the predictors of risk have been identified, behavioural recording must take place. Section 4 of the risk assessment is the pro forma for reviewing the evidence of risk.

It is possible in this chapter to give only a limited example of the risk assessment process. Only a brief extract from the manual is given and anyone interested in adopting the model should gain a copy of the full manual from the authors.

Conclusion

Although the functional analysis model is effective in assessment of violent offenders, there are methods available which allow assessment on a wider scale so that all violent offenders can be assessed and given the opportunity for treatment. Those offenders who come into the angry aggressive/under-controlled group are eminently suitable for anger control training, and detailed assessment of the specific triggers to violence are elicited during the course of the treatment programme. Evaluation of the effectiveness of the treatment is best carried out by means of the Situations-Reactions Hostility Inventory (Blackburn and Lee-Evans, 1985) and, in situations where disciplinary reports are used consistently, these are a valid measure of behaviour change. Where these are an unsuitable measure for regime reasons, staff-report may be used, but a more independent measure is desirable and it is recommended that the assessment model described for offenders with infrequent violent behaviour is more appropriate. This allows an officer to monitor behaviour objectively, and is more independent, not being directly related to the treatment initiative and therefore not so readily open to bias.

Some incentive-motivated aggression which happens on a habitual basis may also be amenable to anger control training, as an aggression control element is included in the programme (McDougall 1988). A short course, described by McDougall and Boddis (1991), is also appropriate. These incentive-motivated aggressive offenders can be differentiated from those with an anger problem by means of the Situations-Reactions Hostility Inventory (SRHI).

Offenders whose violence is infrequent are not amenable to the same kind of assessment as those showing frequent violent behaviour, although this may become appropriate at a second stage when an underlying behaviour pattern is identified. If the behaviour pattern is associated with an angry reaction to provocation, it would then be appropriate to refer the inmate to an anger control training programme and subsequently to monitor behaviour in the establishment for ability to control that underlying behaviour pattern.

References

Bandura, A. (1973) *Aggression: A Social Learning Analysis.* Englewood Cliffs, New Jersey: Prentice Hall.

Blackburn, R. (1982) The special hospitals assessment of personality and socialisation (SHAPS) and the personality deviation questionnaire (PDQ) Unpublished manuscript, Park Lane Hospital.

Blackburn, R. (1985) Cognitive-behavioural approaches to understanding and treating aggression. Paper presented at the *Second Leicester Conference on Forensic Psychology: Clinical Approaches to Aggression and Violence.*

Blackburn, R. (1988) Cognitive-behavioural approaches to understanding and treating aggression. In K. Howells and C.R. Hollin (eds) *Clinical Approaches to Aggression and Violence, Issues in Criminological and Legal Psychology,* 12. Leicester: The British Psychological Society.

Blackburn, R. and Lee-Evans, J.M. (1985) Reactions of primary and secondary psychopaths to anger-evoking situations. *British Journal of Clinical Psychology,* 24, 93–100.

Caine, T.M., Foulds, G.A. and Hope, K. (1967) *Manual of the Hostility and Direction of Hostility Questionnaire (HDHQ)* London: University of London Press.

Clark, D.A., Fisher, M.J. and Thomas, M.E. (1991) *The Assessment of Risk: A Guide.* Unpublished manuscript, HMP Wakefield.

Crawford, D. (1977) The HDHQ results of long-term prisoners: Relationships with criminal and institutional behaviour. *British Journal of Social and Clinical Psychology,* 6, 391–394.

Deffenbacher, J.L., Demm, P.M. and Brandon, A.D. (1986) High general anger: Correlates and treatment. *Behaviour Research and Therapy,* 24, 481–489.

Deffenbacher, J.L., Story, D.A., Stark, R.S., Hogg, J.A. and Brandon, A.D. (1987) Cognitive – relaxation and social skills interventions in the treatment of general anger. *Journal of Counselling Psychology, 34,* 171–176.

Endler, N.S. and Hunt, J.McV. (1968) Sources of variance in hostility and anxiety inventories. *Journal of Personality and Social Psychology, 9,* 309–315.

Foulds, G.A., Caine, T.M. and Creasy, M.A. (1960) Aspects of extra and intra-punitive expression in mental illness. *Journal of Mental Signs, 106,* 599–609.

Glick, B. and Goldstein, A.P. (1987) Aggression replacement training. *Journal of Counselling and Development, 65,* 356–362.

Hazaleus, S.L. and Deffenbacher, J.L. (1986) Relaxation and cognitive treatment of anger. *Journal of Consulting and Clinical Psychology, 54,* 222–226.

Howells, K. (1981) Social relationships in violent offenders. In S. Duck and D.R. Gilmour (eds) *Personal Relationships III: Personal Relationships in Disorder.* New York: Academic Press.

Howells, K. (1988) The management of angry aggression: cognitive behavioural approaches to anger and its management. In W. Dryden and P. Trower (eds) *New Developments in Cognitive Psychotherapy.* London: Sage.

Kettlewell, P.W. and Kausch, D.F. (1983) The generalisation of the effects of a cognitive-behavioural programme for aggressive children. *Journal of Abnormal Child Psychology, 11,* 101–114.

McDougall, C. (1988) Anger Control Programme. *Home Office Directorate of Psychological Services Report, Series II, No 160.* London: Home Office Prison Service.

McDougall, C. (1989) *Anger Control.* Unpublished D. Phil. Thesis. University of York.

McDougall, C. and Boddis, S. (1991) Discrimination between anger and aggression: Implications for treatment. In M. McMurran and C. McDougall (eds) *Issues in Criminological and Legal Psychology, 17, Vol II.* Leicester: The British Psychological Society.

McDougall, C., Barnet, R.M., Ashurst, B. and Willis, B. (1987) Anger Control. In B.J. McGurk, D. Thornton and M. Williams (eds) *Applying Psychology to Imprisonment.* London: Her Majesty's Stationery Office.

McDougall, C. and Clark, D.A. (1991) A Risk Assessment Model. In S. Boddis (ed) *Proceedings of the Prison Psychology Conference.* London: Her Majesty's Stationery Office.

McDougall, C., Venables, P.H., Boddis, S. and Roger, D. (in press) Anger control with young offenders: research and practice. London: HMSO.

Megargee, E.I. (1966) Under-controlled and over-controlled personality types in extreme anti-social aggression. *Psychological Monographs, 80,* (Whole No.611).

Moon, J.R. and Eisler, R.M. (1983) Anger control: An experimental comparison of three behavioural treatments. *Behaviour Therapy, 14,* 493–505.

Novaco, R.W. (1975) *Anger control: The Development and Evaluation of Experimental Treatment.* Lexington, Mass: Heath Sand Co.

Novaco, R.W. (1978) Anger and coping with stress. In J.P Foreyt and D.P. Rathjen (eds) *Cognitive Behavioural Therapy.* New York: Penguin.

Oldham, H., McGurk, B. and Magaldi, R. (1976) Hostility and assaultiveness. *Home Office Directorate of Psychological Services Report, Series I, No 7.* London: Home Office Prison Service.

Schlichter, K.J. (1978) An application of stress inoculation in the development of anger management skills in institutionalised juvenile delinquents. *Dissertation Abstracts International, 38,* (12-B).

Spielberger, C.D., Gorsuch, R.L. and Lushene, R.E. (1970) *Manual for the State-Trait Anxiety Inventory (Self-evaluation questionnaire)* Palo Alto, California: Consulting Psychologists Press.

Spielberger, C.D., Jacobs, G., Russell, S. and Crane, R.S. (1983) Assessment of anger: The state-trait anger scale. In J. Butcher and C.D. Speilberger (eds) *Advances in Personality Assessment, Vol. II.* Hillsdale, NJ: Lawrence Erlbaum.

Appendix 4.1 Situations-Reactions Hostility Inventory (Blackburn and Lee-Evans, 1985)

The purpose of this questionnaire is to determine how you would feel and react in certain situations. On each page there is a description of a particular situation in which you might find yourself. Below it are listed twelve feelings or reactions you might have in the situation.

Read the description of the situation carefully, then indicate how much or how intensely you would experience each of the reactions by circling the appropriate phrase (not at all, slightly, etc)

Remember, what is required is an indication of how strong you think your reaction *would* be in that situation and not what you think it *should* be. Don't miss out any of the situations and give an answer for all feelings and reactions.

Summary of Situations

S1 You are talking to someone who does not answer you.
S2 You are trying to watch TV and someone next to you is talking loudly.
S3 You have just found out that someone has been telling lies about you.
S4 You have done your best at a job but are told it is not good enough.
S5 Someone calls you a dirty name.
S6 You are waiting in a queue and someone you know pushes ahead of you.
S7 You accidentally spill hot tea over yourself.
S8 Someone you do not like bumps into you on purpose when you are eating a meal.
S9 You have just been blamed for something you did not do.
S10 Someone is making fun of you.
S11 You are watching an exciting film on TV and the set breaks down.
S12 Someone owes you money but says he does not.
S13 Someone threatens to beat you up.
S14 You are wearing a new coat you have bought yourself and someone burns it with a cigarette.

Reactions

1. **You feel tense.**
   Not at all Slightly A fair amount Quite a lot Very much
2. **You swear.**
   Not at all Slightly A fair amount Quite a lot Very much
3. **You feel angry.**
   Not at all Slightly A fair amount Quite a lot Very much
4. **Your heart beats faster.**
   Not at all Slightly A fair amount Quite a lot Very much
5. **You want to hit someone or something.**
   Not at all Slightly A fair amount Quite a lot Very much
6. **You grind your teeth.**
   Not at all Slightly A fair amount Quite a lot Very much
7. **You lose your temper.**
   Not at all Slightly A fair amount Quite a lot Very much
8. **You sweat.**
   Not at all Slightly A fair amount Quite a lot Very much
9. **You want to get your own back.**
   Not at all Slightly A fair amount Quite a lot Very much
10. **Your hands shake.**
    Not at all Slightly A fair amount Quite a lot Very much
11. **You want to shout.**
    Not at all Slightly A fair amount Quite a lot Very much
12. **You lash out.**
    Not at all Slightly A fair amount Quite a lot Very much

Scoring

The Situations-Reactions Inventory is made up of 14 different situations and 12 possible reactions. The reactions are the same for each of the 14 situations.

Of the 14 situations, nine are 'Attack' situations (3,5,6,8,9,10,12,13,14) and five are 'Frustration' situations (1,2,4,7,11)

Of the 12 possible reactions to each situation, five make up the 'Aggression' scale (5,7,9,11,12) three make up the 'Anger' scale (1,2,3) and four the 'Arousal' scale (4,6,8,10)

The SRHI, therefore, has 6 scales: Attack – Aggression, Anger, and Arousal; and Frustration – Aggression, Anger, and Arousal.

The subject registers how intensely he would react in the suggested way to a particular situation: 'not at all' is scored 0 for that particular situational reaction; 'slightly' is scored 1; 'a fair amount' 2; 'quite a lot' 3; and 'very much' 4.

Scores may be summed separately for attack and frustration or split into response headings. Before and after comparisons of scores can be used as a means of evaluation of anger control courses.

Appendix 4.2. Risk Assessment Proforma

(This is a worked example. Reponses are shown in underlined italics)

Section 1. Offence Information

Name .... Daley
Number AB1234
Index Offence ... Manslaughter

1. Using material in the prisoner's file, assess the offending behaviour of the individual under the following headings. Remember that the ultimate aim of the assessment is to produce 'Risk Factors' which can be measured through observation of prison behaviour. Therefore try to give as specific details of behaviour as is possible.

   (a) Was the offence one of arson? YES *NO*

   If the answer to (a) is YES GO TO to (d)

   (b) **Victim**

   (i) Was the victim Male or Female? *Male*/Female

   (ii) How old was the victim? Please underline.
   0–10 11–16 17–25 26–40 *41–60* 60+

   (iii) Was the victim known to the offender? *YES* NO
   If YES, what was their relationship?
   Wife, co-habitee, lover, sibling, girlfriend, *parent,* relative, neighbour, friend known vaguely, other...
   Victim was the offender's father
   Evidence:
   Police Report 13/3/1987
   If NO, how did the offender and the victim come into contact? (e.g. selected at random, met in pub, during burglary, in the street)
   Evidence:

   (c) **Weapon**

   (i) Was any weapon used? *YES* NO
   If YES: What weapon? *Two knives*
   Was the weapon habitually carried? *YES* NO
   Evidence:
   One weapon was kept under the offender's pillow. (Probation Service Post-Sentence Report)
   Was the use of the weapon spontaneous? YES *NO*
   (e.g. Was the weapon something that 'just came to hand')
   Evidence:
   Offender selected weapon before challenging victim.
   If NO, did the offender use physical force? YES *NO*
   Did the offender threaten violence? YES *NO*
   Evidence:

   (ii) Did the offender use both weapon and physical force? YES *NO*
   Evidence:

(d) **Co-accused**

(i) Was the offender alone in perpetrating the offence? YES NO
If NO, how many others were involved?
What were the relationships (if any) of the co-accused to the offender/victim?
Is there evidence that this offender was the leader?
Is there evidence that this offender was a follower?

(e) **Planning**

How much planning was there in the offence?

(i) **Spontaneous** – no planning (e.g. *sudden attack after argument,* response to an unforeseen situation)
Evidence:
Use of the weapon to confront victim was not spontaneous, however use of the weapon on the victim was. (Police Report 13/3/1987)

(ii) **Some general planning** (e.g. offender set out to look for some victim, *intended to confront victim,* took job, engineered situation to make offending behaviour more likely)
Evidence:
Offender returned home from the pub and believed that on returning his father had been interfering with mail in the offender's bedroom. (Police Report 13/3/1987)

(iii) **Specified/detailed planning** (e.g. offender planned offence with others, fantasised about offending behaviour, set out to commit offence, arranged alibi, equipped himself with a weapon)
Evidence:

(f) **Use of Violence**

Was the use of violence in the offence extreme? Did it include any of the following? State exactly what occurred:

(i) **Loss of control** (e.g. *multiple stabbing,* excessive blows to the victim, kicks)
Evidence:
Stabbed victim numerous times in the chest. (Police Report 13/3/1987)

(ii) **Sadistic violence** (e.g. torture, attempts to dominate, inflict unnecessary pain)
Evidence:

(iii) **Mutilation** – either before or after the death of the victim
Evidence:
If YES, was the mutilation part of pleasure derived from offending or was it done in order to conceal evidence?

(g) **Motivation**

What class of motivation best describes this offender's behaviour?

(i) **Sexual gratification**
Evidence:

(ii) **Financial gain**
Evidence:

(iii) **Over-reaction to events**
Evidence:
Felt paranoid about his father's behaviour over a long period of time (Probation Service Post-Sentence Report)

(iv) **Over-reaction to an individual**
Evidence:

(v) **Over-reaction to long-term circumstances** (e.g. *relationships,* depression, psychotic breakdown)
Evidence:
Offender had a long held belief that his father was victimising him. This led to a build-up of tension (as (iii) above)

(vi) **Cold-blooded/no apparent motive**
Evidence:

(h) **Earlier Antecedents**
Any recent changes in lifestyle/circumstances which may have led to offending behaviour. Please underline.
Release from prison/institution
Living away from home
Marital problems
Divorce
Cash problems
Redundancy/Sack
Change of work
Psychological problems
Medical problems
Death of loved one Grandmother murdered
Accident
Non-conformist lifestyle
Relationship difficulties
Other (please be exact):

(i) **Trigger Events**
Any other specific events in the offence environment which may have triggered offending behaviour. More than one may be present. (e.g. the way the victim looked, *what they said, how they acted,* expectations thwarted, *argument,* shock)
Evidence:
When offender confronted victim, victim became agitated. Offender felt threatened when victim moved towards him. (Probation Service Post-Sentence Report).

(j) **Alcohol and Drugs**
Were alcohol or drugs involved in the offence in any way? *YES* NO
If YES, please circle:
taken for courage
to relieve stress
reduced inhibition
offence to gain cash for drugs/alcohol
altered mental state
aroused perverse desires

(k) **Bizarre Aspects**
Did any of the following occur during the offence? (tick)
Ask personal questions Talk continuously
Satanic overtures to behaviour Discard own clothes
Took photos Defecation
Sado-masochism Urination Other
Maintained 'normal' lifestyle, appearance during commission of prolonged offence (e.g. kept victim bound whilst offender followed usual daily routine)

(l) **Behaviour after the Offence**
In what way did the offender behave immediately after committing the offence?

(i) Were attempts made to conceal the offence? (please circle)
None Hid body Ran away Destroyed body
Fabricate evidence Arranged alibi
Committed further offences to conceal first one
Returned to usual lifestyle

(iia) At what stage did the offender admit the offence? Please underline.
Never *When arrested* *During police interrogation*
To family To a friend In casual conversation
In a note/letter

(iib) If admission occurred, how long after the offence did it occur?
Shortly after offence Within one year Over one year

(iic) If admission occurred, does the offender still refuse to admit to certain aspects of offending behaviour? YES *NO*

(iid) If 'YES' to (iic) state which aspects:

(iii) Did the offender show signs of shock or regret? *YES* NO
Evidence:
Very depressed in Remand Centre – concern over mental state expressed by two Medical Officers. Depressive state. (Medical Report CPS)

(m) **Blaming**
How does the offender explain his behaviour in terms of fault?

(i) **Blames the victim**
Evidence:
Offender maintains that over a period of years his father victimised him. (Probation Service Post-Sentence Report)

(ii) **Blames co-accused**
Evidence:

(iii) **Blames circumstances**
Evidence:

(iv) **Blames other factors**
Evidence:

(v) **Blames self**
Evidence:

(vi) **Blames family background/upbringing**
Evidence:
Brought up by his grandmother's next-door neighbour until age of 13. Only then did his parents take him back. Feels his father always hated him.

The behavioural account of the offence is now complete. Risk factors can now be extracted from the account. This is the next section of the Risk Assessment process.

Section 2. Risk Factors

From the preceding analysis of offending behaviour, select those areas which appear to be of MAJOR relevance to the offence. Try to select at least three or four. Under each Risk Factor give supporting evidence for your selection. Indicate evidence from offender's background (if available) which would suggest the Risk Factor was consistently present. Evidence may come from previous convictions or reports of similar, earlier behaviour.

1. CHANGE OF BEHAVIOUR FOLLOWING ALCOHOL CONSUMPTION.
   Evidence from offence:
   Became violent and aggressive following drinking.
   Evidence from personal history to indicate the presence of a behavioural pattern prior to this offence:
   Previous examples of changes in behaviour following drinking reported in Social Enquiry Report.
2. PREOCCUPATION WITH KNIVES.
   Evidence from offence:
   Had knife under pillow. Also had knife collection in bedroom.
   Evidence from personal history to indicate the presence of a behavioural pattern prior to this offence.
   Has collected knives as a hobby since the age of 12.
3. SUDDEN CHANGES IN ATTITUDE TOWARDS INDIVIDUALS.
   Evidence from offence:
   Had been 'okay' with victim for time preceding offence.

Evidence from personal history to indicate the presence of a behavioural pattern prior to this offence:
Girlfriend, mother and friends reported unstable nature of offender. Also psychiatric reports indicate unstable, abnormal EEG. (Breech birth)

4. PARANOID THOUGHTS ABOUT BEHAVIOUR OF OTHERS TOWARDS HIM.
   Evidence from offence:
   Believed victim had been picking on him.
   Evidence from personal history to indicate the presence of a behavioural pattern prior to this offence:
   Many instances of paranoia towards victim documented.
5. COPES WITH STRESS BADLY.
   Evidence from offence:
   Stressed by believed/perceived behaviour of victim.
   Evidence from personal history to indicate the presence of a behavioural pattern prior to this offence:
   When relationship with girlfriend ended became heavy drinker.

Section 3. Manifestation of Risk Behaviour in Prison

Predict how the behaviour associated with each risk factor could appear in everyday life in prison. The same Risk Factor could lead to several Predicted Behaviours.

1. **Risk Factor**
   Change in behaviour following alcohol consumption.
   Predicted Behaviour(s)
   (i) May become aggressive if gets involved with drugs.
2. **Risk Factor**
   Preoccupation with weapons.
   Predicted Behaviour(s)
   (i) May receive relevant literature.
   (ii) May draw pictures of knives.
   (iii) May be found in possession of a weapon.
3. **Risk Factor**
   Sudden changes in attitude and behaviour.
   Predicted Behaviour(s)
   (i) Few friends due to unstable nature.
   (ii) May exhibit mood fluctuations: depression/activity.
4. **Risk Factor**
   Paranoid thoughts.
   Predicted Behaviour(s)
   (i) Make requests/complaints about being victimised by staff/inmates.
   (ii) Talk about victimisation in interview.

5. **Risk Factor**
   Copes with stress badly.
   Predicted Behaviour(s)
   (i) Suicidal gestures.
   (ii) Violent outbursts during stressful periods (e.g. anniversary of offence)

The Risk Assessment is now complete. At future reviews of the inmate's behaviour, evidence for predicted behaviours needs to be recorded.

Section 4 – 'Review of Evidence for Predicted Risk Behaviour' is designed for this purpose.

Section 4. Review of Evidence for Predicted Risk Behaviour

Name Daley Date 23/8/91
Number AB1234

* The Predicted Behaviour is possibly only one of a number of ways in which the Risk Factor could manifest itself. If the Actual Behaviour differs slightly from the prediction, but still indicates Risk, then state Actual Behaviour, but describe how this relates to the original Risk Factor. In addition, state if the Actual Behaviour indicates a reduction in Risk, or not)

Predicted behaviour: May become aggressive if involved with drugs.
Actual behaviour: Acts aggressively, known drug user, on normal location.
Comments (as per '*' above):

Predicted behaviour: May receive literature on knives/weapons.
Actual behaviour: Doesn't order magazines of any sort.
Comments (as per '*' above):

Predicted behaviour: Draw knives.
Actual behaviour: No evidence for drawing knives but draws many small illustrations of people, cars etc.
Comments (as per '*' above):
May draw knives or weapons – no evidence due to lack of information.

Predicted behaviour: Possessing weapons.
Actual behaviour: No evidence of attempts to conceal weapons.
Comments (as per '*' above):

Predicted behaviour: Few friends due to unstable nature.
Actual behaviour: Said to be introvert, occasionally mixes, but not often.
Comments (as per '*' above):

Some evidence he is a loner, self-dependent.

Predicted behaviour: Mood fluctuations.

Actual behaviour: Evidence of periods of calm, not mixing followed by outbursts of violence.

Comments (as per '*' above):

Predicted behaviour: Make complaints/requests about being victimised.

Actual behaviour: Has made numerous petition/complaints about many matters, including transfer, privileges, victimisation, asked for wing change because of victimisation.

Comments (as per '*' above):

Predicted behaviour: Talk about victimisation.

Actual behaviour: In interview talks about victimisation outside by father. Claims in interview other inmate and staff are victimising him.

Comments (as per '*' above):

Predicted behaviour: Suicidal gestures.

Actual behaviour: Self-inflicted injuries e.g. banging head against cell door.

Comments (as per '*' above): Self-injury – not suicidal.

Predicted behaviour: Violent outbursts.

Actual behaviour: Yes, assaulted member of staff severely, damaged property, verbal abuse.

Comments (as per '*' above):

Predicted behaviour: Unable to cope with termination of relationships.

Actual behaviour: When girlfriend left him became depressed and started using drugs.

Comments (as per '*' above):

CHAPTER 5

Assessment of Fire-Setters

HOWARD F. JACKSON

'He that can make a fire well can end a quarrel'

Proverb

Despite folklore suggesting that it was man's use of fire that separated him from the animals, there has been little empirical data in the psychological literature to explain the natural fascination man has with fire, the characteristics of individuals who repeatedly commit arson, and the psychological factors involved.

Theories of 'pathological arson' cover the full breadth of psychological orientations from the dynamic to the behavioral. Macht and Mack (1968) have pointed out that 'fire-setting is a complex phenomenon with multiple determinants and multiple intrapsychic functions for the individual'. Given such complexities, it is most likely that a full understanding of fire-setting will come from the interface of different theoretical approaches rather than adherence to only one viewpoint. However, an integration of different orientations is likely to create a rather chaotic picture of fire-setting and the fire-setter. Thus, although I may stray unerringly into areas generally claimed by other orientations, this attempt at a synthesis of empirical evidence and theoretical views of 'pathological arson' is predominantly cognitive and behavioural. The aim is to be pragmatic and provide a basis, if not a formula, for developing an assessment approach.

The sources of the views expressed within this chapter are from the available literature, my own empirical studies, and seven years' clinical experience with pathological arsonists detained under the Mental Health Act in one of Britain's four Special Hospitals and a smaller number of cases in the community. I have generally found the approach to be applicable to offenders in other settings such as psychiatric and mental handicap hospitals and hostels, prisons and remand centres, youth treatment centres, and the community.

In considering assessment, it is important to have at least a basic understanding of the nature of that which is being assessed. Different theorists consider pathological arson in vastly different ways; for example, the dynamic psychotherapist may be concerned with sexual fantasies, parental relationships, and psychodynamic defences, whilst the criminologist may be concerned with factors such as social-economic status, age and other offence history. In some ways, single levels of explanation are misleading. It is insufficient to explain pathological fire-setting as simply poor super-ego control of impulses since situational factors are ignored. Similarly, social and environmental factors, although relevant, do not provide sufficient explanation of fire-setting since psychological factors are omitted. Psychological factors need to be superimposed on environmental determinants for the best explanation.

There are two major questions to answer initially in assessment of 'pathological arson': (1) What distinguishes pathological from non-pathological arson? and (2) What are the predictors of recidivism? Answers to these two questions are most often required for medico-legal purposes and will often determine the course of action taken in response to the arsonist, which in itself may have a considerable impact on the offender's future potential for reoffending.

What Puts the Pathological in Pathological Arson?

Distinguishing pathological from non-pathological arson is not so simple. Most attempts, in some form or another, have implied that arson is pathological when it is motiveless or not understandable. Thus, individuals who set fire to their own homes or businesses as part of an insurance fraud would not be considered pathological since there is a clear and understandable motive. Similarly, the individual who sets fire to cars in a riot would not be considered pathological since the fire-setting is viewed as purposeful destruction within a context of group aggression and destruction. The motives for setting fire may be seen in terms of political or social statements and in this sense they are understandable. Such cases would be dealt with by the penal system (perhaps rightly so).

The Diagnostic and Statistical Manual of the American Psychiatric Association (DSM III; American Psychiatric Association, 1980) describes 'pyromania' as a *disorder of impulse control, the major characteristics of which are a recurrent failure to resist impulses to set fires and an intense fascination with setting fires and seeing them burn in the absence of economic, social or political reasons. Arsonists are excluded from the DSM III diagnosis of pyromania if there is also evidence of organic mental disorder, conduct disorder, anti-social personality disorder or schizophrenia.* Several authors have pointed to the inadequacy of this definition. Koson and Dvoskin (1982) were unable to find any arsonists in their sample who could be diagnosed under the DSM III criteria. Similarly, Yesavage *et al.* (1983) reported that fire-setters meeting the DSM III criteria were very rare.

From my own experience, none of the arsonists I have encountered could be diagnosed as pyromanic using these criteria, despite the fact that some have set in excess of 50 serious fires before the age of 25. This was mainly because most suffered from personality disorder, conduct disorder, cognitive impairment, or psychiatric illness in some form or another. Indeed, several studies have pointed out the applicability of many psychiatric labels to pathological arsonists (e.g. Lewis and Yarnell, 1951; Robins and Robins, 1967). Such psychiatric labels may not be particularly helpful, however. Arson is rarely a direct symptom of mental handicap or psychotic illness, although such problems may influence the presentation and causes of the fire-setting and therefore need to be included within an assessment procedure.

A further restriction of the above diagnostic criteria is the implication that pyromanic firesetting is an irrational, impulsive and unthinking act. Hurley and Monahan (1969) reported that in their sample of Grendon Prison arsonists fire-setting was unplanned and impulsive. In contrast, my experience tends to suggest quite the opposite in that fire-setting is often well-planned and ritualistic. In recidivistic fire-setters, there is a tendency to choose the same type of target (e.g. deserted warehouses, residential property, hospitals, family home). The offence often occurs generally under the same setting conditions (e.g. at night, after passing the target several times). Furthermore, a relatively high percentage of arsonists, especially those in care or hospital, tend to make threats of setting fire. Whilst acts of pathological arson do not seem to be entirely motiveless, without evidence of planning, this is not to say that such fire-setting behaviour is always rational and controlled. Indeed, I have noted, as has been reported by Hurley and Monahan (1969), that fire-setting often follows a build-up of tension and may be explosive or disinhibited in nature, often accompanied with excessive alcohol consumption.

Although not a direct test of impulse control, Keval (1989) tested impulsivity in arsonists using the Matching Familiar Figures Test (Kagan, Moss, and Seigel, 1963) comparing arsonists and violent offenders in Moss Side Special Hospital classified as Psychopathic Disorder under the Mental Health Act, with non-offender controls. The results indicated that whereas violent offenders were significantly more impulsive than non-offender controls, arsonists did not differ significantly from either group. It was concluded that pathological arsonists did not present as a particularly impulsive group but that they were cognitively immature.

I and my colleagues (Jackson, Glass, and Hope, 1987) have adopted a pragmatic approach to the definition of pathological arson, which although clearly imperfect allows for a more meaningful concept from the clinical view point. In essence, we defined pathological arson by five central criteria:

1. Recidivism.
2. Fire to property as opposed to fire against persons.
3. Fire-setting alone or repetitively with a single identified accomplice.
4. Evidence of personality, psychiatric, or emotional problems.
5. The absence of financial or political gain as a motive for fire setting.

Obviously, the first of these criteria may present some problems since often the question is whether a single episode of fire-setting is likely to result in others. This may be particularly pertinent in cases of children who have set one major property fire which is their first offence; are they likely to set further fires? A twenty year cohort study of arsonists by Soothill and Pope (1973) suggested that the percentage of reoffending amongst first-offence arsonists was only about 5 per cent and of this small number an average time lag of 13 to 15 years separated their arson offences. Thus, the evidence suggests that recidivism after a single arson attack is rare. Whilst this does not particularly help in determining whether recidivism is likely at the individual level, it nevertheless suggests that an *a priori* criterion of recidivism is not unwarranted with respect to classifying arsonists as pathological. Deciding upon the likelihood of an individual reoffending will depend on a number of factors ranging from personal history, the nature of the arson attack, the individual's psychological characteristics, and future environmental circumstances.

The second of our criteria for defining pathological arson is designed to eliminate those individuals who use fire as a direct weapon against an individual, in which case the act is not considered to be one of arson but of physical assault. Pathological arson is therefore an offence against property.

The third criterion is setting fire alone, which is, I believe, important in determining the pathological nature of fire-setting. Stewart and Culver (1982) reported that children whose primary offence was arson tended to set fires on their own and these fires were of a serious nature. Setting fires as part of a group in which other members take an equal role in the offence is not a matter for individual psychology but is rather more concerned with group dynamics, and examination of the characteristics or diagnosis of the individual are therefore not useful except in terms of their role within the group. The purpose of including within this criterion the qualification 'or repeatedly with a single identified accomplice' allows for those rare cases of *folie à deux* in which a common pathology is shared between two people who appear to act as one. In general, setting fires alone may not only present a useful classification criterion but also provide a component explanation in the emergence of pathology from a developmental standpoint. The very act of secrecy may eliminate or minimise those aspects of the fire-setting which originally provided principal motives. As a consequence, the arsonist is caught in a developmental process which leads to greater and greater risk-taking in the form of larger fires and greater involvement in the events surrounding the fire. This point is discussed in more detail below; however, at this stage it is interesting to note that Hurley and Monahan (1969) reported that a surprisingly large proportion of their sample actually gave themselves up to the police or confessed to the fire-setting.

Contrary to DSM III criteria, an underlying psychological disorder is necessary to our definition. This does not have to be recognised within the standard psychiatric nomenclature; it simply represents the concept that pathological arson results against a background of psychological problems and these problems influence both the genesis and nature of the arson.

Finally, exclusion of individuals from the pathological category on the basis of financial or political motivations, as with the DSM III criteria, is retained. However, motives for fire-setting which have social significance would fall, in my opinion, within the pathological category. The underlying assumption for this amendment is that all behaviour, whether arson or otherwise, has a motive. The concept of motiveless behaviour is quite foreign to one schooled principally in the cognitive-behavioural sciences. Furthermore, the retention the concept of 'motive' permits a greater understanding of the psychological processes involved in the arsonist.

This is not to say that the motive is clear to the clinician or even to the arsonist. Indeed, if the motives for fire-setting were clear to the offender, the issues would not be so complex, and perhaps the concept of 'pathological arson' would be undermined and society's response to arsonists would be quite different. A number of studies have attempted to catalogue the motives for fire-setting amongst arsonists. In most cases these have been 'stated motives' although others have tended to surmise motive from their psychological analysis of the individual. Schmid (1914) suggested that revenge was a common motive. Hurley and Monahan (1969) also reported that the stated motive of arsonists was predominantly revenge, although in their interpretation they included jealousy, destruction of own effects, and release of tension, with the release of tension being marginally more common in their sample than revenge. Whilst Hurley and Monahan (1969) found only about 7 per cent of arsonists with a stated motive of attention seeking, Bradford (1982) reported that nearly 30 per cent of his sample set fires for this reason whilst revenge accounted for only 13 per cent. Kaufman, Heims and Reiser (1961) noted that fire-setting children often perceived the fire as a restitutive process bringing back together separated persons, such as parents. It is interesting that Hill *et al.* (1982) found that most arsonists were unable to verbalise their motives for fire-setting and often those who were able to state their motives gave numerous and complex reasons.

Despite the fact that the motives for pathological arson are unclear, complex and numerous, the inclusion of the concept of motive is an important one. The motives may well be irrational or pseudo-rational in the sense that the arsonist has some ill-formed expectation of a consequence to such action; nevertheless the major point is that fire-setting is somehow motivated. Listed below are a number of motives which I have encountered through clinical studies. This list is not exhaustive but is presented to indicate the variety of motives that may present:

- to please peers
- to force authorities to move residence
- to force father back into the home
- to be taken into care for pragmatic reasons
- to alert authorities to sexual/physical abuse within the family or hostel
- to avoid discharge from hospital
- to be a hero/improve self-esteem
- to upset parents/friends/professional
- to seek protection
- to divert punishment from another member of the family
- to provoke a caring response from parents
- to resolve guilt
- to seek notoriety/fame
- to protect other member(s) of the family by diversion
- to seek reassurance from parents

- to exact revenge against an institution
- to experience thrill.

The antithesis to a motivational analysis of arson is the concept of impulse or drive that is inherent within the DSM III criteria and embraced by psychodynamic viewpoints. These theories seem to adopt four basic types of drive: (1) arson as an irrational, psychotic act; (2) arson as a primary drive resulting from an abnormal fascination with fire; (3) displaced libidinal drives; and (4) displaced aggressive drives. The assumptions underlying these theoretical viewpoints are addressed in turn.

(1) Arson as a product of psychosis

A theory of motiveless arson results from claims that arson is the result of psychotic experiences; however most pathological arsonists are not mentally ill. Lewis and Yarnell (1951) suggested that schizophrenia accounted for 10–30 per cent of all arson cases. McDonald (1960) suggested that 13.4 per cent of adult male arsonists were psychotic. Bradford (1982) found only about 9 per cent of their sample claiming any psychotic motive for fire-setting. Only 16 per cent of all arsonists were diagnosed as suffering from a psychotic disorder in Hill *et al.'s* (1982) study. Hurley and Monahan (1969) reported only 18 per cent presented with 'schizoid' personality, whereas by far the majority presented with neurotic symptoms and/or inadequate/aggressive personality traits.

It is important to note that the presence of psychotic symptoms may be simply an artifact of fire-setting rather than playing any causal role. That is, because the individual is psychotic it does not necessarily follow that such symptoms play any part in promoting fire-setting behaviour. The involvement of hallucinatory or delusional experiences in the act of fire-setting is rare. There may be only indirect links with the mental illness, with the mental illness being a setting condition rather than a direct precursor.

In Virkkunen's (1974) sample of 30 schizophrenic arsonists, hallucinations or delusions appeared to be the principal 'motive' in only 30 per cent of the cases. Geller (1984) reported a spate of arson attacks in the process of initiating community-care alternatives for psychiatrically ill hospitalised patients, yet in only four of the 14 cases cited did the patient state any psychotic symptoms associated with the act (e.g. 'The voices told me to do it'). It is interesting that none of these patients presented with fire-setting behaviour prior to the process of deinstitutionalisation. Furthermore, in some of these cases the patient's account was highly unreliable, with different stories given to different people. There is a very strong possibility that claims of hallucinatory experiences provide a useful method for abrogating any personal culpability or avoiding potential punishment. Thus, there is the possibility that many psychotic symptoms are over-reported as a function of an avoidance of potential retribution for the fire-setting.

My experience of arsonists within a Special Hospital (where it may be expected that a bias towards schizophrenic conditions may be found) indicates that the importance of psychosis as a causal factor has been greatly over-estimated. Within the Special Hospital, individuals are classified under the Mental Health Act into one of three groups; Psychopathic Disorder, Mental Illness, and Mental Impairment. Arsonists in Moss Side Hospital (now part of Ashworth Hospital) classified as suffering from Mental Illness are the smallest group, with about 16 per cent being so classified, a figure not dissimilar to that in most other studies cited above. Of these patients, it is interesting to note that 64 per cent were female, which is highly unusual. Most studies have found that male arsonists outnumber female arsonists in a ratio of about 9:1. Furthermore, closer examination of arsonists classified as Mentally Ill reveals that many of them have not presented with active psychotic symptoms and even fewer claimed that their fire-setting was related to hallucinatory or delusional symptoms. Indeed, one young male arsonist denied ever having suffered from psychotic symptoms, claiming that he simulated symptoms in order to avoid prosecution and a prison sentence. Our results are very similar to those of Bradford (1982) who reported that antisocial personality disorder was the most common clinical problem presented by arsonists.

Arson and 'Manic' Symptoms: The Control Paradox

Whilst it is not suggested here that there is any specific relationship between manic psychiatric disorders and fire-setting, the processes underlying these patients' behaviour are of interest since they illustrate a number of potentially important points relating to fire-setting generally. Gunderson (1974) suggested that fire-setting may be a product of poor management of patients with mania. Gunderson presented a number of cases outlining the relationship between the manic patients' disorder, its management, and the fire setting. Although not empirically tested, some of the characteristics identified in Gunderson's patients seem to have a direct parallel in many arsonists which I have assessed in the Special Hospital setting, if the symptoms of mania are considered as a continuum rather than a discrete disorder.

Gunderson noted that fire-setting in these manic patients was always related to a provocative event. Of interest is that Gunderson identifies the provocative events as a failure to enforce external control (e.g. diminished medication, being allowed to keep stolen money). For the manic patient, the loosening of external control appeared to invoke heightened grandiosity, panic, and eventually fire-setting. This is an interesting point since it suggests that, although manic patients often actively complain of being subjected to capricious and inconsistent masters, their behaviour suggests that they require external control rather than greater freedom, that is they demand '... an omnipotent, authoritarian parent' (Gunderson, 1974, p.145).

For these 'manic' arsonists, the dilemma is a desire for self-determination along with a desire for external control. We have identified a similar phenomenon amongst some arsonists in the Special Hospital. Such patients complain vigorously about restrictions, yet when these restrictions are lifted they become more anxious, volatile, and demanding. One may hypothesise as to the processes involved in this paradox. In the first instance, the need for external control may result from a number of factors (e.g. poor or inconsistent parenting, uncontrollable experiences, lack of self-esteem or self-confidence, an external locus of control) all of which undermine the arsonist's confidence and ability to control their world and/or themselves. A potential solution to this problem may lie in the abdication of power to others (e.g. parents, staff).

This is a vulnerable position since it heightens the need to control the external controllers to ensure that they will provide adequate protection. This in turn leads to excessive demands, complaints, and indirect manipulations. Also, each time personal control is relinquished to others, it reinforces the arsonist's sense of helplessness and vulnerability. Attempts by others to hand back this power prematurely (e.g. proposing discharge, offering greater freedom) are perceived as a threat in the sense of a burden of responsibility with which the arsonist is unable to cope. An excessively capricious and inconsistent style of management by others simply undermines the arsonist's confidence in the omnipotence of the external control, leading to further insecurity. Hence, many of our arsonists appear to have an intolerance of ambiguity and uncertainty. In my experience, uncertain, inconsistent, and unpredictable management is common in institutional settings where there is relatively high staff turnover and authority is shared across several individuals.

At the other end of the spectrum, excessively restrictive and punitive management by authority figures will undermine the perceived protection that relinquishing power to an external authority provides. As a result, arsonists may feel particularly vulnerable, since they cannot place any faith in themselves or others.

There is some tentative empirical support for this analysis of pathological fire-setting. Kaufman, Heims and Reiser (1961) suggested that fire-setting was an attempt to reinstate parental bonding and ensure a cohesive family unit which provides external control and security for the child. Geller (1984) reported a study of arsonists admitted to a state hospital over a 200-day period which involved 14 patients and 17 fires. He noticed that the process of deinstitutionalisation provoked fire-setting. It may be that deinstitutionalisation invoked a sense of vulnerability by removing familiar supportive services to the patients, resulting in greater demands on the patients' personal abilities to cope. The 'communication' in the fire-setting may well have been for more external control. This may also apply to other psychiatric groups.

In an attempt to examine the coping strategies of arsonists, Keval (1989) administered the Ways of Coping Questionnaire (Folkman and Lazarus, 1980) to matched male arson and violent offenders detained in Moss Side Special Hospital with a classification of Psychopathic Disorder, and non-offender controls. The Ways of Coping Questionnaire provides six factors identifying different strategies for dealing with daily problems. The only significant difference was that arsonists rated themselves higher on the problem focused/help seeking factor than the controls. Thus, it was suggested that arsonists tend to be more directly focused on their problems and primarily seek help from others. My experience is that arsonists seek help in indirect ways. Their fears and complaints are rarely overtly or directly expressed, often for fear of rejection or embarrassment. Thus, arsonists repeatedly place themselves in situations where the help they require is never conveyed to the helper in ways which would result in adequate help being given. A major challenge to the professional is to identify the 'hidden' fears of the arsonist.

It is not suggested that arson is a consequence of mania. This would be an overly simplistic and reductionistic argument. However, the problems highlighted by manic fire-setters seem to represent the psychological processes of many arsonists whom I have assessed and treated. Furthermore, this type of analysis identifies a number of important concepts for the analysis of arson. First, pathological arson is motivated, although the motives may not be readily apparent. Second, the issue of fire-setting as a means of control (in a number of senses) demonstrates that arson attacks are, at some level, strategic. Third, arsonists may present with fundamental problems of personal self-efficacy. Finally, as described by Segal (1985), 'helping behaviour' elicited by help-seeking can reinforce personal inadequacies and create a vicious cycle in which the 'helper' is perceived idealistically. The central question raised by this analysis is what processes have led to these psychological dilemmas? In this sense the analysis moves from one of diagnosis to functional relationships.

(2) Arson as abnormal fascination with fire

There is an unequivocal statement in DSM III that pathological arson is the result of an *excessive fascination* with setting fire and seeing things burn. For this reason, psychiatric and psychological assessments very often contain some reference to an early childhood interest in fire. Indeed, many of the arsonists within the hospital are admitted on the assumption that they have an abnormal interest in fire, yet in therapy groups the only individuals to deny that they find fires exciting are the arsonists. Similarly, ward staff have pointed out that when a fire engine passes sounding its siren, the arsonists on the ward can be identified because they are the only ones who do not look out of the window. Arsonists may, in fact, be combating an interest in fire which is found in most people.

Lewis and Yarnell (1951) suggested that children's fascination with fire is far greater than statistics would lead us to believe, and Kafrey (1980) detected an almost universal fascination with fire amongst children aged between five and ten years. I would contend that this interest in fire is retained by adults, although it is muted by social inhibition. Consider the attraction that bonfires have for all ages and the reactions of adults in passing a fire in fields. Virkunnen (1974) in a retrospective study of the mental examination reports of schizophrenic and non-schizophrenic arsonists found that, at most, one third could have been regarded as having acquired some 'unconscious pleasure from watching the fire'. Thus, for the majority there were no indications of an excessive pleasure taken from the setting of the fire. Even in those for whom some 'unconscious pleasure' may have been present, it is by no means certain that the fire was the principal source of pleasure.

Perhaps the most cogent argument against pathological arson resulting from an intense fascination with fire is the choice of target for fire-setting. It would surely be safer (in the sense of being more socially and legally acceptable) for the arsonist to find waste ground away from any property or persons and set fire to waste material under controlled conditions. However, this rarely constitutes the *modus operandi* of pathological arsonists. Bradford (1982) found that out of a sample of 34 arsonists referred for psychiatric pre-trial examination, over 80 per cent set fire to property, usually of a residential nature. Out this total sample, 29.4 per cent set fire to their own homes and most (55.9%) set fires within a one mile radius of their home. Similarly, Soothill and Pope (1973) found that 68 per cent of their sample set fire to property, and the remainder, coming from rural locations, set fire to haystacks. Thus, the act is most often against property, which is highly likely to present a risk of prosecution. An analysis of pathological arson based on an intense fascination to set fires cannot explain this common bias in the choice of target.

(3) Arson as displaced sexual drive

The dominance of Freudian approaches to psychopathology in the earlier part of this century had an impact on theories of pathological fire-setting in two major ways. First, the notion of unconscious 'base' drives for human behaviour led to the assumption that fire-setting was an expression of a repressed unconscious drive. Second, the concept of the uncivilised id and associated libidinal drive led to the association between fire-setting and repressed sexual drive. Within our culture, the association between fire and libido is apparent. This is reflected in the symbolism of our language, with phrases such as 'flames of desire' and 'fires of passion'. So pervasive is the concept that pathological fire-setting results from a sexual drive that by far the most common item within psychiatric reports relates to sexual fantasies and questions regarding masturbation at the scene of the fires.

To some extent, arsonists themselves may collude with this assumption. In the first instance, the arsonist may not be sure at all why he or she set the fire and may be prepared to accept the psychiatrist's notion of displaced sexual drive as an answer. A prime example is the case of a young man in Ashworth Hospital who reported to a psychiatrist that he had masturbated to his fires and that his sexual fantasies tended to include fires as a central theme. However, within psychotherapy sessions, it emerged that he had been lying about the sexual aspects of his fire-setting. When asked why he had lied he replied that if he denied any sexual element to his fire setting then the psychiatrist would ask him more questions and eventually leave looking unhappy. However, if he admitted to having sexual fantasies involving fire, the psychiatrist would stop asking so many questions and would leave much happier. 'Either way', he said, 'I stay here'.

Within Ashworth Special Hospital, there is only one patient who has a history of sexual offending and arson; however, a high proportion have sexual and social relationship problems. Many have been abused sexually, although the majority appear to have suffered mainly physical and emotional abuse. Fry and Le Couteur (1966) found a similar picture in Broadmoor Special Hospital. There is no doubt a higher incidence of sexual problems amongst pathological arsonists than found in the general population. Hurley and Monahan (1969) found an incidence of heterosexual difficulties and homosexuality in 54 per cent of their sample, however this is not significantly greater than that found amongst other psychiatric populations and indeed amongst the criminal population. Hill *et al.* (1982) compared property offenders, arsonists, and violent offenders on the Clarke Sex History Questionnaire and found that there was no overall difference in sexual experience, and sexual anomalies were absent in most cases.

Lewis and Yarnell (1951) reported cases of arsonists masturbating to fire, although such cases tend to be very much in the minority. Macht and Mack (1968) reported a case of homosexual excitement and fantasy associated with the fire-setting. Stekel (1924) reported that in some cases pyromaniacs may dream of fires, and that these tend to be pleasurable, frequently culminating in seminal emission. None of the sample of arsonists assessed by Bradford (1992) reported any sexual gratification or erotic motives for their fire-setting. As Hill *et al.* (1982) have suggested, it may well be that concepts such as sexual excitement are only inexact labels for a poorly understood general excitement evidenced in arson. Many arsonists do claim that the act of arson was an exciting event, although as mentioned above a simple excitement-seeking explanation for pathological arson would not explain the predominance of property as a target.

We (Jackson, Glass, and Hope, 1987) have suggested that for those cases where there is some apparent sexual excitement associated with fire-setting, this may arise as a confusion between sexual arousal and other experiences of excitement. This may represent a problem of mislabelling of the experience in the developing young arsonist in such a way that sexual excitement and fire become associated. The important distinction made here is that sexual excitement is a product of fire-setting rather than a causal influence in its genesis.

For the majority of arsonists libidinal motivation is rarely a significant factor. The unfortunate prominence which the psychiatric profession places on unconscious sexual motivation provides little solace for the impressionable arsonist, who may already suffer from an inhibited and/or confused sexual identity. Most arsonists whom I have dealt with are well aware of the seriousness and criminal nature of their offences and the association of this criminal act with unconscious sexual drives merely serves to exacerbate an already confused emotional attitude towards sex. The dangers of the arsonist further repressing his/her sexual drive in order to eradicate fire-setting behaviour are clear to see.

(4) Arson as displaced aggression

The propensity to set fires predominantly to property perhaps led to the notion that fire-setting was a form of displaced aggression (McKerracher and Dacre, 1966). Also, some research has suggested that the majority of fires are set within a one mile radius of the arsonist's home (Bradford, 1982). Arson is often considered to involve an act of revenge and many researchers and theorists have noted that revenge is a common motive. Hurley and Monahan (1969) reported that 26 per cent of their sample of arsonists set fires as an act of revenge; however, an equivalent number (28%) reported that they set fire as a means of releasing tension. Also, Hurley and Monahan found that mental status and personality testing did not reveal abnormal aggressive traits amongst their sample of arsonists, whereas in contrast anxiety was found to be high in 68 per cent of cases. Conversely, Koson and Dvoskin (1982) reported that the MMPI (Minnesota Multiphasic Personality Inventory) profiles of their sample of arsonists revealed high levels of aggressiveness and hostility.

Arson has been considered as a displaced form of sadism (Stekel, 1924). Yarnell (1940) reported cases of young arsonists who described fantasies of burning some member of the family who had withheld love or had become a rival for affection within the family. Hellman and Blackman (1966) suggested a triad of fire-setting, enuresis, and cruelty to animals as a predictor of dangerousness; however, a later prospective study failed to confirm this hypothesis. Hill *et al.* (1982) found a higher incidence of cruelty to animals amongst arsonists and violent offenders compared to property offenders. There was a slight but non-significant trend for incidence of cruelty to animals to be greater amongst arsonists. The psychological significance of the possible relationship between cruelty to animals and pathological fire-setting remains obscure. However, one may hypothesise that faced with frustration and anger together with inhibition of conflict resolution by interpersonal means, the arsonist may vent his or her frustrations on animals. We have noted cruelty to animals in the histories of a significant proportion of arsonists within the Special Hospital, although there is little data to confirm the higher incidence in pathological arsonists compared to other mentally abnormal offender groups.

Hill *et al.* (1982) reported a study contrasting arsonists with violent and property offenders. In terms of number of criminal charges for assault, the arsonist fell midway between the violent and the property offenders but on other measures, such as family background, diagnosis, sexual behaviour and drug abuse, the majority of arsonists aligned with property offenders. Interestingly, Hill *et al.* (1982) achieved 90 per cent accuracy in discriminating between property and violent offenders based on only three variables: other reported violence, alcohol abuse, and having a diagnosis. When the discriminant equations were applied to arsonists, 60 per cent were found to be classified as property, as opposed to violent, offenders. Thus, the evidence would suggest that arson is not simply an alternative expression of violence. Furthermore, Stewart and Culver (1982) reported that children whom they described as primary arsonists (i.e., arson was their main offence) tended to be less aggressive than secondary arsonists (i.e., where arson was overshadowed by other offences). This is not to say that anger plays little functional role in the genesis of fire-setting; it merely means that it is neither necessary nor sufficient to explain the behaviour.

A particular facet of aggression which I wish to address is the notion that aggression, like libido, is a form of drive. Assuming the displaced aggression hypothesis of arson and the hydraulic aspects of dynamic psychology, one may expect that once denied the opportunity to set fire, the arsonist would necessarily be forced to release the drive in a more direct form (i.e., physical aggression). Contrary to this hypothesis are the observations that arsonists often present as model prisoners (Hurley and Monahan, 1969). A more direct assessment of the hypothesis was made by Jackson, Hope, and Glass (1987). Arsonists and violent offenders in Moss Side Special Hospital were assessed in terms of their previous offences of violence and the number of violent assaults within the hospital. Table 5.1 shows the results of this study.

Table 5.1: Mean Number of Recorded Assaults prior to and since admission to Moss Side Hospital

Assaults	*Arsonists*		*Violent Offenders*	
	Mean	*S.D.*	*Mean*	*S.D.*
Prior to admission	1.44	0.45	5.11*	1.11
Since admission	1.83	1.04	7.83**	1.13

NB * p<.01 ** p<.0005

It can be seen that violent offenders had a significantly greater incidence of violence than arsonists prior to admission to the hospital and that this difference was maintained after admission. Thus, there is little reason to suppose that if arson is a form of displaced aggression, such aggression is a drive. Finally, considering the seriousness of some fires and the potential uncontrollability of fires, it is surprising that so few people are hurt. This point has also been noted by Stewart and Culver (1982). Most of the pathological arsonists in Moss Side Hospital whom we have assessed report that they were very careful to avoid risk to any person and that they would find it very difficult to live with the idea that anyone was hurt in a fire for which they had been responsible. At a simplistic level, arson does not appear to be simply a violent act, although it may contain elements of anger, revenge, and frustration.

The Target for Arson

The choice of target for the arson attack is important since it may well provide some indication of the underlying motive. We have noted that, contrary to the impulse/drive theories which suppose that the target for arson will be random, most pathological arsonists generally set fires in a prescribed manner and against similar targets. Many will have rehearsed the arson attack at least in imagination and perhaps have visited the target prior to the fire setting episode. In some cases, the act can appear quite ritualistic. The emotions aroused both before and after each arson attack are generally the same. There are, of course, occasions when fire-setting is based mainly on opportunity. However, even the opportunistic type of arson usually fits a set pattern with specific and idiosyncratic targets.

Virkkunen (1974) has reported some differences between schizophrenic patients who set fire and non-psychotic arsonists. Alcohol abuse was found to be an important factor, more so in non-psychotic arsonists. Expression of hate directed towards family and acquaintances was found in non-psychotic arsonists and hence the target of the arson in such cases was predominantly residential. In contrast, schizophrenic arsonists tended to set fires to empty buildings where there were very unlikely to be any residents. It was concluded from this evidence that the psychotic arsonist's motives could be a desire to see fire and/or an impulsive action in a psychotic state. However, an alternative explanation for these findings may be that, whereas non-psychotic arsonists tended to set fires as an act of hate against individuals, the psychotic arsonist set fires as an act of hate against society.

My experience is that the targets for pathological arsonists tend to be property as opposed to people. Within our Special Hospital sample (Jackson, Hope, and Glass, 1987), property was by far the most common target (80%). In most cases, these were hospitals, hostels, schools, warehouses, businesses and other official buildings. In a smaller number of cases, there was evidence that these were attacks aimed specifically at an individual or the family, in which case they were classified as assault on a person (6%). Other cases (10%) involved fires set to their own rooms or property. One case was considered to be a suicide attempt. Amongst the small number of arsonists diagnosed as suffering from mental illness, two of the eleven set fire to their own rooms, five set fires to either the hostel or hospital in which they were resident, and the remainder set fire to empty property.

Arson as a Resolution to a Problem: The Only Viable Option Theory

Jackson, Glass, and Hope (1987) adopt the view that arson is an adaptive response, at least regarding short-term consequences. In essence, this theory proposes that arson provides a highly effective means of escaping or changing difficult-to-tolerate circumstances where other means have proved impossible or excessively difficult, been inhibited, been ineffective or perceived as ineffective.

The difficult-to-tolerate circumstance may be external, for example social situations, or internal in the sense of unexpressed feelings, helplessness, unwanted thoughts, low self-concept, or perceived injustice. Arson may have a positively reinforcing effect in increasing the likelihood of maintaining or enhancing current positive circumstances, social engagement, or attention. Alternatively, it may have a negatively reinforcing effect in avoiding or escaping from undesirable social circumstances, mood states, or cognitions. It is usual for there to be a combination of both internal and external functions and arson may serve multiple functions for the same individual. This functional approach more readily encompasses findings which suggest that there is a bias towards property as a target and also avoids the complications of attaching arson to any specific drive state such as sexual arousal or aggression. This model is not dissimilar to Arlow's (1978) hypothesis that arson provided a vehicle by which to redress grievances. Also, Soothill and Pope (1973) suggested that fire-setting was a 'pathetic' attempt to provide a solution to a problem and Vreeland and Levin (1980) suggested that fire-setting may represented a kind of control over the environment unobtainable in other ways.

The model also contains a developmental component which may explain the transition from fire-play to pathological arson observed in some cases. Whilst assuming that there is a form of rationality underlying all acts of arson, this does not necessarily imply that the rationale is available to the arsonist, and the development component can account for this lack of awareness in its three tenets:

1. Arsonists are personally, psychosocially and/or situationally disadvantaged to the extent that they are faced with the strong need to resolve internal or external problems. These disadvantages are the roots of pathological offending of many types, arson being one example.
2. Arsonists are prevented from being able to resolve these problems in socially acceptable ways due to lack of opportunity, skill, or confidence, and therefore resort to the socially unacceptable action of arson. The question raised is why are other socially unacceptable options not adopted?
3. The factors leading to the use of fire may be relatively slight or appear insignificant in the wider scheme. In this sense, the emphasis for both assessment and treatment is diverted from fire-setting as a central feature to the underlying psychological and situational problems.

The basic core elements of the model are presented diagrammatically in Figure 5.1. A particular feature of this model is that whilst arson may provide effective short-term resolutions to problems, the long-term consequences of fire-setting tend to exacerbate such problems. The elements of this model are discussed in greater detail below.

Setting Conditions for Offending: The Absence of Socially Acceptable Options

In a review of the literature on demographic characteristics of arsonists, Jackson, Glass, and Hope (1987) pointed out that many pathological arsonists suffer from considerable psychosocial disadvantage which is formed by an interaction between personal inadequacies and adverse social conditions. With respect to the former, Inciardi (1970) has noted that arsonists as a group fall into a number of diagnostic categories reflecting considerable psychological impairments. Thus, a higher than expected incidence of schizophrenia, alcoholism, antisocial personality disorder, affective or neurotic disorders, organic brain disorder, drug dependency and personality disorder have been associated with this group. Whilst none of these may be of specific value in understanding the psychological process of pathological arson, they do reflect the psychological distress and disorganisation suffered by such individuals.

Arsonists as a group have been found to have low normal or borderline IQs (Lewis and Yarnell, 1951; Yarnell, 1940) and poor prognosis has been associated with mental retardation. It is clear that fire-setting is not simply a function of intellectual ability, although individuals with borderline intellectual abilities may be particularly vulnerable through failure to acquire the personal ability to cope effectively in a social world, whilst not gaining the protection, support, sympathy and understanding provided to the more overtly intellectually impaired.

Lewis and Yarnell (1951) noted a high incidence of physical abnormality amongst arsonists. Like the findings for borderline IQ, the type of physical abnormality was usually minor (e.g. cleft palate, hare lip, small stature).

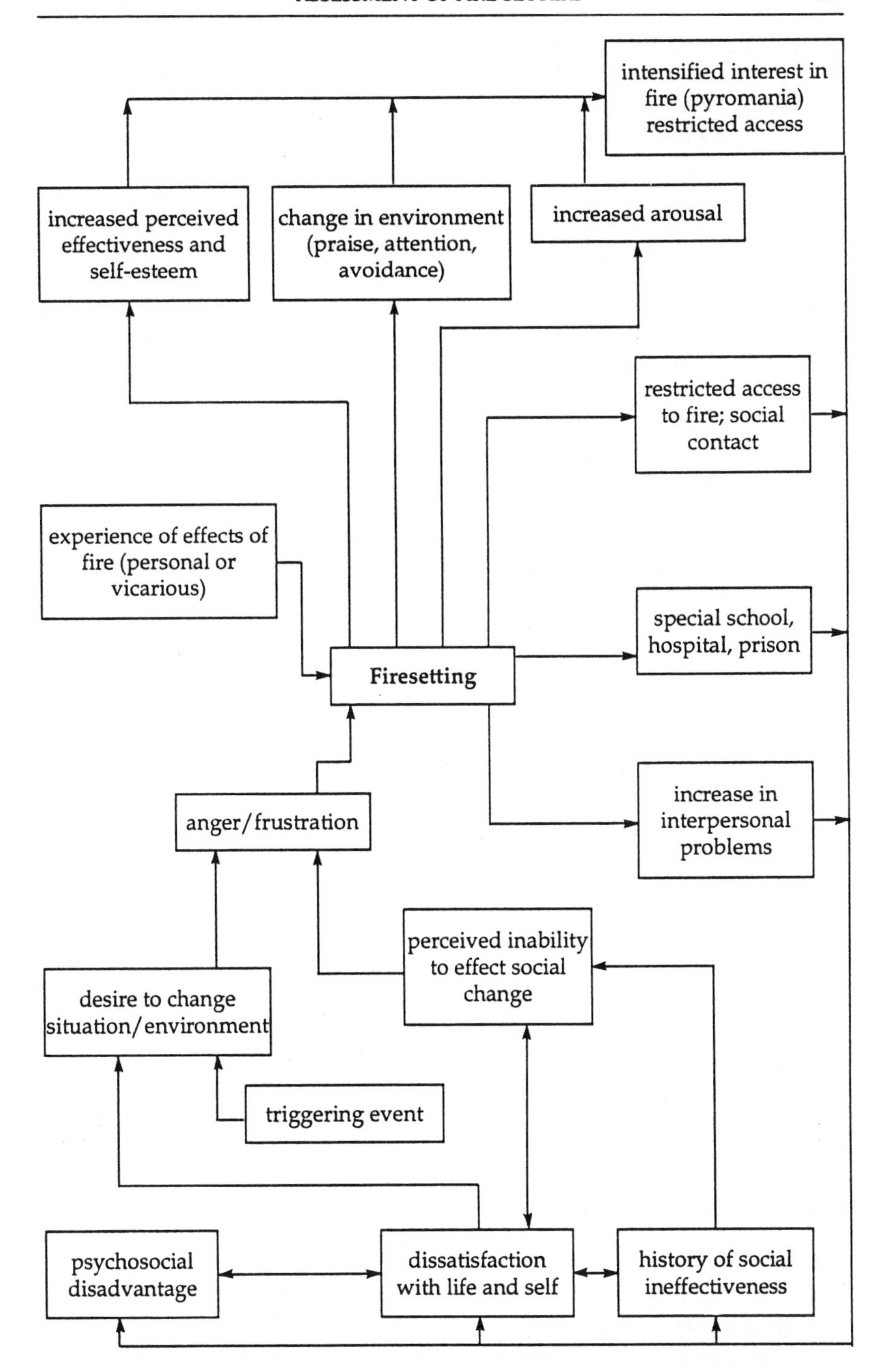

Figure 5.1: A formulation of recidivistic arson (From Jackson, Glass, and Hope, 1987)

Again, the impact is to make the arsonist appear unusual and inferior without evoking sympathy and support. Such factors may explain the almost universal history of teasing, bullying, and peer rejection which we have detected in interviews with arsonists in the Special Hospital (Jackson, Glass, and Hope, 1987).

Neurological abnormality has been suggested to be higher amongst arsonists compared to other groups, in particular, the incidence of temporal lobe abnormality. Bradford (1982) found four cases of temporal lobe EEG abnormalities in their sample of 34 arsonists whereas none was found in a control group. However, Hurley and Monahan (1969) reported non-significant EEG findings in their arsonist sample, apart from a slight to moderate excess of slow wave abnormality in the resting record. In Moss Side Hospital, we examined those patients for whom neurological disorders had been unequivocally identified, ten of whom suffered from temporal lobe epilepsy, and compared them with the remaining population. Despite the small numbers, temporal lobe epilepsy was not found to be associated particularly with arson (although there were a few cases). In contrast, temporal lobe epilepsy appeared to be associated more with interpersonal violence. Similarly, acquired brain injury (traumatic brain injury, meningitis, cerebral anoxia, encephalitis) did not appear to be related specifically to arson but this brain injured group reflected the general offence ratios across the hospital.

Neurological disorders rarely have any direct relationship with pathological arson; however, they may impair social and emotional functioning. It is known that injury to certain parts of the brain such as the frontal and temporal lobes affects problem-solving ability and abstract thinking (e.g. Goldstein, 1939). Injury to these areas has also been associated with psychopathic disorder (Gorenstein, 1982) and psychiatric disorder (Lishman, 1968). In such cases, impairments of problem resolution may occur, increasing the tendency to manifest offending behaviour. Such deficits may impair abilities to appreciate, or even consider, the wider possible implications and long-term consequences of fire-setting.

At a psychological level, several studies have noted a high incidence of depression amongst arsonists (e.g. Tennent, McQuaid, Loughnane, and Hands, 1971) and a high incidence of suicide attempts (McKerracher and Dacre, 1966). Jackson, Hope, and Glass (1987) found that whereas there was no difference between violent offenders and arsonists on the Zung Depression Scale (Zung, 1965), both offender groups significantly rated themselves as more depressed than controls.

Jackson, Hope, and Glass (1987) examined the attitudes of arsonists, violent offenders and normal controls to the seriousness of property and interpersonal offences. Subjects were asked to rate the relative seriousness of two offences, one property and one person offence. Whilst there was no difference between the groups regarding whether property offences were more or less serious overall than person offences, a greater inconsistency of responding was found amongst the offender groups, particularly arsonists. This was interpreted as arsonists having less stable or less clearly defined constructs regarding moral judgements.

Considering the above-mentioned limitations regarding the personal qualities of the arsonist, it is perhaps hardly surprising that Wolford's (1972) study revealed that the MMPI profiles of arsonists were indicative of 'persons undergoing psychic stress'. Furthermore, Hurley and Monahan (1969) reported problems of social isolation in 74 per cent of their sample, pointing out that such social isolation was often self-imposed because of shyness, inability to make friends, fear of involvement, and social distrust. Vreeland and Levin (1980) have suggested that fire-setting, along with other antisocial behaviours, and sexual, marital, and occupational maladjustment may be considered as indicators of a general lack of social skills.

In addition to personal inadequacies, arsonists have often suffered from situational disadvantage. Several studies (Bradford, 1982; Kanner, 1957; Nurcombe, 1964; Vandersall and Weiner, 1970) have noted that nearly all children who set fires experienced inadequate relationships with their parents. Indeed, in nearly one quarter of Bradford's sample a biological parent had been absent from the home and child-rearing had been undertaken by another person, and Macht and Mack (1968) found that the father was often absent from the family. Stewart and Culver (1982) reported that over half the fathers and half the mothers of arsonists suffered from antisocial personality and psychiatric disorder respectively. Of note, this study found that two thirds of the child arsonists in their sample had experienced disruption in family life by family fights, divorce or desertion and that 24 per cent had been abused by one or other parent. These proportions tended to be higher in the primary group of arsonists (i.e., those whose offences were predominantly arson), and more in this primary group were likely to have been raised by the mother alone and more were in foster care at their time of admission to hospital.

Nurcombe (1964) also reported that two-thirds of his sample of young arsonists came from chaotic, rejecting and deprived families. Kafrey (1980) noted that fathers of children who engaged in 'fire-play' tended to perceive these children more negatively than did fathers of 'non-play' children and the mothers rated the relationship between father and child more negatively in the fire-play group compared to the non-play group of children. The results from Hill *et al.'s* (1982) study do not differentiate arsonist from violent offenders in terms of physical abuse from the parents, the psychiatric status of either parent, or family discord; however, these two offender groups were differentiated from property offenders in terms of fathers' heavier drinking habits.

The relevant psychosocial factors within the family may lie in the nature of the parenting. Several studies have noted that parents of repetitive fire-setters adopted a punitive response to their child's fire-setting as opposed to the parents of non-repetitive fires-setters who adopted a constructive, non-punitive response (Block *et al.* 1976; Siegelman and Folkman, 1971). It may be that a harsh punitive parenting style in response to arson (and other misdemeanours) would: (1) model poor problem solving; (2) restrict the development of independent problem solving; (3) create a greater fear of rejection or negative evaluation; and (4) engender a greater degree of secrecy in the child.

It may be speculated that poor parenting either in the form of a poor relationship with the parent or the absence of one or both parents has a significant impact on the young (potential) arsonist. This may lead to poor self-esteem, impaired moral and emotional development, feelings of rejection, and a perceived lack of support. In many cases we have noted the arsonist's potential for self-recrimination for the failure of the parental relationship. This potential should not be under-estimated. In one case, a young fire-setter whose father had deserted the family home had developed self-recrimination to the extent that he blamed himself for his mother's epilepsy (which actually resulted from a traumatic head injury).

Wooton (1959) has suggested that, as a rule, delinquents come from large families. Hurley and Monahan (1969) reported that the average family of their arsonist sample contained 4.45 children, which is well above average. It is interesting that Hurley and Monahan reported that previous convictions were noted to be more prevalent in larger families. One may speculate that the larger the family the less individual parental attention and guidance a child may receive. Family size appears to be an indirect factor leading to offending in general rather than arson *per se.*

Jackson, Glass, and Hope (1987) reported that arsonists compared to other offenders were taken into care at an earlier age. It may be that fire-setting behaviour was the primary reason for their admission into care, since age is irrelevant to the potential danger presented by arson and therefore special conditions may have been enforced from a security aspect. Interpersonal violence in young children may not require care conditions since it is relatively easily managed.

Being taken into care at an early age may contribute to a pathological process. First, institutions rarely provide a consistency of care comparable to the family home, and the opportunity to develop interpersonal conflict resolution skills is diminished. Second, institutions diffuse responsibility and authority, often away from the primary care-givers, and therefore the potential young arsonist has to negotiate with the institution rather than individuals. As Hill *et al.* (1982) have pointed out 'one can strike an individual; but one cannot strike an organisation. However, one can burn its property' (p 653).

Arsonists have been reported to suffer from a high incidence of abuse (Stewart and Culver, 1982). Ritvo, *et al.* (1983) reported that many had been abused by burns. Amongst the population of arsonists in the Special Hospital, physical abuse has been found to be common. Sexual abuse was particularly common amongst female fire-setters; however, we have been becoming increasingly aware of sexual abuse towards young male arsonists. Despite these observations, Bradford (1982) reported that their sample of arsonists reported less parental abuse (neglect, physical, and emotional abuse) than their control group of offenders.

In line with findings of low IQ, poor school achievement was noted. Bradford (1982) found that arsonists had significantly less schooling than other offenders and that arsonists came from a lower occupational status. Hurley and Monahan (1969) also reported the poor work record of arsonists.

In summary, there is a high likelihood of psychosocial disadvantage in pathological arsonists including intellectual impairment, physical abnormality, disrupted family history, and poor interpersonal skills.

Setting conditions for fire-setting: The absence of other socially unacceptable alternatives

One question which arises is why do arsonists not use aggression to resolve their problems? Several possibilities emerge. The first is that arsonists are unassertive individuals, fearful of direct face-to-face confrontation. Jackson, Hope, and Glass (1987) found that Special Hospital patients who committed arson as their primary index offence rated themselves as significantly less assertive on the Ratthus Assertiveness Scale than patients who had violence as their primary offence and no history of arson.

This finding has been replicated in an unpublished study by Jackson, O'Kane, and Hossack (1991). Male violent offenders (N=15) and male arsonists (N=15), matched for age, IQ, and duration of residence in Moss Side Special Hospital were assessed on five measures: the Gudjonsson Suggestibility Scale; the Ratthus Assertiveness Scale; the Social Desirability Scale; the Fear of Negative Evaluation Scale; and the Social Avoidance and Distress Scale. As can be seen in Table 5.2, there were no significant differences in terms of suggestibility or social desirability between violent offenders and arsonists, suggesting that both groups were equally reliable (or equally unreliable) in their self-report. They did not significantly differ in terms of social distress and avoidance, both demonstrating relatively high levels. However, arsonists rated themselves much higher in fear of negative evaluation, and significantly lower in assertiveness than did violent offenders. These findings suggest that arsonists may avoid confrontation due to their low confidence in being able deal effectively with face-to-face confrontation and their higher fear of being evaluated negatively.

Table 5.2: Psychological Characteristics of Arsonist and Violent Psychopaths

Measure	*Arsonists (N=15) (N=15)*	*Violent offenders*	*Significance*
Age	25.07	27.27	NS
Gudjonsson Suggestibility Scale	11.40	11.27	NS
Ratthus Assertiveness Scale	16.27	-9.00	p<.04
Social Desirability Scale	14.00	16.33	NS
Fear of Negative Evaluation Scale	20.27	16.33	p<.005
Social Distress and Avoidance Scale	17.20	14.13	NS

The extent of the arsonist's fears are amply demonstrated by the case of a 19-year-old arsonist in Moss Side Special Hospital with a classification of Psychopathic Disorder. The hospital operated a staged reward scheme for all patients. Every two weeks patients were reviewed by the clinical team and a decision was made either to raise the patient a stage, drop a stage, or remain the same. For several months, this patient was on the lowest stage. Closer evaluation revealed that, although his behaviour was reasonably good for most of the time, he would perform some antisocial act (usually minor) which actively prevented him acquiring any recommendations for an increase in his stage. During counselling, it transpired that he had been quite consciously keeping his stage at the lowest possible level, despite this meaning less money for personal effects (e.g. batteries, tobacco, sweets). His rationale was that, by being on the lowest possible stage all the time, he could not be criticised or 'punished' further. This nihilistic strategy for avoiding confrontation, punishment, and negative evaluation has been seen in many arsonists in different guises.

We did not find any significant difference between violent offenders and arsonists in terms of suggestibility. This is surprising in that clinical impressions tend to suggest that arsonists are over-compliant, often providing answers which they consider the listener wants, even to the point of making false confessions.

One young arsonist confronted with the dilemma of, on the one hand, denying that he committed a particular offence with the consequence of further questions and interrogation, or on the other hand, confessing to the offence and therefore opening himself to potential conviction and confinement, chose a middle path, stating that he 'might not have' committed the offence. I like to think of this as the 'Man For All Seasons Defence' since it resembles Thomas Moore's approach to the dilemma of signing a proclamation recognising Henry VIII as the rightful head of the Church in England. For Thomas Moore, to sign the proclamation was an act against his faith and the Holy Church in Rome which would result in eternal damnation. However, to refuse to sign the proclamation would be an act against his King, treasonable and punished by death. Faced with such a dilemma, Thomas Moore's defence essentially involved him saying that he did not deny that Henry VIII was the rightful King of England but that for reasons of his own which he would not divulge he would not sign the proclamation. The young arsonist when accused chose a similar 'middle ground' stating that he 'might not have' committed the offence.

This example provides a clear illustration of many arsonists' fears of confrontation and the dilemmas produced by such fears. Indeed, it may well explain, in part, the high incidence of problems of anxiety detected in this group and identified by Hurley and Monahan (1969). The inhibition of interpersonal conflict resolution is an important component of 'The Only Viable Option' theory of pathological arson.

It may well be that many arsonists do not consider themselves capable of interpersonal aggression and therefore feel particularly vulnerable in cases where interpersonal violence is likely. If there is poor conflict resolution in the home, then the arsonist may not have had the experience of observing successful face-to-face conflict resolution. Studies of the families of firesetters (Kazdin and Kolko, 1986; Regehr and Glancy, 1988) suggest a high degree of conflict with inefficient negotiation of solutions, weak parental coalition, and unreceptiveness towards the opinions of others. Clearly, such families are unlikely to provide the social and psychological environment for the children to develop the social interaction skills for conflict resolution. Rather, the dynamics in many families of fire-setters seem to generate conflict with little appropriate modelling or experience of successful resolution. Perhaps such family environments and dynamics also engender in the young fire-setter a need for a powerful other (the symbolic father figure) to provide a degree of protection. Macht and Mack (1968) reported several cases of arsonists setting fires in order to re-establish a lost relationship with the father, whilst distancing themselves from an overwhelming mother. Furthermore, Lewis and Yarnell (1951) suggested that firesetting was an indirect expression of aggression against adults who were perceived as rejecting.

Keval (1989) examined the inhibition of interpersonal conflict resolution using the Levenson Locus of Control Questionnaire (Levenson, 1973), which provides three elements of locus of control: chance, powerful others, and internal (personal) locus of control. Both violent offenders and arsonists considered their world to be controlled by powerful others and by chance to a greater extent that did non-offender controls. Violent offenders felt they had a greater internal locus of control than non-offenders, and arsonists fell between the two groups and were not significantly different at the formal statistical level from either. Although speculative and only weakly supported by empirical data, it appears that both violent offenders and arsonists consider themselves to live in a world controlled by powerful others and only the violent offenders believed that they had a high degree of personal control. Under these circumstances, it may be that the arsonists do not attempt direct face-to-face conflict resolution since they have little confidence in their own abilities to alter events or circumstances by such means.

Hill *et al.* (1982) suggested that one potential reason arsonists do not engage in interpersonal conflict or violence may be due to their relatively good abilities to empathise with others. Hill *et al.* cite the doctoral dissertation of Pollack (1980) which reported that violent offenders were less able to take the role of others than non-violent offenders. We have examined this possibility in some detail using the Facial Affect Slides from Ekman and Freisen (1976) to test emotional recognition in different offender groups (Jackson, Ashcroft, Williams, and Hope, 1993). Three groups of mentally abnormal offenders (violent offenders, arsonists, sex offenders) from Ashworth Hospital were assessed and compared with a large sample (N=112) of normal British subjects. The offenders were found to be significantly poorer than normals in emotional recognition. Significant differences were not found for basic emotional categories (e.g. happy, sad) or for slides where no emotion was present (neutral) but were found for categories of fear, anger, surprise, and disgust. Moreover, significant differences were found between the three offender groups. Arsonists were better than sex offenders and violent offenders in the recognition of facial expressions of disgust. Sex offenders were more impaired than the other two offender on slides depicting fear. Thus, there is some tentative empirical evidence to support Hill *et al.'s* (1982) hypothesis that arsonists may be able to empathise better than other offenders.

Overall, there appear to be many reasons why interpersonal conflict may not be (or not considered to be) a viable option for the arsonist in resolving problems. Finally, other options which avoid interpersonal conflict such as bogus telephone calls, self-mutilation, and suicidal gestures may offer some avenue for effective impact for the pathological arsonist. Indeed, Grunebaum and Klerman (1967) have noted that wrist-slashing often results from conflict-laden situations. Similarly, Ross and McKay (1979) have suggested that self-mutilation may result from the subject experiencing a sense of helplessness in an undesirable situation and that encouraging autonomy and self-efficacy reduces the incidence of self-mutilation. Our experience is that these 'other solutions' are frequently found in many arsonists' behavioural histories, fire-setting being only one of a myriad of such behaviours.

Developmental aspects: The potential for addiction in fire setting

It is speculated that there may be three psychological processes underlying the 'addiction' to fire-setting. These are: (1) Addiction rooted in attempts to relive the emotional experience involved in fire-setting; (2) Addiction based on the intermittent reinforcement effect; and (3) Addiction based on the positive short-term consequences despite the long-term negative consequences of fire setting.

Hodge (1992) proposed that violence may be maintained by a process of addiction. He referred to Peele's (1985) theory which defines addictions, not in terms of addiction to a substance or event as is commonly assumed, but addiction to an *experience*. Hodge (1992) suggested that processes underlying addiction might play a part in many types of criminal behaviour such that the core element of the crime is to achieve an experience. Applying this concept to pathological arson might explain some of the difficulties in identifying the motives for some acts of fire-setting. It is notable that many of the motives reported in previous research relate not to a tangible outcome, but to an experience (e.g. relief from tension, excitement). Could it be therefore that arson also progresses to a point where it is the experience rather than the event which is of central importance? It is known that pathological arsonists describe a range of emotional experiences immediately prior to, during, and immediately after fire-setting which mainly involve excitement (Bumpass, Fagelman, and Brix, 1983). I would hypothesise that this type of addiction occurs in the latter stages of a fire-setting career and may incorporate other related behaviours such as false alarms, calling the fire brigade, and fighting the fire. Also 'addiction' of this nature perhaps resembles most closely the DSM III criteria for pyromania and perhaps, in part, explains some reports that the arsonist felt a compulsion. However, in the initial stages of the fire-setting career the motives for the fire-setting are perhaps more instrumental, rather than related to this type of addiction.

Regarding the second possible mechanism for 'addiction', I have noted that I consider solitary fire-setting as an important factor. We interviewed 35 arsonists within the Special Hospital regarding the circumstances of their first and last fire, finding a progression towards solitary fire-setting, with first episodes of fire-setting being committed predominantly with others and later fires being set alone. I have hypothesised that the progression to setting fire alone reflects intermittent reinforcement processes which underlie addiction and may, in part, explain the apparently motiveless aspects of pathological arson.

Intermittent reinforcement is likely to occur if an important aspect of the fire-setting is dependent upon the arsonist being found out. For the arsonist, the effect and impact of the act of fire-setting is highly dependent on others being aware who was the perpetrator. This may come in the form of kudos from peers, avoidance or escape from situations, or the 'manipulation' of others. Indeed, one may hypothesise that there would be only meagre advantages if the arsonist were not caught.

At the same time, arsonists, aware of the possible punitive measures which may befall if they are caught, will seek to avoid detection. One way in which detection can be avoided is to set the fire alone and in secret. The fundamental problem is that secrecy fails to reproduce the desired consequences. Thus, an intermittent reinforcement effect is established. The arsonist then engages in an escalating 'game', where the risk of detection increases (i.e. larger fires, more public fires, greater involvement with the fire), until they are eventually caught.

The third possible mechanism involves the assumption that, whilst the short-term consequences promote a desired effect (such as avoidance of or the resolution of a problem), the long-term outcomes create or exacerbate problems, thus initiating a vicious cycle. The short-term consequences of arson have been described above and in many instances arson may be successful resolution. For example, the young arsonist sets a fire in order to reinstate the parental relationship. In the short-term this may be successful in that the father returns to the family home to resolve the problem. In the long-term this is likely to add further stress and impair relationships within the family. Eventually, the result of arson is the removal of the child from the family and a further barrier to an important relationship. Similarly, a young arsonist who sets fires with others for the kudos of peer recognition may actually achieve that recognition in the short-term but then become ostracised as others mature and avoid contact with the arsonist who becomes seen as a potential source of trouble. The arsonist who sets fire as a means of resolving conflict in a non-interpersonal way, eventually is placed in direct face-to-face confrontation, usually with police and other authorities, resulting in the arsonist being moved to an ever restrictive institutional setting. The potentially detrimental consequences of being in an institution have been mentioned above with respect to the processes considered to underlie pathological arson. The essential point here is that learning conditions in which the short-term solution to a problem provokes longer-term exacerbation of that problem may lead to a form of psychological addiction.

Why fire?

The question still remains as to why fire particularly is chosen as the vehicle for problem resolution when this behaviour runs so many risks for the arsonist (and others). I have suggested that the events or psychological factors which steer the arsonist to the use of fire may be apparently insignificant, although having dramatic consequences. This is in direct contrast to those theories which place the symbolic nature of fire and fascination at the centre of the model. In my opinion, the processes which lead to fire-setting do not involve any special significance of fire (at least in the embryonic stages), any more than the knife is significant to the murderer. All that is required is that the arsonist's attention is drawn to fire-setting, or more exactly the effects of fire-setting. It is likely simply by chance that some contact with fire will lead to it being considered as a vehicle for impacting on a situation where no other methods are, or seem, possible.

Vicarious experience of fire may influence those predisposed to its pathological use. For example, it has been noted that inclusion of a single arsonist into a vulnerable community can lead to an epidemic of fire-setting (Boling and Brotman, 1975; Rosenstock *et al.* 1980). We have noted that a number of arsonists can recount experiences of fires which they had not set and the effects that such fires had on the community. Ritvo *et al.* (1983) found that fire had been used as a means of physical abuse against young arsonists and suggested that the emotional effects of such associations led to the recognition of fire as a potent weapon. We have found that some arsonists have been the victims of fires, receiving severe burns.

Some studies have suggested that fire-setters originate from rural areas where large field fires are likely to be seen (Wolford, 1972), although our experience is that the majority originate from inner cities. Some of these have had experience of fire being set in riot situations and have been party to such urban riots. Some studies have suggested that fire may have a significant symbolic association with an important other (e.g. father); for example, Macht and Mack (1968) found that fire was often an important component of the father's occupation. Finally, we have suggested that normal childhood fascination with fire may be the only significant association.

A Standardised Assessment Approach?

Considering the variability that exists in the genesis, development and maintenance of pathological arson, it is perhaps overly ambitious and potentially misleading to suggest a standardised assessment approach. Clearly, a thorough investigation of the idiosyncratic characteristics of each arsonist is required. However, as a summary and perhaps as an initial guidance to developing an individual formulation I have listed below a number of factors in different domains which may be considered to represent high-risk factors which are likely to be important in assessment. I make no excuse for the speculative nature of some of these factors, but offer them in the hope that further empirical investigation will modify this list.

1. *Personal demographic characteristics*

   (a) Physical/Psychiatric Disorders

   - Low or borderline IQ
   - Mild physical abnormality

  - Psychiatric disorder
  - Neurological disorder
  - Antisocial personality disorder
- (b) Psychological Disorders
  - Unassertive personality
  - Social avoidance or avoidance of conflict
  - Excessively insecure personality, perhaps exposed by over-defensiveness
  - History of self-mutilation and/or suicidal gestures
  - Low self-esteem
  - Over-compliance/High suggestibility
  - Cruelty to animals
  - History of substance abuse
  - High fear of negative evaluation
- (c) Social/Family Problems
  - History of being bullied
  - History of physical, emotional, or sexual abuse
  - A high number of different institutional placements
  - Taken into institutional care at an early age
  - Unrealistic ambitions
- (d) Offending History
  - History of aggressiveness
  - History of property offences
  - Truancy from school, home, or hostel
- (e) Fire Related Factors
  - History of fire-play
  - Personal experience of fire
  - Symbolic significance of fire
  - Vicarious experience of fire

2. *Family characteristics*

- High number of siblings
- Father absent
- Family excessively punitive and rigid
- Mother–child coalition and overprotectiveness
- High family disruption

- High expressed emotion
- Fire associated with family member (actually or symbolically)
- Personality disorder in father
- Mental illness in mother
- Emotional neglect in family
- Poor conflict resolution in the family

3. Fire-related behaviour

- Ambiguity of relationship between the target and overt motive
- Lack of insight into motive
- Solitary fire-setting
- Developmental history of larger fires
- Fire to property
- Threat to life
- Fire to own property
- Offender involved in 'fire-fighting' (e.g. calling the fire-brigade, etc.)
- Fire preceded by related threats of violence or fire
- Early developmental history of fire-setting
- History of similar targets and evidence of 'ritualistic' fire-setting
- Predictable emotional states preceding fire (anger, rejection, boredom)
- Fire set under conditions of high psychological stress or distress

None of the above items within the checklist is entirely necessary or solely sufficient to explain pathological fire-setting. Furthermore, the list is not exhaustive and other factors may, in individual cases, play a crucial part. This checklist, therefore, should be considered only as a guide to full assessment. The information gathered in assessment should then be integrated into a problem formulation, based on an understanding of the psychological processes precipitated by each of the above items.

Implications for Treatment

The 'Only Viable Option' theory of pathological arson suggests that treatment should be aimed at helping pathological arsonists:

1. Attain greater insight into the psychological motives for fire setting.
2. Attain alternative strategies and abilities for personal problem solving.
3. Overcome inhibitions or handicaps that may prohibit the use of such alternatives.
4. Tolerate unsolvable problems and direct efforts towards attainable goals.

Furthermore, it supposes that the important indices for prediction of dangerousness lie not in any psychiatric diagnosis or indeed in the nature of the fire-setting *per se,* but in the underlying psychological factors which lead to distress and helplessness. This approach is in contrast to the dynamic theories which suggest cathartic dissipation of internal drives (aggressive, sexual), and the antithesis of those approaches which seek to extinguish the interest in fire by satiation.

This enabling approach to treatment requires a careful balance between external control which provides safety and security for the arsonist, and the development of internal and personal control. The aims of therapy should be to increase the arsonist's tolerance of failures and the shortcomings of external control agents, and increase self-sufficiency. The roots to pathological fire-setting are emotional and interpersonal. In this sense emotionally distant and impersonal approaches to their management should be avoided. Authority should be given to a single, clearly identified individual (as opposed to an amorphous body) who will encourage and prompt negotiation of that authority with the arsonist. The development of interpersonal skills for problem-solving is essential and thus it is often necessary to use group therapy and training approaches. The outline of a group therapy course developed and employed at Ashworth Hospital is provided below.

Group Therapy Course

Aims of the course

1. To explore with repetitive offenders of any diagnosis, the functions served by their offences of arson and possible alternative coping strategies.
2. To explore with the group their current coping strategies and problem-solving abilities, using peer confrontation to challenge avoidance and denial of personal responsibility and to facilitate positive acceptance and insight.
3. To examine with the group possible misconceptions about their offence and reactions to fire setting and education regarding the potential effects of fires and others' reactions to fire.
4. To help members of the group develop better positive coping strategies and skills for conflict resolution, social problem-solving, and emotional control.
5. To help members of the group develop a sense of personal effectiveness, self-esteem, and comprehension of human rights in social situations.
6. To help members of the group tolerate and cope with anxiety, disappointment, depression, anger, and unresolvable dilemmas.
7. To help the group consider the roles of members of their family, their role within this system, and the relationship of these factors to their offending behaviour.

8. To help members of the group develop realistic plans for the future (both short-term and long-term) which involve planning for the attainment of social, professional, and financial support.
9. To investigate behaviours and problems related to fire-setting (e.g. alcohol/drug abuse, suicidal inclination, self-mutilation, interpersonal violence, false 999 calls, threats of fire setting).
10. To assess dangerousness, potential for future fire-setting, and alternative coping abilities.

Course outline

The arson course is divided into four major sections. Not all clients would be willing or able to take advantage of all these sections and therefore they operate as separate courses within an overall framework. In addition, weekly homework assignments are given in each of the sessions and reviewed at the beginning of the following session.

Section 1: Educational and information components

1. Dangers of fire
2. Fire prevention
3. Others' reaction to fire
4. Others' reaction to fire-setters
5. Personal beliefs about the above

Section 2: Alternative skills training

1. Assertiveness skills training (including effective communication skills development)
2. Social problem solving training
3. Anxiety management
4. Negotiation skills training
5. Conflict resolution strategies
6. Coping with insoluble situations

Section 3: Self-awareness and self-esteem

1. Human rights
2. Realistic expectations of self and others
3. Ideal self; Current self; Acceptable self
4. Sources of self-esteem
5. Developing trust and trust engendering
6. Current coping strategies

Section 4: Family and related issues

1. The function of fire-setting to the family and institutional system
2. Realistic appraisal of family members
3. Family life cycle
4. Drugs, alcohol, unemployment
5. Abuse and abusing
6. Sexuality

Finally, it needs to be stated that research and treatment into pathological arson is considerably hampered by the absence of facilities for such offenders. Indeed, the high number of different placements which our patients have suffered has been a direct result of the unwillingness of either health or social authorities to provide for arsonists. The eventual outcome is to place arsonists in the most restrictive of environments which provides little opportunity for personal efficacy and which also exposes these often vulnerable and suggestible individuals to further threat from aggressive offenders. In this sense, the response of society not only further rejects the arsonist but colludes in the pathological processes underlying arson.

References

American Psychiatric Association (1980) *Diagnostic and Statistical Manual of Mental Disorder*, 3rd Edition. APA: Washington, DC.

Arlow, J.A. (1978) Pyromania and the primal scene: a psychoanalytical comment on the work of Yukio Mishima. *Psychoanalysis Quarterly, 47*, 24–51.

Block, J.H., Block, J. and Folkman, W.S. (1976) *Fire and Young Children: Learning Survival Skills.* USDA Forest Service Research Paper, PSW-119.

Boling, L. and Brotman, C. (1975) A fire setting epidemic in a state mental health centre. *American Journal of Psychiatry, 132*, 946–950.

Bradford, J.M.W. (1982) Arson: A clinical study. *Canadian Journal of Psychiatry, 27*, 188–193.

Bumpass, E.R., Fagelman, F.D. and Brix, R.J. (1983) Intervention with children who set fires. *American Journal of Psychotherapy, 37*, 328–345.

Ekman, P. and Friesen, W.V. (1976) *Facial Affect Slides.* Palo Alto: Consulting Psychologists Press.

Folkman, S. and Lazarus, R.S. (1980) An analysis of coping in a middle aged community sample. *Journal of Health and Social Behaviour, 21*, 219–239.

Fry, J.F. and Le Couteur, B. (1966) Arson. *The Medico-Legal Journal*, XXXIV, 108–121.

Geller, J. (1984) Arson: An unforeseen sequel of deinstitutionalization. *American Journal of Psychiatry, 141*, 504–508.

Goldstein, K. (1939) *The Organism.* New York: American Book Co.

Gorenstein, E.E. (1982) Frontal lobe functions in psychopaths. *Journal of Abnormal Psychology, 88*, 605–610.

Grunebaum, H.Y. and Klerman, G.L. (1967) Wrist Slashing. *American Journal of Psychiatry, 124,* 527–534.

Gunderson, J.G. (1974) Management of manic states: the problem of fire setting. *Psychiatry, 37,* 137–146.

Hellman, D.S. and Blackman, N. (1966) Enuresis, firesetting and cruelty to animals: A triad predictive of adult crime. *American Journal of Psychiatry, 122,* 1431–1435.

Hill, R.W., Langevin, R., Paitich, D., Handy,L., Russon, A. and Wilkinson, L. (1982) Is arson an aggressive act or a property offence? A controlled study of psychiatric referrals. *Canadian Journal of Psychiatry, 27,* 648–654.

Hodge, J.E. (1992) Addiction to violence: A new model of psychopathy. *Criminal Behaviour and Mental Health, 2,* 212–213.

Hurley, W. and Monahan, T.M. (1969) Arson: The criminal and the crime. *British Journal of Criminology, 9,* 4–21.

Inciardi, J.A. (1970) The adult firesetter: A typology. *Criminology, 8,* 145–155.

Jackson, H.F., Ashcroft, J.B., Williams, K. and Hope, S. (1993) Emotional recognition in mentally abnormal offenders: I Assessment. *Criminal Behaviour and Mental Health,* (in press).

Jackson, H.F., Glass, C.A. and Hope, S. (1987) A functional analysis of recidivistic arson. *British Journal of Clinical Psychology, 26,* 175–185.

Jackson, H.F., Hope, S. and Glass, C. (1987) Why are arsonists not violent offenders? *International Journal of Offender Therapy and Comparative Criminology, 31,* 143–152.

Jackson, H.F., O'Kane, A. and Hossack, A. (1991) Comparison of violent offenders and arsonists special hospital patients: Suggestibility, Fear of Negative Evaluation, Social Desirability and Social Avoidance. Unpublished paper: Ashworth Hospital.

Kafrey, D. (1980) Playing with matches: Children and fire. In D. Canter (ed) *Fires and Human Behaviour.* New York: John Wiley and Sons.

Kagan, J., Moss, H.A. and Seigel, I.E. (1963) Psychological significance of style of conceptualisation. In J.C. Wright and J. Kagan (eds) *Basic Cognitive Processes in Children.* Monographs of the Society for Research in Child Development, 28, 2, Serial No. 86.

Kanner, L. (1957) *Child Psychiatry.* Springfield, IL: Charles C. Thomas.

Kaufman, I., Heims, L.W. and Reiser, E. (1961) A re-evaluation of the psychodynamics of firesetting. *American Journal of Orthopsychiatry, 31,* 123–136.

Kazdin, A.E. and Kolko, D. J. (1986) Parental psychopathology and family functioning in childhood firesetters. *Journal of Abnormal Child Psychology, 14,* 315–329.

Keval, N. (1989) Cognitive Style in Recidivistic Arson. Unpublished Master's Dissertation, Department of Clinical Psychology, University of Liverpool.

Koson, D.F. and Dvoskin, J. (1982) Arson: a diagnostic study. *Bulletin of the American Academy of Psychiatry and the Law, 10,* 39–49.

Lewis, N.D.C. and Yarnell, H. (1951) Pathological firesetting (pyromania) *Nervous and Mental Disease Monographs,* No. 82.

Levenson, H. (1973) Multidimensional locus of control in psychiatric patients. *Journal of Consulting and Clinical Psychology, 41*, 397–404.

Lishman, W.A. (1968) Brain damage in relation to psychiatric disability after head injury. *British Journal of Psychiatry, 114*, 373–410.

Macht, L.B. and Mack, J.E. (1968) The firesetter syndrome. *Psychiatry, 31*, 277–288.

McDonald, J. (1960) *FBI Law Enforcement Bulletin*, July, 3–9. Washington D.C.

McKerracher, D.W. and Dacre, J.I. (1966) A study of arsonists in a special security hospital. *British Journal of Psychiatry, 112*, 1151–1154.

Nurcombe, B. (1964) Children who set fires. *Medical Journal of Australia, 18*, 579–584.

Pollack, N. (1980) The relationship between criminal behaviour and constricted role-taking activity. Unpublished PhD thesis, University of Toronto.

Regehr, C. and Glancy, G. (1988) Families of firesetters. *Journal of Forensic Psychiatry, 2*, 27–36.

Ritvo, E., Shanok, S.S. and Lewis, D.O. (1983) Firesetting and non-firesetting delinquents: a comparison of neuropsychiatric, psychoeducational, experimental, and behavioural characteristics. *Child Psychiatry and Human Development, 13*, 259–267.

Robins, E. and Robins, L. (1967) Arson with specific reference to pyromania. *New York State Journal of Medicine, 67*, 795–798.

Rosenstock, H.A., Holland, A.L. and Jones, P.H. (1980) Fire setting in an adolescent inpatient unit: An analysis. *Journal of Clinical Psychiatry, 41*, 20–22.

Ross, R. and McKay, H.G. (1979) *Self-Mutilation*. Lexington, Mass.: D.C. Heath and Co.

Schmid, H. (1914) Zur Psychologie der Brandstifter. *Psychologische Abhandlungen Bd., 1*, 80–179.

Segal, J. (1985) *Phantasy in Everyday Life: A Psychoanalytic Approach to Understanding Ourselves*. London: Penguin Books.

Siegelman, E.Y. and Folkman, W.S. (1971) Youthful firesetters: An explanatory study in personality and background. USDA Forest Research Note, PWS-230.

Soothill, K.L. and Pope, P.J. (1973) Arson: a twenty year cohort study. *Medical Science and Law, 13*, April.

Stekel, W. (1924) Pyromania. In *Peculiarities of Behaviour*, Vol. 2. New York: Boni and Liveright.

Stewart, M.A. and Culver, K.W. (1982) Children who set fires: The clinical picture and follow-up. *British Journal of Psychiatry, 140*, 357–363.

Tennent, T.G., McQuaid, A., Loughnane, T. and Hands, A.J. (1971) Female arsonists. *British Journal of Psychiatry, 119*, 497–502.

Vandersall, T.A. and Weiner, J.M. (1970) Children who set fires. *Archives of General Psychiatry, 22*, 63–71.

Virkkunen, M. (1974) On arson committed by schizophrenics. *Acta Psychiatria Scandinavia, 50*, 152–160.

Vreeland, R.G. and Levin, B.M. (1980) Psychological aspects of firesetting. In D. Canter (ed) *Fires and Human Behaviour*. New York: John Wiley and Sons.

Wolford, M. (1972) Some attitudinal, psychological and sociological characteristics of incarcerated arsonists. *Fire and Arson Investigator, 22*, 1–30.

Wooton, B. (1959) *Social Science and Social Pathology.* London: George Allen and Unwin.

Yarnell, H. (1940) Firesetting in children. *American Journal of Orthopsychiatry, 10,* 282–286.

Yesavage, J.A., Benezech, M., Ceccaldi, P., Bourgeois, M. and Addad, M. (1983) Arson in mentally ill and criminal populations. *Journal of Clinical Psychiatry, 44,* 128–130.

Zung, W. (1965) Self-rating Depression Scale. *Archives of General Psychiatry, 12,* 63–70.

CHAPTER 6

Forensic Report Writing

ANDY BENN AND CAROL BRADY

It is crucial that forensic reports are accurate, clear and useful. Despite this, reports are often criticised for being hard to understand and of limited usefulness, which is, perhaps, a reflection of the fact that many disciplines have little or no formal training in written communication. Report-writing appears to be a skill which professionals are assumed to 'pick up' in the process of learning the job. The purpose of this chapter is to describe some of the methods of producing clear, credible and persuasive forensic reports.

Several key areas will be covered. First, we will look at some of the reasons why forensic assessment reports may be requested or written. Some of the potential effects of the Access to Health Records Act (1990) and the Criminal Justice Act (1991) will be discussed, as will be the issues of who is the 'client' and who 'owns' the assessment. The research on report writing will be reviewed and the implications for report writing outlined. Considerations which result from the anticipated readership will be highlighted, including format and style of writing. A sample forensic report is provided in an appendix to illustrate points made in the chapter. Whilst there may be some differences in psychiatric, social work, probation, prison, clinical psychology or nursing reports, most of the points made in this chapter are relevant to reports by authors of all disciplines. What is presented is an outline of how the assessments described in the preceding chapters may be presented in report form.

The Purpose of Forensic Reports

The purpose of reports is largely guided by the need to answer these four questions: (1) What problems does the offender experience? (2) What interventions are available? (3) Is intervention likely to be successful? (4) Where should the intervention take place? Requests for assessment often come from courts, since these are the main decision-makers in the process which deals with these four questions. A court may recommend that an offender has a period of assessment in hospital to identify or clarify the offender's problems. In addition, solicitors may request assessments when they believe these would be beneficial to their client's case. Tennent (1990) provides a fuller discussion of this process.

When offenders have reached the destination which the court has decided upon, the decision-makers within that system may also request assessment reports to help with decisions about future placement or treatment. Within the prison system, the Local Review Committee would use reports prepared by the personnel who have contact with the prisoner (and the prisoner's own evaluation) to formulate its recommendations to the Parole Board. A Mental Health Review Tribunal (MHRT) will refer to reports on offenders subject to Mental Health Act (1983) legislation during its decision-making process. How the four questions may be addressed in forensic assessment reports is illustrated below.

(1) What problems does the offender experience?

The report needs to describe what problems the offender experiences, along with what resources the offender possesses. The report should differentiate psychiatric problems (e.g. depression and delusions), psychological problems (e.g. poor problem solving skills and poor anger control), and social problems (e.g. unemployment and social isolation). In addition, the report should state any clear relationships among the problems (see later section on Formulation).

(2) What interventions are available?

After problems have been identified, the report needs to specify what possible interventions would be available to address those problems or to prevent those problems becoming worse. The court is unlikely to make recommendations for treatment when the assessments have been unable to identify interventions.

(3) Is intervention likely to be successful?

Even where interventions are available, courts are unlikely to recommend the offender receives these if it is unlikely that the offender will benefit from them. Reports should detail factors that suggest whether the offender would or would not benefit from an intervention programme, including response to previous interventions

(4) Where should the intervention take place?

When placement decisions have to be made, reports should specify in what setting the intervention could take place. In many cases the setting can only referred to in a broad sense (e.g. community versus custody). In addition, reports may recommend movement within a system (e.g. between wards in a special hospital), between different parts of a system (e.g. transfer from one prison to another), or between different systems (e.g. transfer from a prison to a regional secure unit). The Parole Board may use the recommendations in a report to decide where future treatment should take place as part of a parolee's licence. Similarly, a MHRT may use the information to review the need for continued intervention and the necessary security level.

Legislation

The Access to Health Records Act (1990) enables individuals to have access to information entered in their medical records. The information which can be disclosed includes hand-written notes as well as formal reports. The professions included within the scope of the Act are medical practioners, registered nurses, and clinical psychologists. Information which may not be disclosed includes: (a) that which is likely to cause serious harm to the physical or mental health of the patient or of others; (b) that which has come from sources other than the patient and which could identify that person (unless their consent for its release is obtained); and (c) records made before the commencement of the Act on 1 November 1991. The applicant does not have to be informed when information in the above categories has been withheld.

The Act 'allows for inaccurate information to be challenged' (British Medical Association, 1990). On producing evidence demonstrating errors, the patient can request that factual inaccuracies are corrected. The professional is not obliged to accept the patient's version but must record the patient's statement about the disputed information.

The Criminal Justice Act (1991) has introduced open reporting for offenders serving life sentences ('lifers'). Woodward (1992, p.11) remarks that the 'expectation is that reports written on lifers will be disclosed to them'. However, many social workers, probation officers, prison officers and prison psychologists already write their reports with the understanding that offenders (not only lifers) may see those reports. Woodward (1992, p.11–12) expects that the 'commitment to openness... will in the foreseeable future be expected to apply to all prisoners'.

The main conclusion for report-writing which flows from the introduction of these Acts is that 'records should be compiled on the assumption that they will be opened to the patients' (NHS Management Executive, 1991).

Who is the Client?

In forensic situations the professional may be working for the Prison Service, Probation Service, National Health Service, Special Hospitals Service Authority, or the Department of Social Services. Reports are the property of the author's employer, and, through their employing institutions, these professionals are accountable to the courts and ultimately the public.

Where a solicitor requests an independent assessment, the professional is then working for the solicitor and his or her client (or for the Crown, if the request has come through the prosecution solicitor). In such cases, a solicitor may accept and use a report including all the professional's findings, or inform the professional that their written report is not required if it seems the report is unlikely to be favourable to their client. What cannot happen is for parts of the report to be selected for presentation in court.

An ethical dilemma can be created for the professional where, for example, assessment results may be unfavourable to a client but have implications for the client's potential dangerousness to other people. Where the assessment results are unfavourable to the client and the client's solicitor does not use the report, the professional is unable to inform the court of assessment results without breaking confidentiality. To prevent this difficulty arising, a useful strategy is for the professional to offer an assessment *provided that the report is used* and solicitors can then accept or decline this offer (Glasgow, 1992).

Where a report is made as part of assessment in an institution (e.g. prison, offenders' centre, hospital, secure unit) by an employee of the institution for the institution, the document may be used by the care team or Parole Board regardless of its favourability to the client. For example, an offender in a secure psychiatric unit may welcome the submission to a Mental Health Review Tribunal of reports written about them by the various members of the clinical team when the reports are known to be favourable. However, in a case where the reports are less favourable, the offender's Responsible Medical Officer may refer to or submit reports by other professionals, or the author may attend the Tribunal to support the contention that the offender remains in need of treatment within a secure setting.

Research on Report Writing

Written communication about clients is central to the provision of forensic services. Whether the services are team-based or a network, written communication provides the basis for sharing information on problem definition, assessment, problem formulation, interventions, and outcome. Key components of writing assessment reports may be identified as: (1) describing the client and the client's problem; (2) recording the results of the assessment; (3) organising and integrating old and new information; (4) presenting conclusions based on the current assessment and previous information; (5) recommending an appropriate course of action; and (6) communicating the results of the assessment to interested persons. Ownby (1987) believes that the report should also serve an influencing function in persuading the reader either to alter beliefs about the client, or to take a particular course of action with regard to the client. The way of achieving this is by providing statements that are credible and persuasive, that is, effective report writing. How well then do professionals do at report-writing?

There is little research on psychological report-writing and even less on reports written by other professional groups. To our knowledge, there are only three research studies on multidisciplinary views of psychological reports, all of them from 1959. A further study from 1983 looks specifically at the use of jargon in forensic psychology reports (Dietz *et al.* 1983). No similar studies looking at reports from other professions could be located. Given the importance of reports in the process of decision-making by courts, Mental Health Review Tribunals, clinical teams, Local Review Committees, the Parole Board, and others, the paucity of research is surprising.

Several book chapters and a few books on report-writing in general are available (Groth-Marnat, 1984; Ownby, 1987; Sternberg, 1988; Tallant, 1986), as are some which deal with forensic reports in particular (Bowden, 1990; Haward, 1981; Trick and Tennant, 1981; Weiner, 1987). The latter provide advice for writing forensic reports and are mainly orientated to reports for court. Only two authors base their advice on research on report writing (Groth-Marnat, 1984; Ownby, 1987).

Ownby (1987) provides an overview of the available research on psychology reports. His review shows that psychological reports in clinical settings: (1) are sometimes considered useful by the people receiving the reports; (2) are often criticised on the grounds of content and style by the professional groups receiving the reports; and (3) may or may not make substantial contributions to the client treatment planning. Criticisms of psychological reports include: excessive speculation; failure to include data from which inferences are drawn; and vagueness and ambiguity in writing style. However, psychologists have also criticised reports by other professional groups for failure to include the behavioural data from which inferences are drawn and for stylistic problems including vagueness and the use of jargon.

Tallant and Reiss (1959a) found that psychologists, psychiatrists, and social workers had much in common regarding what they thought important to include in reports, as well as important differences. All three professional groups thought that descriptions of general personality, dynamic defences, interpersonal relationships, and intellectual status were appropriate content. However, psychiatrists and social workers appeared to be more interested in receiving statements about intelligence than the psychologists were in reporting it. Most of the psychologists (74%) thought that recommendations for treatment were appropriate in reports, while few psychiatrists (14%) thought that this was so. It is likely that these opinions have changed since the 1959 research. The changing role of the professions, advances in assessment methods, and developments in theories about psychological problems and mental illness will have influenced the content of reports through both the writer having something different to offer and the reader coming to expect something different.

In a study looking at what 'the trouble with psychological reports is', psychologists, psychiatrists, and psychiatric social workers alike stressed the need for the 'responsible' interpretation of data and complained of expressive deficiencies in the reports (Tallant and Reiss, 1959b). The irresponsible interpretation of data included under- and over-interpretation and use of statements which appeared to reflect the examiner's personality more than the client's. Under-interpretation of the data presented in a report leaves the reader unsure about how the author has used the data in forming the conclusions and the report is thus open to misinterpretation. Over-interpretation of the data involves drawing unwarranted conclusions. Statements reflecting the author's personality include descriptors which are overly positive or negative (and may even be pejorative). Two implications for report-writing follow from these observations. First, if data are presented in a report, these data should be explained and possible interpretations outlined for the reader. Second, the report should detail conclusions which are consistent with the data presented and not based on the professional's personal thoughts or reaction to the client.

Expressive deficiencies refer to wordiness, the use of jargon, and ambiguity in content. Each of these has implications for report-writing. Wordiness lengthens the report, slows the reader down, and gives the impression that the report writer is unsure of how to state the conclusions in a concise manner. Writers should be mindful of the importance of being succinct. Technical terms should be explained when they are introduced in reports; it *is* possible to explain technical terms in plain English (Dietz *et al.* 1983). After this has been done, the technical term can thereafter be used as a short-hand description of a concept. Finally, ambiguity in the content of a report suggests that the writer has not focused on specific issues. Within the introduction to a report, a clear statement should be made about the issues addressed in the assessment, and thereafter the content of the report should focus on these issues.

Hartlage and Merck (1971) suggest that 'reports can be made more relevant to their prospective users merely by having the psychologists familiarise themselves with the uses to which their reports are to be applied' (p.460) and that psychologists and other report-writers should 'evaluate their own reports in terms of what these reports contribute to the operation of their unique settings rather than continue to grind out reports with good theoretical consistency, but little decisional value' (p.460). Ownby and Wallbrown (1983) suggest that report-writers should request feedback about their reports as a way of improving them. A questionnaire accompanying a report, asking whether the report answers the referral question and whether any parts of the report require further explanation, will provide useful feedback for the report writer.

We recently carried out a survey in Rampton Hospital, asking what it was about reports that made them useful and what made them unhelpful (Brady and Benn, 1992). Questionnaires were sent to the principal consumers of forensic reports in the hospital (consultant forensic psychiatrists, social workers, specialist nurses, ward nursing staff, and clinical psychologists). Of the 76 questionnaires sent out, 23 were returned, a response rate of 30 per cent.

The results of this survey suggest that reports judged as particularly useful tell the reader something new, or present the reader with information which leads them to view the situation in a new light. Useful reports were those which used headings, were brief, used simple language, answered the referral question, and provided a summary of the report.

Reports that were judged as not helpful were described as having no clear purpose and making no conclusions or recommendations. In addition, reports in which the structure was unclear, used jargon, were too long and rambling, or too detailed were also judged as not helpful. Those reports which focused mainly on the negative aspects of the offender and reports that contributed nothing new to the readers' understanding were also judged as not helpful. Suggestions for improving reports included stating the reason the report was being written, omitting jargon, explaining technical terms, using headings to structure the text, and improving the presentation and layout.

In summary, the consumers of reports in this survey wanted short reports, which state and answer the referral question, provide new information, use jargon-free and simple language, and are well structured with headings. The consumers also wanted a summary of the report, including conclusions and recommendations.

Terms of Reference of the Report

The first step in producing a useful report is to decide the terms of reference of the report. Two questions are relevant; what is the purpose of the report, and who is going to read it? The answers to each of these will influence the content of the report.

(1) Purpose

The purpose of the report will determine the information included, since the report should attempt to answer the referral question. The purpose should be made clear at the start, and the necessary information provided to answer the questions posed and to justify opinions and recommendations. Beyond that, the author should avoid any tendency to be overinclusive; information should only be included if it increases understanding.

(2) Readership

The report not only needs to be relevant to the needs of the readership but also readable by them. Prior to writing any report a 'readership analysis' could be carried out in order to facilitate the production of a report in which the author is writing 'for the readers'. Points to consider include the readers' previous knowledge of the subject, and the use to which they might put the information. Additionally reports, though aimed at a 'primary reader', also have an audience of 'secondary readers' who require consideration.

Contents of the Report

Ownby (1987, Chapter 3) makes three proposals based on the observation that readers want a well-reasoned explanation of how the report writer arrived at the conclusions.

(1) Concepts are used to explain the client's behaviour, therefore both the writer and reader should have a shared understanding of any terms used in the report. The writer should briefly explain terms which may be unfamiliar to the report reader the first time they are used.

(2) Conclusions are regarded as evaluative statements about the degree or extent of the concept in question. The conclusions must be supported by data presented in the report. To increase the understanding of the non-professional reader, with particular reference to court reports, Haward (1981) suggests not only stating what procedures were carried out during assessment, but also why these assessment procedures were seen as appropriate. This demonstrates the relevance of the assessment.

(3) Recommendations must be logically related to the explanatory concepts and conclusions stated in the report. The rationale for any recommendation should be contained in the preceding sections of the report.

It is necessary to present the data, concepts, conclusions, and recommendations for the report to have some degree of credibility and persuasiveness. Sources of information (e.g. client self-report, witness statements, previous reports, psychometric tests) should be acknowledged and clearly differentiated from the professional's inferences and interpretation of the information. Following the above guidelines increases the reader's understanding of the issues. Ownby (1987, p.40–41) gives an example of a statement not following the above guidelines: 'Visual-motor skills are poor, and work on remedial tasks such as puzzles and tracing are recommended'. An example of one which *does* follow the guidelines is: 'The client had difficulty with several tasks such as copying drawings and putting together puzzles of common objects [data]. These difficulties suggest that the client has poor [conclusion] visual-motor skills [concept], and that work on tracing tasks and putting together puzzles may help her develop these skills [recommendations]'. Use of these logical guidelines makes reports more credible and persuasive.

Reports should contain only statements which the authors are confident enough to defend in an adversarial situation (e.g. court). The possibility of reports being used at a later date, for purposes other than that for which they were originally written, makes it crucial that information and conclusions are expressed clearly. Haward (1981) comments: '...it is incumbent upon the report-writer to ensure that his report is understandable to all who might have legitimate access to it...' (p.193). To ensure that the professional's conclusions are to be held valid only while certain conditions remain constant, the report-writer is urged to '...qualify any statements which refer to transitory conditions by reference to the possibility of temporal changes' (Haward, 1981, p.193).

Style and Format

Consideration should be given to spelling, grammar, and the construction of sentences in producing readable reports. Reports written in poor English make reading more difficult, and they may not convey the intended information. The reader may also doubt the accuracy of the facts if the report is badly written. A comprehensive guide to improving the readability of reports is given in Sternberg (1988, p.58–69). He urges authors to avoid digression, the use of unnecessary qualifying words and phrases, and inclusion of redundant material. These make reports longer and may distract the reader from the essential points an author wishes to make. He encourages the use of simple words and sentences over those which are more complicated. Sternberg also gives advice about grammatical errors which are common in reports. Although the ideal report is concise, the aim is also to make it sufficiently interesting to hold the reader's attention. This may be achieved by varying the vocabulary and the length of sentences. The use of a thesaurus, which provides alternative words, can be an aid if used judiciously.

The best way to avoid rambling and incoherence is to attend to the format of the report. Information sensibly 'chunked' makes the content easier for the reader to assimilate, and information easier to find. Examples of possible structures for forensic reports are given in Bowden (1990, p.188), Haward (1981, p.187) and Trick and Tennent (1981, p.186–188). One possible format is suggested here as a logical way of presenting assessment results, and a sample report is appended to this chapter.

(1) General information

There is a range of information which it is useful to find at the beginning of a report. This includes the name of the subject of the report, age, where they are being held, the source of the report, and the offence which they are accused of or have committed. It is useful to have a standard layout for the front sheet, as shown in the example (see Appendix 6.1). This section enables the reader to see at a glance the present circumstances of the offender and a brief offending history.

(2) Introduction

This section is intended to set the scene for the report. The sources of information (e.g. other reports, depositions) and the methods of assessment (e.g. interview, psychometric tests) can be described. Some description of how the offender responded to the assessment procedure may be given; the individual's state of mind, emotional state and level of cooperation are all relevant. Separate sections for (a) information sources, (b) assessment methods, and (c) presentation at assessment may be useful.

(3) Background information

A range of information might be relevant in this section including: family background; education; occupational history; social and sexual history; and psychiatric history. It is likely that much of this information will be contained in other reports, and it is tempting simply to draw on these. Beware of repeating information without checking other sources; failure to do so can result in the repetition of a mistake in a whole series of reports. A great deal of background information is likely to be available from interview and other sources, and it is important to include only that which is relevant to the purpose of the report. If other reports are informative, and bearing the above caveat in mind, the writer may refer the reader to these, thereby keeping the report brief and concentrating upon new information.

The relevance of the areas of inquiry listed above will vary amongst offenders. The offender's sexual history is an area of particular sensitivity. Whilst this has obvious relevance in the case of sexual offences, it may also have relevance in the commission of other types of offence where a lack of success in sexual relationships may be a contributing factor. However, if this is not so in the individual case, it is ethically doubtful to give a detailed account of the offender's sexual history beyond commenting that this has been investigated. Care must be taken to exclude material not relevant to the purpose of the report.

(4) Offending history

The author should aim to describe the individual's history of offending, tracing the development of offending behaviour over time. It is vital to report as objectively and as accurately as possible, and corroboration of the offender's report should be based on other sources, such as witness statements.

The index offence should be described in detail, with close attention paid to the antecedents to the offence and the immediate consequences for the offender. This section is primarily aimed at describing what happened and how, rather than providing an explanation for it, therefore a factual account should be presented.

(5) Assessment of current functioning

This section should contain information concerning the individual's current behaviour, mood, intellectual functioning, and social skills relevant to the questions to be answered. Results of specific assessment techniques may be used, including standardised psychometric tests, self-report questionnaires, and observation records kept by staff. It is important to keep the reader in mind when reporting such data to ensure that technical information is easy to understand. No test result should be included without an explanation of what the test is designed to measure and the meaning of the result. Some statement should also be made about the likelihood of change with regard to what is measured. Decisions will be different depending upon whether the reported characteristic is easy or difficult to change.

(6) Formulation

In this section, an attempt is made to answer the referral question using the information available from the offender's history, current behaviour, and test results. The facts will be construed within the theoretical framework of the author to make what is essentially an 'educated guess' at the causes of the offender's behaviour. Further assessment may be necessary to clarify the picture, and it is important to make this clear rather than make claims which cannot be substantiated.

(7) Recommendations

The formulation should then lead into a set of recommendations for how the target behaviour could be changed. This section should be short and clear; what is required is that recommendations for disposal, further assessment, or treatment are clearly stated in a set of numbered points.

(8) Summary

A brief summary should conclude the report. This should include a re-statement of the purpose of the report, the assessment methods and results, the formulation, and recommendations.

References

British Medical Association (1990) *Guidelines on the Access to Health Records Act (1990): Guidance Notes – Ethics.* No.1, pp.1–8. London: British Medical Association.

Brady, C. and Benn, A.W. (1992) What makes a useful forensic report. Rampton Hospital: Unpublished manuscript.

Bowden, P. (1990) The written report and sentences. In R. Bluglass, and P. Bowden (eds) *Principles and Practice in Forensic Psychiatry.* Edinburgh: Churchill Livingstone.

Dietz, P.E., Cooke, G., Rappeport, J.R. and Silvergleit, I.T. (1983) Psychojargon in the psycholegal report: Ratings by judges, psychiatrists, and psychologists. *Behavioral Sciences and the Law, 1,* 77–84.

Glasgow, D. (1992) *Personal communication.*

Groth-Marnat, G. (1984) *Handbook of Psychological Assessment.* New York: Van Nostrand Reinhold Company Inc.

Haward, L. (1981) *Forensic Psychology.* London: Batsford.

Hartlage, L. and Merck, P. (1971) Increasing the relevance of psychological reports. *Journal of Clinical Psychology, 4,* 481–483.

National Health Service Management Executive. (1991) *Health Service Guidelines: Access to Health Records Act (1990)* HSG (91)6. London: Department of Health.

Ownby, R.L. (1987) *Psychological Reports.* Brandon, Vermont: Clinical Psychology Publishing Co. Inc.

Ownby, R. L. and Wallbrown, F. (1983) Evaluating school psychology reports, Part I: A procedure for systematic feedback. *Psychology in the Schools, 20,* 41–45.

Sternberg, R.J. (1988) Rules for writing the psychology paper. In R.J. Sternberg (ed) *The Psychologist's Companion.* Second Edition. Cambridge: Cambridge University Press.

Tallant, N. (1986) *Psychological Report Writing.* Englewood Cliffs, New Jersey: Prentice-Hall.

Tallant, N. and Reiss, W.J. (1959a) Multidisciplinary views on the preparation of written psychological reports: I. Spontaneous suggestions for content. *Journal of Clinical Psychology, 15,* 218–221.

Tallant, N. and Reiss, W.J. (1959b) Multidisciplinary views on the preparation of written psychological reports: III. The trouble with psychological reports. *Journal of Clinical Psychology, 15,* 444–446.

Tennent, G. (1990) The Parole Board. In R. Bluglass and P. Bowden (eds) *Principles and Practice of Forensic Psychiatry.* Edinburgh: Churchill Livingstone.

Trick, H. and Tennent, I. (1981) *Forensic Psychiatry.* London: Pitman.

Weiner, I.B. (1987) Writing forensic reports. In I.B. Weiner and A.K. Hess (eds) *Handbook of Forensic Psychology.* New York: John Wiley and Sons.

Woodward, R. (1992) The Criminal Justice Act and life-sentence prisoners: Some implications for psychologists. *Division of Criminological and Legal Psychology Newsletter,* No. 32, 10–16. Leicester: The British Psychological Society.

Appendix 6.1. Sample report.

Ramford Hospital Psychologist's Report

Date of report: 12 May 1992

Name: Anthony Harris

Date of birth: 26 October 1960

Responsible Medical Officer: Dr V. Clarke

Date of admission: 17 March 1990

Location: Eastwood Ward

MHA Classification: Psychopathic Disorder

MHA Section: 37/41

Index offence: Mr Harris was convicted of indecently assaulting three girls between 9 and 11 years of age. The offences took place over a period of four weeks during August 1989.

Previous convictions:

5.07.1983: Indecent exposure – fined.

6.09.1983: Indecent assault on a female x 2 – 4 months imprisonment.

7.02.1984: Attempted rape, indecent assault – 4 years imprisonment.

6.09.1988: Indecent exposure x 3–4 months imprisonment.

Previous hospital admissions: None

Reason for referral: Mr Harris was referred by Dr Clarke for an assessment of his sexual offending and to determine what treatment could be offered by the Psychologist.

Aim of report: This report provides a psychological assessment of Mr Harris's sexual offending. Based on assessment findings, suggestions are made for future treatment options.

Introduction

(a) Sources of information

The following reports were read: Dr R. Hudson, Prison Medical Officer (15.08.83); Dr S. Ramsay, (17.01.84); Ms J. Rice, Prison Psychologist (13.07.87); Dr V. Clarke (10.01.90); Ms G. Hunter, Social Worker (21.01.90) I have also read the depositions, and nursing records.

(b) Assessment methods

Mr Harris was interviewed on six occasions between March and April 1992. During this time ward staff kept records of his attention to young girls on the television and in magazines. Mr Harris kept a daily mood rating scale and an activity checklist. He was also given the Beck Depression Inventory.

(c) Presentation at assessment

Mr Harris was co-operative and communicative in interview. He was initially reluctant to take part in the written assessment procedures, which we soon discovered was due to his embarrassment about his poor reading and writing. After designing rating scales and checklists which Mr Harris was easily able to complete, he was fully co-operative with all aspects of the assessment.

Background Information

(a) Family background

Mr Harris was born the youngest of five siblings. His father left home when he was four years old. Since his mother was unable to cope with caring for all the children, Mr Harris was taken into local authority care at the age of five. He remained in a children's home for three years before being placed with foster parents. The placement broke down within the year when Mr Harris's coercive sex-play with a six-year-old girl was discovered. The girl, a neighbour, told her mother about the sex-play, and the allegations were reported to Mr Harris's foster father. At this time Mr Harris's foster father developed multiple sclerosis and his foster mother decided that her husband and son required her full attention. At the age of nine, Mr Harris was returned to the care of the local authority where he remained for another two years before being fostered once more.

He remained with his second set of foster parents for five years, from the age of 11 until he left home at sixteen. He describes life with this couple as 'stormy'; there were many arguments between his foster parents, and between himself and his foster parents. He remembers his foster father as an aggressive, sometimes violent, man who used to hit his wife and Mr Harris. Mr Harris was also physically violent towards his foster mother on a number of occasions. When he left home at 16, it was after an argument with his foster father about coming home late at night. He has no contact with them since leaving home, and he is not in contact with his natural parents or siblings.

(b) Education

Mr Harris attended school from age five, and said he enjoyed junior school, although he had some difficulties with reading and writing. At secondary school he found the work harder, and his low literacy became more of a problem. At the age of twelve he began to truant and attended school as little as possible. He did not sit any examinations or gain any qualifications.

(c) Occupational history

After leaving home, Mr Harris spent some time living rough before obtaining a place in a Salvation Army Hostel and a job washing dishes in a cafe. He left this job after a few months because he had a fight with the manager over time-keeping. He then had a series of casual jobs in catering, and lived in a number of hostels. Mr Harris's last employment was as junior storeman at a local footwear factory. He was dismissed from this post following several unexplained absences from his duties.

(d) Relationships

Mr Harris describes himself as a 'loner', having had few friends at school or since. He feels that he has difficulty in getting on with adults of both sexes, and that he usually gets 'picked on' and used. This was especially so in the hostels where other residents stole his property and played practical jokes on him.

(e) Sexual history

Mr Harris's foster-brother (aged nine at the time) introduced Mr Harris (then aged eight) to sex-play with the daughter of a neighbour. This took the form of looking at each others' genitals. While his foster brother appears to have grown out of the sex-play, Mr Harris continued his contact with the young girl. Mr Harris reports that initially he provided biscuits and drinks to ensure that the girl would meet with him, but when she later became reluctant to meet him he used threats to ensure that the meetings continued and remained secret.

Mr Harris describes himself as heterosexual. As an adult, he has always had difficulty talking to women and has never had a girlfriend. He has never had sexual intercourse. He says that his most 'successful' relationships are those he has had with young girls. His definition of 'success' is when the girl lets him give her small gifts in exchange for looking at and touching her genitals. He believes that it is natural for girls to protest about being touched and attributes this to them not wanting to seem too 'easy'. He reports that he masturbates to fantasies of young girls.

Offending History

(a) Previous offences

Mr Harris reports that he molested at least five young girls in the neighbourhood of his second foster home and hostels over a period of eight years, and these went undetected. He claims that the incidents were very similar in nature, with victims being girls between eight and ten years old. In each case he offered the girl chocolate to go with him, usually to a local park. He then began to play what he calls his 'tickling game', which involves touching the girl's body outside her clothing at first, then putting his hands under her clothing, gradually moving towards her genitals. When chocolate failed as lure to get the girls to meet him again, he would use threats to ensure compliance. A commonly used threat was that he would tell the girl's mother what she had done with him last time. When a girl did not arrive for his meeting, he avoided her street for up to a year for fear of getting caught. During this time he would seek out and befriend another victim.

The indecent exposure offence (5.07.83) is described by Mr Harris as a misunderstanding. He claims to have been urinating behind a bush in a local park only 15 yards from a group of young girls. However, a witness saw Mr Harris at the side of the bush and reported that he had an erection.

Later that year (6.09.83) Mr Harris assaulted two young girls (aged 7 and 9) in a secluded spot in the formal gardens at St John's Park where he was sleeping rough at the time. He gave them two bars of chocolate each in exchange for playing his 'tickling game'. The incident came to light when the mothers of the two girls asked them where they got the chocolate. Mr Harris was arrested on suspicion following descriptions of the place and of Mr Harris by the two girls. He confessed to the indecent assault, although he claims that the girls encouraged him.

During his four months imprisonment, Mr Harris apparently received informal 'sex education' from another inmate. Following this, Mr Harris appears to have formed the belief that he was charged because touching young girls was considered perverted. He thought that if he penetrated a young girl with his penis he would not be charged because this is the 'normal way'.

At the town carnival on 7.02.84, Mr Harris found a girl in tears because she had lost her parents in the crowd. Mr Harris offered her an ice-cream and said that he would take her to her parents. He led her some way from the carnival, took her behind a caravan, and attempted rape. Someone heard the girl screaming and saw Mr Harris hurrying away from the caravan. Mr Harris was charged with attempted rape and imprisoned for four years.

Mr Harris was arrested again on 6.09.88 following complaints that he had been exposing himself to junior school pupils. The complaints included three separate occasions when Mr Harris displayed his erect penis to pupils during their break-time and lunch-time. He was charged with three offences of indecent exposure and given four months imprisonment.

(b) Index offences

Mr Harris was convicted of indecently assaulting three girls aged between 9 and 11 years. The offences took place over a period of four weeks during August 1989. In each case, he approached the girl while she was walking alone in a park, grabbed her, threw her to the ground, and attempted to remove her clothing. In one case, the girl struggled free and ran off. On the other two occasions, the child's screaming brought passers-by to the scene; on the second of these occasions a witness apprehended Mr Harris, restraining him until the police arrived. When he was arrested for the third offence, he admitted the other two offences.

At the time of these offences, Mr Harris was employed as a storeman at a local footwear factory. He told me that his employment left him with little time to meet potential victims. As a result, he had tried to rush several young girls into accompanying him. At least four girls refused his advances, and he felt rejected, deskilled and angry at his lack of success. He reports fantasising about getting what he wanted without having to be 'pleasant'. Mr Harris thought that by asking the girls to go with him, he was giving them the opportunity to say 'No' to his requests, therefore he decided to go ahead and undress and touch the girls to see if they would let him continue. He said he had seen several films on television where adults had met and the man had undressed the woman without receiving a rebuff.

Assessment of Current Functioning

(a) Intellectual assessment

An intellectual assessment was conducted by Ms J Rice (psychologist) at HMP Barton while Mr Harris was there on remand. Full details can be found in her report (19.09.89) Mr Harris's results on the Wechsler Adult Intelligence Scale (Revised) indicate that he is functioning within the 'borderline' level of ability, that is, between dull-normal and impaired. He scored poorly on those subtests likely to be affected by education and breadth of experience, namely: Information, Picture Completion, Comprehension, Similarities, and Vocabulary.

(b) Interest in young girls

Nurses monitored Mr Harris's attention to young girls on television and in magazines. Mr Harris currently spends about 60 minutes a day watching programmes with children in lead roles, and 80 minutes watching programmes with adults in the lead role. Since most of the television programmes shown on the ward have adults in lead roles, these results suggest that the time he spends watching programmes with children in lead roles is disproportionately high. Quantifiable results from the monitoring of his use of magazines depicting young girls proved to be impractical to collect. However, nursing staff thought that his frequency of looking at girls in magazines was higher than other patients on the ward with similar offences.

(c) Mood

During the period of assessment, Mr Harris reported feeling low in mood, and having difficulty sleeping. He expressed feelings of guilt, and uncertainty and pessimism about his future. He was particularly distressed when he thought about the length of time he would be spending in various institutions over the next few years. He denied any thoughts of self-harm, and has no recorded history of self-harm. The Beck Depression Inventory (BDI) was administered verbally. This assesses the severity of depression in adults, and Mr Harris's score of 22 suggests a moderate level of depression (moderate range = 19–28).

Mr Harris was asked to rate his overall mood each day. His mood appeared to be relatively stable over the assessment period as a whole. For six days, he was asked to complete an hourly mood rating scale along with an activity checklist. His mood rating varied markedly in relation to his viewing of sexually arousing materials (mainly television programmes and magazines) and his masturbation, both of which considerably elevated his mood.

(d) Insight

Mr Harris appears to understand that his sexual assaults were unlawful, but is unclear why. He made a connection between the young girls' screaming and them being upset by his sexual assault, but he was unsure why they did not enjoy his sexual attentions. Mr Harris reported that he was fearful about where his behaviour was leading and that he wanted to receive help.

He said that he very much wants a sexual relationship, but that women of his own age do not like him and he finds it difficult to talk to them. He finds young girls more approachable. Mr Harris appeared to understand that the 'good' feelings (the mood lift and orgasms) he gains from looking at young girls and masturbating to fantasies of young girls contribute to maintaining his sexual interest in this age group.

He accepted that it would take time and effort to learn how to stop thinking about young girls, and to learn to like and get on with adult women. He reported that he was interested in attending the psychologist's individual and group therapy sessions described to him in order to find ways of managing his problems.

Formulation

Mr Harris's early background was one which militated against the development of good social skills. He was taken into care at the age of five and then fostered to two families. The second foster family was one where arguments and violence were common. In addition, Mr Harris did not fit in well at school owing to his poor literacy and during his adolescence he avoided school as much as he could.

It is apparent both from interviews and previous reports, that in adulthood Mr Harris is underassertive, suffers from considerable social anxiety, and has difficulties in relating to people of his own age in general and to women in particular. He describes himself as isolated, feeling inferior to others, and feeling painfully shy in the presence of women. He has never had a girlfriend, and has never had sex with a consenting partner of his own age.

As a young boy, Mr Harris was introduced to sex-play with a young girl by his foster brother. He learned then that threats were likely to secure the girl's compliance in sex-play. Rather than grow out of such sex-play, this continued into adulthood. His ability to coerce girls into sex appears to have made Mr Harris feel successful in this one area of his life. His sexual interest in young girls has been maintained through these feelings of success, along with the absence of appropriate heterosexual relationships.

Mr Harris seeks out material from television and magazines depicting young girls, and also masturbates to orgasm using fantasies of young girls. Along with the reinforcing effect of orgasm, he also experiences mood enhancement, both of which strengthen his sexual interest in young girls.

It can be seen in the description of his offences that there is an escalating degree of physical assault. He has become less concerned with gradually grooming the children for sex. A number of factors have contributed to this. Mr Harris had found employment which did not allow him the time to befriend and groom potential victims. He did, however, take some time off work to seek out young girls, and these absences eventually led to his dismissal. The job was of particular importance to him, being the first job he had managed to hold down for longer than a few weeks. He felt that he was starting to 'belong' at the factory, and had recently begun to socialise occasionally with his work colleagues. He experienced his dismissal as a rejection by his managers, and found difficulty coping with the loss of status and social contact.

Around this time, Mr Harris reported that he made a number of unsuccessful approaches to young girls. This led to a loss of confidence in his ability to manipulate young girls into allowing him to touch them. He also reported feeling angry with the girls for refusing him and frustrated at not being able to get what he wanted. In order to reduce the frustration, he decided to 'take' what he believed he should have. He modelled his approach on adult behaviour which he had seen in television drama.

Mr Harris has little insight into the reasons that sex with young girls is prohibited. His concern to change his future behaviour is at present based on his despondency about having to spend time in institutions.

Recommendations

Given the above, it seems that the following may prove practicable and effective strategies for reducing the likelihood of Mr Harris offending in future.

(1) Education about the age of consent, and why children need to be protected. This will be done in the Sex Education Group.

(2) Empathy training to increase his understanding of the effects of his sexual assaults. This will be addressed in the Sex Offender Rehabilitation Programme.

(3) Social skills training, including assertiveness and inter-personal problem solving training. This will be done in the Social Skills Training Group.

(4) Retraining in the use of age-appropriate sexual fantasies together with covert-sensitization to fantasies of young girls (i.e., pairing aversive images with sexual fantasies of girls) This will be done in individual therapy.

(5) A relapse prevention programme will be developed to help Mr Harris identify and cope with situations where there is a high risk of offending. This will be met by the Sex Offender Rehabilitation Programme.

The success of these interventions will be monitored by: (a) penile plethysmography assessment, which will monitor his levels of sexual arousal to both appropriate and inappropriate stimuli; (b) masturbatory and fantasy diaries; and (c) staff observation of interest shown in young girls on television and on escorted trips out of the hospital.

Summary

Mr Harris was referred for assessment of his sexual offending. Mr Harris has a long history of sexual offences against young girls, showing a gradual increase in severity and culminating in the three offences of indecent assault on young girls which led to his admission to Ramford Hospital.

Based on material gathered from reports, interviews, staff observation, and self-report diaries, the following conclusions were drawn. His offences against children are based upon feelings of isolation from the adult world, and lack of any appropriate social or sexual contact with women. Sexual 'success' with young girls makes him feel in control, confident and able to assert himself. His sexual arousal to young girls is maintained by masturbation to sexual fantasies involving young girls.

Whilst Mr Harris's insight into the effects of his behaviour on his victims is limited, he is prepared to work towards change.

The recommendations are:

(1) Education

(2) Empathy training

(3) Social skills training

(4) Sexual fantasy re-training

(5) Relapse prevention training

John Smith
Principal Clinical Psychologist
Ramford Hospital

CHAPTER 7

The Psychologist as an Expert Witness

GISLI H. GUDJONSSON

Psychologists have been providing expert testimony to the Courts for about a century (Gudjonsson, 1991). Since that time their role has expanded considerably both in criminal and civil proceedings (Haward, 1981, 1990; Bartol and Bartol, 1987; Gudjonsson, 1986). This has resulted in various professional issues being raised about psychological evidence in relation to admissibility, confidentiality, and the independence of psychologists as experts (Gudjonsson, 1985, 1987a).

In the 1960s most psychologists were referred cases from their psychiatrist colleagues and their findings were commonly incorporated into the psychiatrist's report (Gudjonsson, 1985). More recently, the contribution of psychologists as expert witnesses, which is often unique and highly specialised, is better recognised and more accepted by the Courts (Gudjonsson, 1992). This chapter provides an insight into the types of contribution psychologists can make to judicial proceedings. This is discussed within the context of the English Legal System and the types of problem that may arise when giving evidence in Court.

The Legal Framework in England

In English law cases can be divided into civil and criminal cases. Most commonly, criminal cases are brought against defendants by the Crown Prosecution Service, who are acting on behalf of the State. Civil action involves all those cases brought before the court which are not criminal. Action is typically brought against another individual with the intention of seeking financial compensation for such matters as a breach of contract or personal injury. Civil cases may also involve family issues (e.g. child care proceedings, divorce) and property disputes.

The majority of civil litigation is dealt with by the County Court. However, the Magistrates' Courts, which deal with about 98 per cent of all criminal cases, also process some civil cases, including those related to domestic matters. The Crown Court deals with the most serious criminal cases and provides defendants with a trial by jury in contested cases. The Crown Court also deals with cases committed for sentence by magistrates. When defendants wish to appeal against the decision of magistrates, then this is heard in the Crown Court. Further appeals are heard in the Court of Appeal, which is divided into Civil and Criminal Divisions. Final appeals, which are generally on points of law and of general public importance, are heard in the House of Lords.

Psychologists most typically give evidence in the Crown Court. This is because they tend to be instructed in the most serious cases. However, psychologists do often give evidence in the Magistrates' Court, particularly in juvenile and domestic cases (Lane, 1987; Parker, 1987).

The Roles of the Forensic Psychologist

Haward (1981, 1990) describes in detail the four roles that psychologists may fulfil when assessing psychological evidence for the purpose of judicial proceedings. He describes in detail the various types of Court where psychologists may find themselves giving evidence. The four roles are referred to by Haward as the 'clinical', 'experimental', 'actuarial' and 'advisory' roles. I shall discuss each of these roles briefly.

The *clinical role* is typically fulfilled by practising clinical psychologists. This is the most common role among psychologists who have been instructed to prepare a court report (Gudjonsson, 1985). In many ways it resembles the principal role fulfilled by our forensic psychiatrist colleagues. Indeed, in the clinical role there is often a considerable overlap between psychological and psychiatric evidence. Here, the psychologist interviews a client and carries out the required assessment, which may include extensive psychometric testing (e.g. the administration of tests of intelligence, neuropsychological functioning, personality, mental state) and collecting behavioural data (Gudjonsson, 1985). The nature of the assessment will depend upon the instruction of the referral agent and the type of problem being assessed. The client may need to be assessed on more than one occasion and sometimes informants need to be consulted to provide corroboration and further information. Previous reports, including school reports and previous psychological and psychiatric assessments, should be obtained whenever they are likely to be relevant to the present assessment.

In the *experimental role,* the psychologist performs unique functions which are typically outside the expertise of our forensic psychiatrist colleagues. Here, human behaviour is studied by experimentation rather than by a clinical interview. Often this requires the ability and knowledge to apply psychological principles and techniques to unique forensic problems. Haward (1981, 1990) provides many excellent examples of this particular role in civil and criminal cases.

Gudjonsson and Sartory (1983) used an experimental procedure involving the polygraph as an aid to the diagnosis of blood injury phobia. A young man had been arrested for speeding and was suspected of driving whilst under the influence of alcohol. He failed two breathalyser tests and admitted to having consumed three pints of beer that evening. He was asked to provide a specimen of blood, which he claimed to be unable to provide. The young man was subsequently convicted in the Magistrates' Court for failing to provide a specimen of blood without a reasonable excuse. He appealed against his conviction on the basis that he was a blood injury phobic and therefore had a reasonable excuse for failing to give a specimen of blood. The case was referred to me for a psychological assessment.

The case presented me with an ideal opportunity to apply recent knowledge about blood injury phobia and polygraph technology to a forensic case. My colleague, Gudrun Sartory, and I set up an experimental procedure that involved testing whether or not the young man exhibited cardiovascular responses on the polygraph which were consistent with blood injury phobia (i.e., bradycardia to critical stimuli in contrast to the usual cardiac acceleration commonly seen in other phobias). The results provided clear evidence of blood injury phobia, which was supported by relevant clinical data. I testified in Court and the defendant's conviction was quashed (Gudjonsson and Sartory, 1983).

In another case, an experimental procedure was applied to a case of alleged rape of a person with a severe mental handicap in order to differentiate between areas of the victim's reliable and unreliable testimony (Gudjonsson and Gunn, 1982). I testified at the Old Bailey and advised the Court about how to evaluate the victim's testimony.

The case had important implications for psychology. First, it provided a methodology for assessing the reliability of testimony for persons with a severe mental handicap, which was subsequently extended into developing instruments for measuring 'interrogative suggestibility' (Gudjonsson, 1992). Second, it opened the Courts' acceptance of psychological evidence in the area of reliability of testimony. Following this case, psychologists came to be increasingly asked to provide Court Reports on the issue of 'suggestibility'. Third, the case illustrated the point that persons with a severe mental handicap, even when they can be demonstrated to be unduly suggestible, can provide reliable testimony about areas which they remember clearly. In this landmark case, I provided the jury with a way of differentiating between the victim's potentially reliable and unreliable evidence.

The *actuarial role* refers to the application of statistical probabilities to events and behaviour. The kind of probabilities and observational data analysed by psychologists include: the probability that a person with a given I.Q. or psychological deficit could earn a living; the probability that a person could have guessed a telephone number by chance; the probability that a person's I.Q. scores fall within certain confidence limits. This role is not confined to psychologists and is commonly used by statisticians and other scientists when interpreting observational and behavioural data.

In one case, a suspect confessed to the murder of a stranger. He told the police that he had looked up the victim's telephone number in the telephone directory in order to arrange a meeting with him. After his arrest and whilst interviewed by the police, he correctly recalled the first four of the six digits in the victim's telephone number. The suspect subsequently retracted his confession and claimed to have given the police random numbers as to the victim's telephone number. A statistician worked out that there was less than one chance in 1,000 that the suspect could have correctly guessed the four digits without some prior knowledge of the victim's telephone number. The suspect was convicted of the murder in spite of his having retracted his confession.

The *advisory role* typically involves psychologists advising counsel how to cross-examine psychologists who are testifying for the other side. For example, the prosecuting counsel may request that a psychologist sits behind him in Court and advises him how to cross-examine the defence psychologist. Increasingly, reports by psychologists are subjected to peer review by an expert for the other side. That expert may have carefully studied the psychological report and, in addition, he or she has sometimes carried out an assessment of the defendant.

Having another psychologist in Court evaluating one's testimony increases the stress experienced by psychologists when they testify (Gudjonsson, 1985). Sometimes there is considerable disagreement between the opinions of psychology experts and this may result in lengthy and stressful cross-examination (Tunstall *et al.* 1982). My recommendation to psychologists is to assume that their report will be subjected to a careful peer review by the other side. Even if it is not, lawyers are becoming increasingly familiar with psychological testimony and are able to ask some very searching questions. The psychologist must be thoroughly familiar with the development and validation of the instruments and tests used.

The Contributions to Criminal Proceedings

In criminal proceedings, the English Legal System involves three distinct stages: *Pretrial, trial* and *sentencing*. The nature and contribution of the psychological assessment will be influenced by the relevant legal issues at each stage of the criminal proceedings. It is important, therefore, that psychologists should be familiar with the nature of these issues.

Pretrial issues

At the pretrial stage, issues about the defendant's fitness to plead and fitness to stand trial are sometimes raised by the defence (Chiswick, 1990). This happens when the defendant's physical or mental state at the time of the trial is such that proceeding with the case may interfere with the due process of the law (i.e., the defendant may not have a fair trial if the case proceeds). The ability of the defendant to give adequate instructions to his lawyers, to understand the charge against him, to distinguish between a plea of guilty and not guilty, and to follow the proceedings in Court are the main legal issues to be decided upon at the pretrial stage. In England, fitness to plead and stand trial issues are generally only raised in serious cases which are of major legal and clinical significance (Chiswick, 1990).

In the United States of America clinical psychologists are actively involved in this area of the criminal proceedings, and here their role overlaps considerably with that of psychiatrists (Blau, 1984; Cook, 1980; Weiner and Hess, 1987). Special psychological instruments have been developed by American psychologists in order to assess objectively the psychological deficits that are relevant to the legal issues (Blau, 1984). In the United Kingdom, on the other hand, psychiatrists are mainly involved at this stage of the proceedings and psychologists only occasionally become involved. However, my experience in recent years is that psychologists in England are becoming increasingly requested by defence lawyers to carry out a psychological assessment in these cases, because it provides the Court with an objective and standardised assessment of the defendant's strengths and weaknesses. This may involve an assessment of the defendant's intellectual and neuropsychological status, as well as an assessment of problems related to anxiety and depression.

In a recent case, I was asked by a defence solicitor to provide an assessment on the mental state of a civil servant who was suffering from a post-traumatic stress disorder following a previous trial. The defendant had been so traumatised by the experience of certain events in Court that, in my view, he would not have been capable of concentrating satisfactorily on the trial proceedings and adequately instructing his lawyers. After hearing my evidence in Court, the prosecution obtained a report from a consultant forensic psychiatrist who agreed with my findings. The trial was postponed for a few months, during which time I provided the defendant with the psychological treatment needed in order to enable him to stand trial. The treatment was carried out on an out-patient basis and involved desensitising the defendant to the original trauma.

Trial issues

In English Law, a criminal offence consists of a number of different elements, which fall into two main categories with distinct legal issues: *actus reus* and *mens rea* (see Leng, 1990, for a detailed review). The former comprises elements relevant to the criminal act itself, whereas the latter typically, but not exclusively, focuses on the mental state of the assailant. During the *actus reus* stage, the prosecution has to prove: (a) that a criminal offence was committed; and (b) that the defendant committed it. Issues related to *mens rea* focus on the state of mind of the accused at the time of the alleged offence and his or her blameworthiness (e.g. whether the offence was committed either intentionally or recklessly).

The criteria for establishing *mens rea* vary according to the nature of the offence. The reason for this is that each offence is defined separately in law and there are no standard criteria for defining *mens rea* across different offences, even among related offences. Some offences do not require an element of *mens rea* for the defendant to be convicted (i.e., they are offences of 'strict liability' and the prosecution only have to prove *actus reus*). However, in such cases a mental condition relevant to *mens rea* can be used as mitigation at the sentencing stage.

Psychologists in England are commonly asked to prepare Court Reports which are relevant to both *actus reus* and *mens rea* issues and their involvement in such cases is expanding rapidly (Gudjonsson, 1986, 1992; Fitzgerald, 1987). Some of their contributions to *actus reus* issues include:

(a) The assessment of severe mental handicap in cases of unlawful sexual intercourse (Gudjonsson and Gunn, 1982). According to Section 7 of the Sexual Offences Act (1956), it is a criminal offence to have sexual intercourse with a person with a severe mental handicap. However, the offender is not guilty in law if he can prove that he did not suspect, or had no reason to suspect, that the woman was a 'defective' (Mitchell and Richardson, 1985; p.1825). Psychologists are sometimes asked, typically by the prosecution, to assess cases of persons with a mental handicap in order to determine whether or not Section 7 of the Sexual Offences Act applies. If the psychologist comes to the conclusion that the woman was a 'mental defective', as defined by the Act, then the culprit may be charged with a sexual offence, in which case the psychologist may have to testify in Court (Gudjonsson and Gunn, 1982).

(b) The assessment of cases involving disputed or retracted confessions (Gudjonsson, 1992). Here, the onus is on the prosecution to prove, beyond reasonable doubt, that the alleged confession was made by the defendant and that it was not obtained in circumstances that are likely to render it unreliable. The psychological assessment of these cases can be complicated and often requires unique experience and skills. I have elsewhere provided a comprehensive framework for the assessment of these cases (Gudjonsson, 1992). The psychologist will generally focus on characteristics and vulnerabilities (e.g. low I.Q., high suggestibility) of defendants that may undermine the reliability of the self-incriminating admission made during police questioning. The demand for a clinical assessment of retracted confession cases is likely to increase in the future with the favourable Court of Appeal Judgement in the case of Engin Raghip (see below).

(c) The assessment of perceptual or identification error (Haward, 1981; 1990). There are a number of circumstances in which psychologists may conduct specific experiments, or refer to experimental evidence, as a way of challenging the *actus reus* of the alleged offence.

The contribution of clinical psychologists to *mens rea* issues complements that of their psychiatrist colleagues (Gudjonsson, 1984, 1986). This may include dealing with issues relevant to diminished responsibility in cases of homicide and the question of intent in cases of alleged shoplifting.

The recent case of *R. v. McGovern* (1991, 92 Cr. App.R.) illustrates well the contribution of the psychological assessment in a murder case. McGovern was a 20-year-old woman who was one of three persons charged with murder. I was asked to assess her with regard to her intellectual functioning and suggestibility. The results from my assessment indicated poor intellectual functioning and the possibility of brain damage. I advised that a neurological assessment be carried out. The results supported arguments for the possibility of brain damage. I gave evidence at McGovern's trial and we argued successfully for diminished responsibility. She was sentenced to 10 years imprisonment whereas her two co-defendants received life sentences for murder. I also argued that McGovern had not understood the police caution which was given prior to the police interview. No solicitor or 'appropriate adult' was present during the police interview. McGovern's case was referred to the Court of Appeal on the grounds that the trial judge should not have allowed her confession statement to go before the jury since she should have been interviewed in the presence of a solicitor. The appeal was successful and her conviction was quashed.

Sentencing issues

Sentencing is the final stage in the criminal proceedings. If the defendant is acquitted by the jury or Magistrates, then he or she is free to go. Where the defendant pleads guilty or is convicted, the judge or the Magistrates have to pass a sentence. Various sentencing options are available, depending on the nature of the offence and the circumstances of the case (Eysenck and Gudjonsson, 1989).

Traditionally, psychologists have been less involved at the sentencing stage than their psychiatrist colleagues. Increasingly, however, they are providing Court Reports about factors which are relevant to mitigation concerning sentencing (Gudjonsson, 1986). This includes offering treatment to persons convicted of sexual offences, compulsive shoplifting (Gudjonsson, 1987b), and car theft (Brown, 1985).

Admissibility

The question of admissibility can arise with regard to any evidence, which includes expert psychological and psychiatric testimony. When lawyers seek to introduce the expert opinion or findings of psychologists, then the judge has to decide on the admissibility of the evidence. Submissions and legal arguments by the defence and prosecution are heard by the judge in the absence of the jury (known as a *voire dire*). The fundamental criteria for the admissibility of expert testimony were stated by Lord Justice Lawton in the case of *Regina v. Turner* (1975, 60 Cr.App.R.80,C.A.). These are: 'An expert's opinion is admissible to furnish the court with scientific information which is likely to be outside the experience and knowledge of a judge or jury' (Mitchell and Richardson, 1985, p.476).

According to the *Turner* principle, it is not admissible for experts, whether psychiatrists or psychologists, to give evidence about how an ordinary person is likely to react to stressful situations. Nor can experts give evidence about matters directly related to the likely veracity of witnesses or defendants. Therefore, English law has a rather restrictive approach to the admissibility of evidence from expert witnesses (Fitzgerald, 1987), which means that psychologists are not allowed to give evidence on such matters as eyewitness testimony, unlike psychologists in America (Davies, 1983). Their evidence, like that of psychiatrists, has to deal with the presence of mental abnormality. When this involves mental illness or mental handicap the evidence is readily admissible.

On occasions, problems may arise when dealing with diagnosis of 'personality disorder' rather than mental illness or mental handicap. For example, in the case of *Regina v. Mackinney and Pinfold* (1981, 72 Cr.App.R. 78) a social psychologist was not allowed to talk about the likely unreliability of the testimony of a 'psychopathic' witness whom he had observed in court but never formally interviewed. The decision to exclude the psychologist's evidence was upheld by the Court of Appeal. It was decided that 'Whether or not a witness in a criminal trial is capable of giving reliable evidence is a question of fact for the jury' (Mitchell and Richardson, 1985, p.420).

Expert evidence is allowed when there is evidence of mental illness or mental handicap. According to the judgement in the case of *Masih* (1986, Crim.L.R. 395), an I.Q. of 69 or below is required for a defendant to be formally classified as mentally handicapped and here the expert evidence would be admissible, whenever it was considered relevant. In the *Masih* case the defendant's I.Q. was 72, which falls at the lower end of the 'borderline range' (i.e., the bottom 3% of the population). Lord Lane's view was that expert testimony in a borderline case will not as a rule be necessary and should therefore be excluded.

The most recent developments on admissibility

The judgement of the Court of Appeal on the 5th December, 1991, in the case of *Regina v. Raghip* has major implications for the admissibility of psychological evidence. Raghip was arrested in 1985 following the Tottenham Riot. He was interrogated by the police in the absence of a solicitor and an appropriate adult. A pretrial psychological report had been prepared on behalf of the defence, but unfortunately the report turned out to be incomplete and misleading so that it was never used at Raghip's original trial (Gudjonsson, 1992). In 1988 I was asked to prepare an independent report on Raghip, where he was found to have a Full Scale I.Q. of 74 and he scored abnormally high on tests of suggestibility, in addition to other psychological vulnerabilities. My report was submitted to the Court of Appeal in December 1988, but Lord Lane refused Raghip leave to Appeal on the basis that Raghip's I.Q. was above the cut-off point of 69 and the Jury would have been in a better position than any psychologist to judge his mental deficiencies and level of suggestibility when he gave evidence.

I testified at Raghip's appeal on the 26th November, 1991. Also testifying were the psychologist who had carried out the pretrial assessment and a third psychologist (Olive Tunstall) who gave an assessment of Raghip's educational background and his significant mental impairment. The pretrial psychologist stated in court that he fully agreed with my assessment. The three judges accepted the psychological evidence and made a ruling which has widened the criteria for psychological evidence. First, psychological evidence is now seen as important in its own right, rather than relying on medical criteria for admissibility. Second, even if defendants have an I.Q. above the cut-off point of 70, the psychological evidence is still admissible. Third, evidence of psychological characteristics, such as suggestibility, was accepted by the Court of Appeal as important and admissible. Finally, psychological evidence is viewed by the judges as being valuable even when the jury has ample opportunity to observe defendants testify in court. That is, expert psychological evidence is needed when defendants have significant psychological deficiencies and the jury is not expected to be in a position to judge the defendant's vulnerabilities.

Confidentiality

Issues relevant to confidentiality often arise when mental health professionals are requested to prepare Court Reports (Eastman, 1987; Gudjonsson, 1987a). Confidentiality typically arises in one of three ways. First, the defendant tells the psychologist about matters that he wants kept confidential (e.g. previous offences). In such circumstances I never make a promise to keep information out of the report. When preparing a Court Report, any information that emerges during the interview may be communicated to the referral agent, and this should be made clear to the defendant at the beginning of the interview. In one case of alleged rape, the defendant told me that he had committed several similar rapes, but wanted me to keep it confidential (i.e., not inform his solicitor). As this information was highly relevant to the assessment, I had no alternative but to inform his solicitor about it.

In England, mental health professionals have no legal obligation to disclose information about past or planned offences provided by their patients or clients, unless they are ordered to do so by a judge, but they may feel morally obliged to do so (Finch, 1984).

The second issue of confidentiality when preparing Court Reports, relates to who 'owns' the report. The report is 'owned' by the referral agent and the psychologist cannot provide other persons with a copy of it, or disclose its content, without the consent of the referral agent (e.g. solicitor) or the patient himself.

The third issue concerns 'test confidentiality'. Most psychological tests are not available to the general public, and if they were it might undermine the validity of the tests concerned. When writing a Court Report, a detailed description of a particular test and its procedure (e.g. the measurement of suggestibility) may undermine the test's future validity if the report is widely circulated. Similarly, disclosing detailed information in Court about the rationale, content and scoring of psychological tests could provide future subjects with information which invalidates the results of the test. My own approach to this problem is not to describe tests in much detail, either in Court Reports or when testifying in Court. Judges are generally quite sympathetic about the potential consequences of breaches of test confidentiality when this is carefully explained to them in Court. Psychologists should be aware of the fact that in many instances defendants will receive a copy of the psychological report from the defence solicitor and they may circulate it to friends, relatives and other defendants.

Differences Between Psychological and Psychiatric Evidence

In my experience, certain differences exist between psychological and psychiatric evidence, both in terms of their respective contributions and in the ways in which the courts evaluate their evidence.

The evidence of psychologists and psychiatrists clearly differs most when the former begin to comment on the development and mental functioning of ordinary individuals. Psychologists do devote more of their training to the understanding of normal human behaviour than their psychiatrist colleagues. They are therefore, in general, better qualified than psychiatrists to testify about how normal individuals might react to unusual predicaments or special circumstances, such as being interrogated by the police. In England, judges are generally reluctant to have psychologists testify about central issues such as those directly dealing with 'reliability' and 'truthfulness'. However, there have been exceptions and I have been allowed by some trial judges to comment on the effects of police interrogation techniques or specific types of questioning, even when the defendants had not been diagnosed as mentally handicapped or mentally ill.

Psychologists are sometimes allowed to testify about personality traits in the absence of psychiatric abnormality. For example, scores from tests of suggestibility or compliance are sometimes allowed in evidence even when they do not fall outside the normal range (Gudjonsson, 1992). The scores obtained on testing can be converted into percentile scores to demonstrate how they compare with respective normative scores. Of course, even when abnormal scores are obtained by defendants these are not always allowed in evidence by trial judges. Indeed, there have been occasions when abnormal personality scores (i.e., those falling outside the 95th percentile rank) have been disallowed by trial judges, even when relevant, because they do not constitute a psychiatric abnormality. This problem with admissibility will probably be made easier in view of the favourable judgement in the case of Engin Raghip, which I discussed earlier in this chapter.

A major difference between psychologists and psychiatrists when testifying in Court relates to the ways in which their respective professions are construed and respected by legal advocates, including judges. The expert contribution of psychologists is sometimes construed by legal advocates as constituting little more than common sense and ordinary knowledge (Tunstall *et al.* 1982). Similarly, psychometric tests are often viewed with scepticism and the importance of the results may be marginalised or rejected out of hand. In my experience, judges sometimes reject detailed and valid psychological findings and opinions in favour of a psychiatrist's unsubstantiated opinion. For example, in one criminal case the judge preferred to rely on a psychiatrist's guess of a defendant's I.Q. than the results from two separate I.Q. tests! The attitude seems to be that psychiatrists, because of their medical training, provide the Court with testimony superior to that of psychologists, even when dealing with issues that are principally psychological in nature.

How to Present the Evidence

Psychological evidence may be presented to the Court in a written form or orally, or both. The normal procedure is for the psychologist to prepare a Court Report, which may be presented to the Court without the psychologist having to give evidence orally. This most commonly happens when the opposing side accepts the Report and does not require to cross-examine the psychologist on it. In the event of the findings being unfavourable, the defence would normally not forward a copy of the Report to the prosecution and the psychologist would not be required to give evidence. If the psychologist has been instructed by the prosecution, then the Report will invariably be forwarded to the defence, irrespective of whether or not the findings are favourable to the prosecution. Normally, if the defence decides to rely on the psychological report, then the report has to be served on the prosecution seven days before the trial.

It is common to find that the psychological assessment consists both of favourable and unfavourable findings. For example, a defendant may prove to possess poor intellectual abilities but score low on tests of suggestibility which, by implication, means that he or she may be able to cope reasonably well with interrogation in spite of limited cognitive abilities. Similarly, the psychologist may recommend treatment as an alternative to a custodial sentence, but he or she may also express reservation about the defendant's motivation to change or about the prognosis.

If the psychological findings are not favourable, then the defendant's solicitors have various options. They can keep the report from the prosecution, they can instruct another psychologist for a report and hope that it will be more favourable, or they can ask the psychologist to delete the unfavourable findings from the report. With regard to the last option, I always refuse to do this and no psychologist should ever be tempted to comply with the solicitors' wishes to alter the report in such a way that it could mislead the court. The only time psychologists should consider altering the report is when the findings or sentences contained within it need to be clarified or when a mistake has been made that needs to be corrected.

It is important that the psychologist's findings are presented clearly and succinctly in the report. The conclusions drawn should be substantiated and made relevant to the issues addressed. When the findings are presented clearly, and are relevant to the legal issues, then the report may be accepted by the respective legal advocates without the psychologist having to give oral evidence. This happens quite often. In only about one fifth of retracted confession cases does the psychologist have to give oral evidence in court, sometimes both during the *voire dire* and the trial proper (Gudjonsson, 1992). The great majority of civil cases involving compensation are settled out of Court so psychologists very infrequently have to testify in person. In some instances the prosecution may even withdraw the charges after considering the psychological findings.

Haward (1981), Carson (1983) and Cooke (1990) provide psychologists with much valuable information about how to present themselves and their findings when testifying in Court. This includes knowing the difference between 'expert' and other witnesses. The former can, with the permission of the legal advocates, sit in Court and listen to other witnesses give evidence before testifying themselves. This is often an invaluable experience, because it provides the psychologist with certain familiarity with the Court's layout and the approach and strategy of the legal advocates. Courts are formal settings where certain rituals and conventions must be followed. For example, the expert witness should be formally dressed and speak slowly, clearly, and confidently. Even when asked questions by different legal advocates, the psychologist should address his or her answers to the judge.

The psychologist first provides evidence in Chief and he or she will then be cross-examined about the evidence, after which there may be re-examination of various matters raised during the cross-examination. When giving evidence, the psychologist can be asked probing and challenging questions by the various legal advocates, including the judge. The psychologist should always be fully prepared by knowing the basic facts of the case, and being intimately familiar with the tests used in the assessment. Notes of the interviews with their client and any psychological test they bring into Court may be closely inspected. Psychologists should think carefully before answering questions. If they consider the question asked as being unreasonable or impossible to answer, which is often the case with hypothetical questions (Tunstall *et al.* 1982), they should not hesitate to say so.

Giving evidence in Court is a stressful experience for most expert witnesses. Attending court and listening to court proceedings before giving evidence is often helpful. The stress will reduce as the psychologist becomes more experienced at giving evidence. However, irrespective of the Court experience of the psychologist, the most important factors are good preparation and clear presentation of the evidence.

Conclusions

The demand for the services of clinical psychologists in the preparation of Court reports is on the increase. The recent Court of Appeal judgment in the case of the 'Tottenham Three' illustrates the increased acceptability of psychological evidence among legal advocates. This Chapter provides clinical psychologists with the basic legal and psychological framework, which will assist them in the preparation and presentation of evidence for judicial purposes.

References

Bartol, C.R. and Bartol, A. M. (1987) History of forensic psychology. In I.B. Weiner and A. K. Hess (eds) *Handbook of Forensic Psychology*. New York: John Wiley and Sons.

Blau, T.H. (1984) *The Psychologist as a Expert Witness*. New York: John Wiley and Sons.

Brown, B. (1985) The involvement of psychologists in sentencing. *Bulletin of the British Psychological Society, 38*, 180–182.

Carson, D. (1983) Developing courtroom skills. *Journal of Social Welfare Law, 12*, 29–38.

Chiswick, D. (1990) Fitness to stand trial and plead, mutism and deafness. In R. Bluglass and P. Bowden (eds) *Principles and Practice of Forensic Psychiatry*. Edinburgh: Churchill Livingstone, pp.171–178.

Cook, G. (1980) *The Role of the Forensic Psychologist*. Springfield: Charles C. Thomas.

Cooke, D. (1990) Being an 'expert' in Court. *The Psychologist, 3*, 216–221.

Davies, G.M. (1983) The legal importance of psychological research in eyewitness testimony: British and American experiences. *Journal of the Forensic Science Society, 24*, 165–175.

Eastman, N.L.G. (1987) Clinical confidentiality: A contractual basis. In G. Gudjonsson, and J. Drinkwater (eds) *Psychological Evidence in Court*. Issues in Criminological and Legal Psychology, No. 11. Leicester: The British Psychological Society, pp.49–57.

Eysenck, H.J. and Gudjonsson, G.H. (1989) *The Causes and Cures of Criminality.* New York: Plenum Press.

Finch, J.D. (1984) *Aspects of Law affecting the Paramedical Professions.* London: Faber.

Fitzgerald, E. (1987) Psychologists and the law of evidence: Admissibility and confidentiality. In G. Gudjonsson and J. Drinkwater (eds) *Psychological Evidence in Court.* Issues in Criminological and Legal Psychology, No. 11. Leicester: The British Psychological Society, pp.39–48.

Gudjonsson, G.H. (1984) The role of the 'forensic psychologist' in England and Iceland. *Nordisk Psykologi, 36,* 256–263.

Gudjonsson, G.H. (1985) Psychological evidence in court: Results from the BPS survey. *Bulletin of the British Psychological Society, 38,* 327–330.

Gudjonsson, G.H. (1986) Criminal court proceedings in England: The contribution of the psychologist as expert witness. *Medicine and Law, 5,* 395–404.

Gudjonsson, G.H. (1987a) The BPS survey and its implications. In G. Gudjonsson and J. Drinkwater (eds) *Psychological Evidence in Court.* Issues in Criminological and Legal Psychology, No. 11. Leicester: The British Psychological Society, pp.6–11.

Gudjonsson, G.H. (1987b) The significance of depression in the mechanism of compulsive shoplifting. *Medicine, Science and the Law, 27,* 171–176.

Gudjonsson, G.H. (1991) Forensic psychology: The first century. *Journal of Forensic Psychiatry, 2,* 129–131.

Gudjonsson, G.H. (1992) *The Psychology of Interrogation, Confessions and Testimony.* Chichester: John Wiley and Sons.

Gudjonsson, G.H. and Gunn, J. (1982) The competence and reliability of a witness in a criminal court. *British Journal of Psychiatry, 141,* 624–627.

Gudjonsson, G.H. and Sartory, G. (1983) Blood-injury phobia: A 'reasonable excuse' for failing to give a specimen in a case of suspected drunken driving. *Journal of the Forensic Science Society, 23,* 197–201.

Haward, L.R.C. (1981) *Forensic Psychology.* London: Batsford.

Haward, L.R.C. (1990) *A Dictionary of Forensic Psychology.* Chichester: MediLaw\Barry Rose.

Lane, D.A. (1987) Psychological evidence in the juvenile court. In G. Gudjonsson and J. Drinkwater (eds) *Psychological Evidence in Court.* Issues in Criminological and Legal Psychology, No. 11. Leicester: The British Psychological Society, pp.20–28.

Leng, R. (1990) Mens rea and the defences to a criminal charge. In R. Bluglass and P. Bowden (eds) *Principles and Practice of Forensic Psychiatry.* Edinburgh: Churchill Livingstone, pp.237–250.

Mitchell, S. and Richardson, P.J. (1985) *Archbold. Pleading, Evidence and Practice in Criminal Cases.* Forty-Second Edition. London: Sweet-Maxwell.

Parker, H. (1987) The use of expert reports in juvenile and magistrates' courts. In G. Gudjonsson and J. Drinkwater (eds) *Psychological Evidence in Court.* Issues in Criminological and Legal Psychology, No. 11. Leicester: The British Psychological Society, pp.15–19.

Tunstall, O., Gudjonsson, G., Eysenck, H. and Haward, L. (1982) Professional issues arising from psychological evidence presented in court. *Bulletin of the British Psychological Society, 35,* 329–331.

Weiner, I.B. and Hess, A.K. (1987) *Handbook of Forensic Psychology.* New York: John Wiley and Sons.

Contributors

Andy Benn is Senior Clinical Psychologist at Rampton Hospital, Retford, and Pilgrim Hospital, Boston.

Carol Brady is Senior Clinical Psychologist with Central Nottinghamshire Health Authority.

David I. Briggs is Consultant Psychologist at Rampton Hospital, Retford, responsible for organisational development.

Danny A. Clark is Principal Psychologist at HMP Wakefield.

Martin J. Fisher is Higher Psychologist at HMP Whitemoor, March.

David M. Gresswell is Principal Clinical Psychologist with North Lincoln Health Forensic Services.

Gisli H. Gudjonsson is Reader in Forensic Psychology at The Institute of Psychiatry, London.

John E. Hodge is Director of Rehabilitation at Rampton Hospital, Retford, and Honorary Lecturer in Clinical Psychology at the University of Leicester.

Howard Jackson is Principal Clinical Psychologist at Ashworth Hospital, Merseyside.

Ilona Kruppa is Principal Clinical Psychologist at Rampton Hospital, Retford.

J. Michael Lee-Evans is Consultant Clinical Psychologist at Kneesworth House Hospital, Royston.

Cynthia McDougall is Head of Prison Service Psychology, London.

Mary McMurran is Consultant Clinical Psychologist at Rampton Hospital, Retford, and Honorary Research Fellow at the University of Birmingham.

Index